21, 14, 47,   5,63, 94, 82, 84, 89 90. 103 144
  152, 154, 200, 210
148, 161

NW

Spiritual
Gems

HUZUR MAHARAJ SAWAN SINGH

Spiritual Gems

Maharaj Sawan Singh Ji

Radha Soami Satsang Beas
Punjab, India

Published by:
Sewa Singh, Secretary
Radha Soami Satsang Beas
P.O. Dera Baba Jaimal Singh
Dist. Amritsar 143204
Punjab, India

First edition, 1958   (includes *Spiritual Letters*)
Second edition, 1960   (includes *Spiritual Letters*)
Third edition (revised), 1965:   5,000 copies
Fourth edition, 1974:   3,000 copies
Fifth edition, 1976:   5,000 copies
Sixth edition, 1980:   5,000 copies
Seventh edition, 1986:   5,000 copies
Eighth edition, 1991:   5,000 copies
Ninth edition (revised), 1996:   10,000 copies

Printed in India at
Baba Barkha Nath Printers
26/7 Najafgarh Road Industrial Area
New Delhi 110 015

CONTENTS

FOREWORD

*T*hese letters, written by Huzur Maharaj Baba Sawan Singh Ji (the Great Master), originally constituted the second part of a bigger book of the same name, *Spiritual Gems*. The first part of that edition consisted of letters written to the Great Master during the days of his discipleship by his venerable Master, Baba Jaimal Singh Ji Maharaj. Those letters have now been printed as a separate volume under the name *Spiritual Letters*. This arrangement, besides separating the letters of each Master into different volumes, has rendered the books handy and of a convenient size.

The Great Master wrote these letters in response to the questions and queries of his American and European disciples and seekers. Nearly all the questions and doubts that typically crop up in the minds of seekers of truth and reality have been amply dealt with in this volume, which makes it extremely valuable. These answers are mainly based on Sant Mat principles; thus they serve as a comprehensive discussion of the teachings of the saints.

Sant Mat—the teachings of the saints—is not a religion, cult, or creed. It does not consist of any rites, rituals, ceremonies, dogmas, priesthood, or church or temple worship. It is a scientific method of entering and realizing the Kingdom of Heaven within us, while we are still living in the here and now. It may be called a school of practical spiritual training for God-realisation. Living in the world and discharging all our obligations towards wife, children, relatives, friends, and humanity, we have simply to turn our heart Godward. The saints' teachings are very simple. They say that all the woe, misery, and anguish that is the lot of the human race are due to our sad separation from God. This world, which we love so much, is not our true home.

Our soul is a drop from the ocean of bliss, life, and energy, from which it separated many millions of ages ago. It is a stranger in this foreign land of agony and grief. There is nothing homogeneous to it here below in this world of earth, water, fire, and air. Unless it returns to its ancient original home, its sorrows and sufferings cannot and will not end. For this purpose, it need not seek anywhere outside of itself. Our body is the temple within which the Lord resides. No one has ever found Him nor will ever find Him outside.

All the saints, sages, and prophets of the world affirm that "the Kingdom of God is within us," and that one is not to wander outside to achieve salvation. The Lord dwells in this "temple of nine gates" (our body). One only needs a teacher or guide who knows the secret of the path to enter this palace, one who can lead us to the presence of the Lord—our loving Father. This is possible only in human life. No subhuman species has this capacity or privilege. A teacher of the science of spirituality is as much needed as is a teacher of any other science or art. This unknown path is so curved, complex, and labyrinthine that one cannot tread it without the help of a guide—an enlightened soul. This guide must be a living Master, who can take us to the highest region, beyond death and dissolution, whence there is no coming back. Such Masters are always present in the world. The Masters who died long ago, or their writings, can be of little help to us.

The method of God-realisation taught by all the saints, to whichever country or religion they have belonged, has always been the same and will ever be the same. It is not designed by man, that it may need alteration,' addition, or modification. It is the Lord's own design and is as old as the creation itself. It consists of three parts:

First is *simran*, or the repetition of Lord's holy names. It brings back our scattered attention to the *tisra til*—the third eye (behind our eyes), which is the headquarters of our mind and soul, in the waking state, whence it has scattered.

Second is *dhyan*, or contemplation on the immortal form of the Master. This helps in keeping the attention fixed at that centre.

Third is *bhajan*, or listening to the Anahad Shabd or celestial music that is constantly reverberating within us. With the help of this divine melody, the soul ascends to higher regions and ultimately reaches the feet of the Lord.

This, in a nutshell, is the gist of the spiritual practices which the saints of all ages and countries have been teaching to their disciples for the purpose of God-realisation. Blessed are those who come across a perfect Master, who takes them back to their original home.

The Great Master, Huzur Maharaj Baba Sawan Singh Ji, has been one of the greatest exponents of these teachings that the world has ever produced. Born in 1858 in a highly respectable Sikh family of Punjab, he showed signs of great spiritual understanding from early childhood. As a boy he could repeat by heart the "Japji Sahib" of Guru Nanak and "Jap Sahib" of Guru Gobind Singh. His great spiritual hunger and thirst for knowledge of truth and reality brought him in contact with Baba Jaimal Singh Ji in 1894, who at the time of initiating him remarked that he had been holding something for him in trust from the Lord, which he had discharged that day.

In 1911, Huzur Maharaj Sawan Singh Ji retired prematurely on pension from the Military Engineering Service, to attend to his real task for which he was commissioned by the Lord. He preached and taught the practice of Surat Shabd Yoga at the Radha Soami Colony, Beas, Punjab, which he named Dera Baba Jaimal Singh, after the name of his Master. Millions flocked to hear his spiritual discourses. He initiated more than 125,000 souls into this mystic path, the largest number in the history of the world ever to be initiated by any saint, sage, or prophet (until that time). He spread the light of Sant Mat, not only in every nook and corner of India, but also carried its torch to the distant lands of Europe, America, Canada, and South Africa.

The spiritual practices taught by him for God-realisation are the same as those taught by Christ, Kabir, Nanak, Paltu, Dadu, Jagjiwan, Tulsi, Maulana Rum, Shamas-i-Tabriz, Hafiz, Mujadid Alf Sani, and other saints of the world. These practices are mentioned in the Vedas as Anahad Marg, by the Muslim mystics as Sultan-ul-Azkar, and in the Bible as the Word or the Logos. The followers of the Great Master included people of all religions, countries, and nationalities. When he started his work, the light of Sant Mat was slowly fading out. People under the influence of priestly classes had taken to rites and rituals and had forgotten the teachings of the saints. Nobody knew what Surat Shabd Yoga was. Now, by his grace, large satsang centres have been established, not only in the length and breadth of India, but throughout Europe, America, Canada, South Africa, and other countries.

His famous book, *Gurmat Sidhant (Philosophy of the Masters)*, consisting of two large volumes of 1,000 pages each, and his *Discourses on Sant Mat*, in two volumes, have been translated into English and many other languages.

He left the mortal coil in 1948, after duly appointing Sardar Bahadur Jagat Singh Ji, retired Vice Principal of Lyallpur Agricultural College, as his successor, to carry on his mission of pointing the way to the abode of bliss.

Charan Singh

Radha Soami Satsang Beas
Punjab, India
1965

PREFACE TO THE NINTH EDITION

*I*t has been more than thirty-five years since *Spiritual Gems* was first brought to light. The publication of its ninth edition gives one pause to think about its continuing relevance. The book is unique in its presentation of letters from the Great Master to his disciples in America during a time when there were no books on Sant Mat available in English. Thus these letters served as the primary link on the physical plane between the Master and his disciples—a bridge to fill the gap between intellectual understanding and personal experience of the great truth of the path which he taught. In these letters, the contemporary reader will find evidence of the Master's love and concern for his disciples, and his careful explanation in logical, scientific terms of the underlying philosophy and spiritual practice taught by the saints. Most inspiring to present-day readers are the accounts of the spiritual progress made by these early disciples, and the Great Master's guidance concerning the various stages and experiences they encountered. These letters are a testimony to the truth of the path; they provide a glimpse of possibility and a promise of success for all who make the effort to achieve the spiritual heights that exist within us all.

In order to enhance the book's readability and usefulness to the modern reader, this edition has been edited to correct many typographical errors and inconsistencies in punctuation. Most Indian-language terms have been defined where they first appear in the text as well as in the glossary. The use of italics has been minimized throughout the book.

It is hoped that the present edition of *Spiritual Gems* will be a source of inspiration to all who labour on the spiritual path.

Sewa Singh
Secretary

Radha Soami Satsang Beas
Punjab, India
1996

Extracts from the Letters of
Huzur Maharaj Sawan Singh Ji
to Seekers and Disciples

1919–1948

THE LETTERS

1. Sant Mat was spread in the Punjab by Guru Nanak Sahib and subsequently by Maharaj Baba Jaimal Singh Ji. Every single line of the Granth Sahib[1] insists upon going in and contacting Nam, but we find very few mahatmas even, who really go in.

Although I was born in a Sikh family, and at the age of ten read Guru Granth Sahib, and afterwards intimately associated with Sikh religious preachers, yet whenever I read *Gur Bani* (Granth Sahib), it struck a strange note in my heart. When I put searching questions to preachers, none could give me a satisfactory explanation.

Gur Mat (Sant Mat) is above all religions. For a long time I associated with Baba Kahan. He usually remained in an ecstatic condition, which he developed after fourteen years of persistent and vigorous practice. I associated with him for several months and during that time he showed supernatural powers on several occasions. When I asked him if he would shower grace upon me by initiating me, he answered: "No, he is somebody else; I do not have your share." I then asked him to tell me who that person was so that I could contact him. He replied: "When the time comes, he will himself find you."

---

1. Granth Sahib: The Sikh scriptures, containing the teachings of the ten Gurus in the line of Guru Nanak and the writings of other Indian saints.

When I was S.D.O. (sub-divisional officer) at Murree Hills and in charge of water supply works, my house was near a *dharamsala*, a free rest-house where sadhus, mahatmas, and others going on their way to the pilgrimage of Amarnath in Kashmir would often stay, and I had the opportunity of talking to them and discussing religious and spiritual problems with them.

In those days Baba Ji came to Murree and put up in the *gurdwara* (a Sikh temple). He held satsang from Granth Sahib and created quite a stir by his novel (or what seemed to be novel) interpretation of Granth Sahib. This was brought to my notice too. One man said that he offers as *prashad* (blessed food) what is left in the plate after eating; another told me that he puts musical instruments in the heads of people. I promptly pulled him up and said: "I am an engineer and I know it is not possible to put any musical instrument in the head of a person."

On the fourth day I went to attend satsang. Baba Ji was at that time explaining the meaning of "Jap Ji Sahib." Well, I started my volley of questions—so much so that the audience got tired and began to feel restless. The sacred book *Sar Bachan*, was lying there and I objected to the name of "Radha Soami," and Baba Ji explained from the book itself what "Radha Soami" meant:

Radha ad surat ka Nam.
Soami ad Shabd Nij Dham.

Translated:

Radha is the name for the first or primal soul.
Soami means the original Shabd of the real home.

Now he wanted to point out the way, but I had read Vedant. When I read Gur Bani, my opinion was different; when I read Gita, my opinion was again different, etc; and I was unable to come to a decision. At last I applied for eight days' leave to enable me to study the teachings of Baba Ji. He advised me to read Kabir Sahib's *Anurag Sagar*. I immediately ordered eight copies of this book from Bombay so that I could also give some to my friends, Babu Hari Ram, Gulab Singh, and others, to read and comment on it.

After several conferences with Baba Ji I was thoroughly convinced and received initiation from him on the fifteenth day of October, 1894.

~

2. The ritualistic part of all religions is blind and misleading, no matter what the religion might be—whether our own or of other people.

As to the good and bad things or the sin and the virtue both becoming meaningless, that may be. When you leave the British Territory (during the days of British occupation in India) and pass into the land of the Pathans, who can ask you to account for your deeds? While you are here in the region of Kal (the lord of judgment), you have to account for all that you do. Once you cross over to the region of Dayal (Merciful), who can touch you? This applies only when you have actually crossed the boundary of Kal. Until then it is only a saying.

But the scroll[1] is torn when you devote yourself to Nam; that is, by practice of Surat Shabd Yoga. To tell the truth, we ignorant people cannot even form an idea of the immense power which the Masters possess. But they do not let supernatural

---

1. Scroll: A metaphorical reference to the record of accounts (of our karmas) kept by Kal.

or miraculous powers even approach them, much less accept
and use them. If filth has to be removed, we do not do it ourselves but utilize the services of sweepers. If the saints were to
exercise these powers, the whole world would run after them.

Kal has obtained three boons from Akal Purush:[1]

1. Saints should not persuade people of this world by
    the use of miraculous or supernatural powers.
2. Nobody here should know anything about his previ-
    ous life. If we knew what sins we committed in the
    previous life, for which we are being punished in this
    life, then we would naturally never repeat them again.
3. Wherever a soul might be placed, it should feel con-
    tented in that condition. For instance, look at the pigs.
    Do they want to die? They also cling to this life.

If the saints were to convert people by performing
miracles, the entire population would be after them because
it would not be difficult at all for them to raise a dead man to
life in one place, restore the sight of another in another place,
etc. But no, that is not the way of the saints; although it is
true that wherever a perfumer stores or displays his goods,
the atmosphere is full of scent. (Wherever saints live, even if
they do not show miracles, people know there is something
extraordinary about them.)

You know how I broke my leg. It is a long story and I
have narrated it several times in satsang (spiritual discourse).
I used to go every Sunday to my Master for satsang. One day
he asked me not to come, and said: "You go straight"; that is,
from visiting my mother at home I should return straight to the
hill station where I was in service, without stopping at Beas

---

1. Akal Purush: Literally, "the timeless being," i.e., the true Lord.

as I usually did. When the train reached the station at Beas, I found Maharaj Ji (Baba Jaimal Singh Ji) standing there on the platform. It seemed as if he wanted to say something, but kept quiet. I proceeded to the hill station and resumed my duty.

It was my habit to catch hold of the mane of my horse and jump on it while it was going by. But my servant, in my absence and without my knowledge, had clipped the horse's mane. I did not notice that and, as I grabbed for the mane, my hand slipped and I fell down and broke my leg. The fracture was painful, no doubt, but much more painful was the fact that I could neither defecate nor urinate. The doctors even thought that it would be difficult for me to survive.

On hearing of this accident, a Muslim overseer, who belonged to my district, came to me and said: "I am your own man, a sort of family member. I belong to your place. Tell me please, how can I help you?" I said, "My children are studying as boarders in a school about eight miles from this place. I do not want them to know of this accident. But I would like you to send a telegram to Maharaj Ji (Baba Ji)." He sent the telegram. And when Baba Ji received the telegram He said: "Well, if the Master wants to take him away, He may, for at least he has got Nam." But my sister in faith, Bibi Rukko, pleaded for me with Baba Ji.

It was Baba Ji's practice to go into meditation when anything important was expected to happen, and then to give out whatever information he received from within. He sat in meditation at 8:00 P.M. or earlier (whenever the information was received by telegram). At about 3:00 A.M. he called Bibi Rukko, and she asked, "Shall I bring your food now?" (He had not taken his evening meal.) Baba Ji replied: "No, but you asked something about Bhai Sawan Singh.[1] Now you can

---

1. *Bhai:* Literally, "brother," a term of affection.

inform Sawan Singh that he is not going, but the karmas were very heavy. It was ordained that he had to suffer for five years but now we will settle the karmas in five months. Is it not something? We shall not go to him just now, but after he has been discharged from the hospital. In the meantime you may acknowledge receipt of his telegram." And the moment Baba Ji's telegram was received, I was able to defecate and urinate.

Saints show their mercy but they never talk about it. Now, while I was reduced to this condition, I had to suffer from the monetary point of view also. I lost my sub-divisional allowance, my horse allowance, and half of my pay too. The Chief Engineer was very kind to me. He said: "If only you could come to the office every day in a *dandi* (a sedan chair), I would consider you on duty." But I was very doubtful and feared that as my leg was still weak, I might slip and have another accident. The Chief Engineer thereupon allowed me one month's leave. I wondered if I would be fit to work after one month. The next morning I saw the Commanding Engineer and he said: "Now you are going for only one month." Prior to this, Baba Ji came to see me and told me that I would be absent from duty for only one more month, but it was hard for me to believe it.

At last the month passed and a letter was received from Baba Ji stating: "We people have not come into this world to do our own work, we have come here by the orders of Maharaj Ji (Soami Ji). If he likes, he will get the work out of us." It is impossible to describe the reach or the power of the saints. I am sure, if the Guru wants, he can make even the stones carry out his work.

~

3.   It is only by great good luck that you meet saints. I will tell you my own story. If now and then we have the good

fortune to come across such people, then we do not believe what they say. Before Baba Ji came here (to Beas), I am told that there used to be an apparently half-witted fellow, but really a very spiritual person (a *mastana*), who would often pick up bricks from far and near and make them into small heaps at the place where the Dera is now situated. He was called Kanhom the half-witted. If people asked him what he was busying himself with, he would stop and say: "This will be a very flourishing place. Splendid houses will be built here. It will be populated just like a city." In those days there was absolutely nothing here—no buildings of any kind. It was all wasteland and desert.

When Maharaj Ji (Baba Jaimal Singh) took his abode here, there was only one very small mud hut—8'x8'. When I stood in it, I could touch the roof with my hand. The story of our Baba Ji is also wonderful. Sometimes I used to ask him very childish questions, but he was never annoyed and always answered most kindly.

When Baba Ji's regiment was ordered to the Frontier District, while there, he would at night go out into the open and dig a small pit in the sandy soil. With his rifle tucked behind his knees, he would sit there in meditation the whole night. In the morning the enemy (the Pathans) would be found sitting around him. As he would get up to leave for his regiment, they would pay him respect and obeisance. Nobody would disturb him, and they would say among themselves: "He is a faqir. We should not touch him." If there were three or four holidays, he would devote all of them to *bhajan* (spiritual practice).

He also taught Gurmukhi to the Colonel of his regiment.[1] He retired on pension after thirty-four years of service. He

---

1. Gurmukhi: The Punjabi language and script.

remained at the Dera (Beas) for fourteen years and passed away on December 29, 1903.

~

4.　I was fond of satsang and *parmarth* (spiritual topics) from my childhood. I often associated with sadhus and religious people, partly because my father was fond of *sadhu seva* (service to holy men). Then, while in service, I read Vedant and discussed Vedant with people, especially with the sadhus who, on their way to Kashmir, stopped at the dharamsala near my house.

Later I was transferred to Murree Hills. One day as I was supervising my work, I saw an old Sikh going up a hill along with a middle-aged lady. When I noticed him, I thought he had probably come in connection with some case in the Commissioner's court. Little did I think that he was to be my Master. He was no other than Baba Ji Himself and the lady was Bibi Rukko. This I did not know at the time, but found out later that Baba Ji said to Bibi Rukko, referring to me, "It is for his sake that we have come here." To which Bibi Rukko replied: "But he has not even greeted you." Baba Ji said to her, "What does the poor fellow know yet? On the fourth day he will come to us."

Baba Ji went to the dharamsala and started satsang from the Granth Sahib. Babu Sukh Dayal, my friend, came to me and told me of the novel explanations of the teachings of Granth Sahib, which were given out by a sadhu who recently arrived at the dharamsala. I was ready to accept the truth from anyone, and so we went together to listen to the satsang. In three or four days my doubts were resolved and I got satisfactory explanations to the various questions which I used to take with me.

At last I asked for initiation, but requested that I might not be told to accept the name of "Radha Soami" as I had never heard of it prior to this. Baba Ji said to me, "Radha Soami implies the highest spiritual power. What objection have you to the name of 'Radha Soami'?" I said, "It does not appeal to me." Then he asked, "How many new names of the one God are mentioned in 'Jap Sahib'?" I replied, "Some twelve or fourteen hundred." Then Baba Ji said, "If you do not object to those names, why do you object to the name of 'Radha Soami'?" Thus, my doubts being resolved, I got initiation.

At Murree Hills my house faced Maksh Puri (a place of Hindu pilgrimage). One day when Baba Ji was visiting me, I pointed in that direction and said, "Look, Sir, what beautiful scenery!" Baba Ji laughed and said, "I have seen it." (Implying that he had seen it long ago.) I asked, "Was your regiment ever posted there?" He replied: "My child, you do not understand these things. We saw this place at a time when these hills and valleys had not yet been formed."

Baba Ji used to be very kind to me, and whenever I came to visit him, he would give me a place in his own room. Once I got down from the Beas station at twelve o'clock at noon. It was very hot and I sat down under a tree for a while. Then I felt that I had come for Baba Ji's darshan, yet here I was seeking comfort and delaying that meeting with the beloved. Even worldly lovers have done much better. The thought troubled me, so I started on foot from the railway station to the Dera.

Meanwhile at the Dera, Baba Ji Maharaj, who was very sensitive to heat, came out and began to pace the open courtyard before his room. Bibi Rukko remonstrated and requested him to go inside his room, out of the hot sun, but he would not. A few minutes before I reached the Dera, he went in and then Bibi Rukko, seeing me coming, exclaimed: "Oh, now I see why Baba Ji was walking in the hot sun." (He had himself absorbed some of that extreme heat so that I would not be overcome by it on the way.) There are so many wonderful things about Baba Ji that if I go on relating them for one hundred years, it would not be possible to finish them all.

~

5. It is only when you go up and see inside what happens, how things are managed, that you really understand these things.

But there are some karmas which cannot be wiped off because if there is too much interference, the deed still stands.

Outward love also is not bad, but the real love and devotion can be manifested only when you rise above the nine doors of the body. Eating sweet things is different from just talking about them. But even talk of sweet things is also interesting. As long as there is any worldly attachment, it is no use. If you want love and grace, then use all your energy in going up. Such people are not non-existent, but they are few.

The soul goes in and when the flame of love bursts forth within, it goes up immediately, and there is only one way. The inner design is not the result of any human effort. It is the design of God. But the formal religions do not even suspect its existence. Even if they conquered the whole world, would it go with them? Of course not.

That true Nam resounds in the sweetest strains in the hearts of all of us. It cannot be written or spoken or read. It is neither Gurmukhi nor Arabic nor Persian nor any other language. It cannot be seen with these eyes nor heard with these ears; for these eyes are mortal and, in order to function properly, they depend upon some sort of light such as sun, moon, or electricity. Guru Nanak Sahib says: "Those eyes are different with which you can see the Lord—your Mother and Father. You speak without the tongue and thus you die in life. And there is no language. If there is no language then there is no room for any Vedas, Shastras, or any other scriptures." That is to say, when one dies in life, then he contacts the true

Nam. This means, when one consciously leaves this house of nine doors and contacts Gur Bani or Shabd, that is the true Nam and it is not the monopoly of any religion.

The real Form of the Guru or the essence of Guru is *Shabd* (the creative power, the Word). Only those people who are extremely fortunate get the opportunity to follow the practice of Shabd. When they enjoy it thoroughly, then lust, anger, greed, attachment, and pride are destroyed. When you control your mind and senses, you enjoy Shabd all the more. Then you have attained salvation in this very life. "Not until you love the Shabd, will there be an end to your coming and going." Now this is a universal law and is for everyone without exception. The trouble is that people do not know what *Satguru seva* is. They think spending wealth or spending money in some good cause is seva. Those who have been able to go in and enjoy the Shabd are true satsangis and they have made full use of their lives. That is real Satguru seva. And this is not the exclusive teaching of Guru Nanak Sahib, but the Muslim saints also say the same thing. Dadu, Paltu and, in fact, all those mahatmas who have reached Sach Khand, say the same thing.

∽

6. Every *jiva* (soul), according to his karmas, is given another birth in some other place. The body into which he has to be put is ready. The body into which he has to be born and the interval between death and rebirth, both depend upon his karmas.

∽

7. The Master showered his grace when he initiated you. Now your duty is to practise concentration and go up. Then love will come automatically.

A loving disciple will not be left in the lurch. For example, if a child gets dirty, the mother washes and bathes it and then again takes it into her lap. In the same way a Satguru, after cleansing the disciple of the effects of his bad karmas and making him pure, takes him up.

Whatever we do in this world, we do according to the dictates of the mind, whether it is eating, drinking, seeing friends, entering into new relationships—all these things are of the mind. In fact, the world does not worship God but worships the mind because it obeys the dictates of the mind only.

～

8.   Many people practise *simran* (repetition), but all credit and all glory to him who practises simran without any desire. If one has not gone up and opened 'the door', then he is no better than an animal.

When we are attending to our daily duties, our mind is usually not occupied with them but is wandering. Saints say, "Hold the reins of the mind tight in your hand throughout the day; then, when you sit in bhajan, concentration will be quick and easy." It is easier to concentrate the mind by simran than by any other practice. Saints do not waste even a single minute but keep their attention fixed either in simran or in *dhyan* (contemplation) or in *Dhun* (Shabd, Sound).

Simran collects and concentrates the mind and the soul. Dhyan helps to keep it at one place, and Dhun or Shabd pulls it up.

Do not let the mind remain idle. When we go up into higher regions, the mind stays back; but when we return, it joins us again on the way back to the body.

"When you begin to enjoy simran, the mind will not go out again?" That can be answered by the following illustration: Moses, thinking that he was a great devotee and lover of

God, requested God to bring him in contact with or point out to him a greater and a better lover of God than himself, and God pointed to a bird upon a tree not far from the place.

When Moses approached the bird and asked if there was anything that it wanted or that he could do for it, the bird replied that it was perfectly satisfied and happy except for one thing. Moses asked what that was. The bird said that it wished it did not have to leave its perch to go for water. Moses was astonished at this and pointed out that the bird was perched on a tree immediately above the water and all it had to do was to fly down a few feet to take a drink. The bird replied, "That is true, but I am always thinking of God, and the time spent in flying down and taking a drink takes me away from the contemplation of my love (God) for a few minutes. That is my only regret." Upon hearing this, Moses felt ashamed and realised that this bird loved God more than he did.

~

9. By simran alone the soul leaves the body and goes up. When concentration is complete, one does not feel the need to change positions or to attend to the calls of nature for hours (eight or ten). Mahatmas who employ various other techniques reach only up to the first stage. Simran is the best. I speak from my own experience.

I did not give dhyan or Dhun to quite a number of Muslim disciples, but only taught them the technique of simran, and they concentrated their mind and soul, and went up. When the simran is complete, one hears the Sound within. If you can vacate (withdraw the current from) even half the body, you will see light inside. I received hundreds of letters to this effect. My work is practical. In order to see how they behaved and how they felt, I initiated them into simran only, but they went up and saw things for themselves. This meets

the objection made by several people; namely, that they see
only what they have been told.

Even after going in, you are not allowed to meditate on
the sun, the moon, and the stars. These are material inside as
well as outside. Till one reaches the Ashtdal Kamal, he is not
fit for true dhyan; that is, contemplation of the Master's
Form. In the primary stages *chitta* (mind stuff) serves as *nirat*
(sight). Real nirat is developed higher up. The *anahad Shabd*
(unstruck music) goes as far as the region of matter and mind.
After crossing Par Brahm the *sar* (true) *Shabd* is heard.

~

10.   Of the three phases of spiritual practice, the first is
simran. With the help of simran we have to vacate the nine
doors of the body. After crossing the sun and the moon, we
need something on which to fix our attention. You can stay
there only with the help of dhyan. After that, you require
Sound or Shabd for going up. The true Shabd begins from
Turiya Pad. The power that has created the entire universe is
Shabd. *Jyoti* (light) is one thing and Shabd is another thing.

The jyoti will automatically come, whether you practise
pranayam (breath control) or Shabd Yoga. In the waking
state the headquarters of the soul is behind the two eyes. If
you happen to be in the middle of a hill and you want to
go up, why need you go down at all? You can go up from
where the concentration of the soul begins. When you cross
the *neel chakra* (blue centre) you will see jyoti. It has one
thousand lights. At the stage where the jyoti is, there are ten
sounds.

The soul has two faculties: the faculty to see and the fac-
ulty to hear. In fact, the body is divided into four parts: Pind,
Anda, Brahmand, and Sach Khand. Sach Khand is immortal.
The six chakras of Brahmand are reflected in the six chakras

of Anda, and these are again reflected in the six chakras of Pind. To try to develop the Pind chakras is a waste of time.

Vedant goes only up to Brahm. That is, the goal or the end of the Vedas is Brahm. It is the second stage according to Sant Mat. Sant Mat takes you to the fifth stage.

Shabd is of two kinds: *varnatmak* and *dhunatmak*. Whatever can be written, read, or uttered or pronounced is varnatmak. First of all, there is the sound which is made by the tongue and then that which is muttered in the throat. The third is that which is spoken in the heart. The fourth is made in the *nabhi* (navel) centre by the yogis, with the help of *pranas* (vital force). These sounds can help you only in concentration, but no further. We have to withdraw the soul out of the nine doors, cross the sun and the moon, and go beyond that.

The humming sounds in the ear you can hear even now. The true Shabd you will hear when you reach the region of jyoti. The body outside is the material body, and the next covering or body is in the region of jyoti and is the *suksham sharir*. There Patanjali ends. Patanjali takes you only to the region of *purusha* and *prakriti* (the first spiritual region). It is only in the region of Par Brahm that you are able to shed the five *tattwas* (elements) and all the body covers. Then the soul's own light will be equal to the light of twelve suns. Then you will realise that you are *atma* (soul). When you have realised that you are atma, you will have a longing to know *Parmatma* (God).

The jyoti or the light exists on account of Shabd. Where there is no Shabd, there is no jyoti or light. This light is mixed with *ahankar* (egotism). Rather, the mind accompanies the soul up to the top of Brahm. You would realise or meet your guru after you have crossed the sun and the moon. But he can take you up only as far as he goes himself. We do not

need the pranas. We only take the mind and soul up. Atma
becomes Parmatma only in Sat Lok.

So far you go with the help of light. Beyond that you go
with the help of Shabd. And in Maha Sunn there is no Shabd
even. It is all dark. It is the region of darkness.

You know that there is a jyoti of tattwas. This jyoti then
of which you speak springs from tattwas. Well, I am glad that
a man living a house-holder's life has achieved so much.
When the dissolution comes, this creation up to Brahm is
destroyed. In the case of the grand dissolution it reaches up
to Sohang, but not to Sat Lok.... At the most, the jyoti will
take you up to the top of Brahm; thence onward you travel
up by means of Shabd.

The lights which you see when you go up are the lights of
the tattwas. The jyoti which springs from Shabd will be further up. Tattwas have their own light, but the real jyoti you
will meet further on.

The trouble is that you are now in the big jail of eighty-
four lakh cells.[1] You cannot be happy even in human life. The
pleasures of the senses are only nominal and short-lived. Besides, everyone has his problems and sorrows: one's daughter is a widow, another's son has left a widow, yet another is
groaning under a load of debt and all types of adversity.

The point is that we are a drop of that great ocean and we
have to go back and merge in it. For innumerable aeons we
have been rotting in this jail. Now, just as we attend to other
affairs of the world, let us devote a couple of hours every day
to this practice also. What is the harm then? Besides, this is a
wealth which you take with you and not leave behind.

When you pierce the veil and go up, the pleasures of this
world appear very low and coarse compared to the bliss you

1. A lakh is 100,000.

enjoy there; in fact, it is like a public latrine when compared
to the inner bliss. This is a thing which cannot be bought nor
can it be had for the asking. Work hard, vacate the body
(withdraw the consciousness) and go up, and you will get it.
It is your inheritance and has been kept for you. This joy is
greater than all worldly pleasures. Now please think, have you
ever attended to your own work?

Yes, one does hear voices inside. These voices come from
two sources: one from the Rehman (Merciful) or God and
the other from the negative power. You should not accept them
at once but first say, "Please come before me. Who are you?"

~

11.   *Sikhi*, or the path of discipleship, is like a sword's edge.
There are two paths in this world: *manmukh* and *gurmukh*.
Gur Bani (what has been written in the Granth Sahib) is wonderful if we give careful thought to it. But, of course, if you
read carelessly it is a different matter. Bani has a medicinal
effect on the mind when read thoughtfully.   .

There is only one remedy to control the mind and that is
within us. When the mind and soul go beyond the six chakras,
cross the sun, moon, etc., reach the Turiya Pad and enjoy the
Shabd which is resounding there, then is the mind brought
under control.

If you think that we should remove all the thorns from
the path first, then walk comfortably, barefooted, that is impossible. Even if you succeed in doing so, next year there will
be more thorns. If on the other hand, you put on heavy boots,
then you can go about as and when you please. Whatever is
to happen has already been ordained, and that will happen.
Tulsidas says: "First the *pralabdh* (destiny) was made, and then
this body. The wonder of it is that we still feel so discontented."
Before a person is born, his entire life or destiny is settled.

A rider wanted to take his horse to drink water. Close by a Jat was working at his persian wheel, so he took his horse there. The creaking sound of the persian wheel made the horse shy and it drew back. The rider thereupon asked the Jat to stop working the persian wheel, and the fellow obeyed. When the wheel stopped, he again took the horse to the gully into which the water had been flowing from the well, but by the time the horse reached there, all the water had run out. The rider then requested the Jat to work the wheel again for a few minutes. The moment he did so, the horse again shied and drew back. This greatly annoyed the rider. The Jat thereupon observed: "Well, sir, it is only during this creaking noise that you can get water for your horse." The rider then whipped his horse and again brought it to the same place. The horse obeyed and drank his fill. And the same is true of our mind. These worldly cares and anxieties will remain. Whatever you have to achieve, you will have to accomplish in the midst of these circumstances.

The three worlds are ruled by Kal. Very few people know this mystery of Kal (the negative power) and Akal (the true Lord, who is beyond Kal).

Yes, Kal also acknowledges Akal as his master. But are you aware that Kal performed great austerities by standing on one leg for seventy *yugas*,[1] and thus worshipped Akal for seventy yugas? It was in return for this that he was given this kingdom of Triloki (three worlds) to rule. (Soami Ji said about Kal that when he asked for the boon, he said: "This kingdom of Sat Purush does not appeal to me. Permit me, Sir, to create another world over which I may rule.")

Kal also obtained three boons from Sat Purush. The first one is that the saints should not induce souls to leave Kal's

---

1. *Yugas:* Ages; great cycles of time.

kingdom and go back to Sach Khand by means of showing miracles or other supernatural performances; but they are free to appeal to them, reason with them, and thus induce them to go back. Otherwise it would have been so easy, for all that the saints would have to do would be to give sight to a blind person or to bring the dead back to life, and hundreds and thousands would follow them. But they are not permitted to do so by Akal Purush.

When you say, "What can we slaves do?" you are talking of the worldly or political slavery. But all of us are slaves of the mind and senses—and the richer and the higher a person is socially, the greater are the bonds of slavery. The saints try to free us from this slavery of the mind and the senses by giving us satsang. But how do we behave? If a sheep pen catches fire, the onlookers—taking pity on the sheep—take them out to safety; but the sheep insist on going back again and again to the same danger zone and there meet their death. The same is the case with us. The worldly wealth, worldly kingdoms are all subject to decay. And, of course, nothing can accompany us after our death. We cannot take any of these things with us. Let alone other things, even our dear relatives have to be left behind. The real wealth which we can call our own is the treasure of Nam, and that is within us.

Yet man does not go within. Indeed, how can he go in till he comes across a Sant Satguru who will show him the way? Then he can work his way up by vacating the body of nine doors and then come in contact with Nam. Everything is within him and everything is inside. Whole continents—even universes—are inside. Nay, the Wahiguru (God) himself is inside. The pity is that people read Gur Bani but they do not reflect on its meaning. I have had occasion to meet prominent people, big national leaders, but whenever we discussed Gur Bani, they would always say: "How is it possible to conceive that all these things are inside?" Several doctors have humorously told me: "We have performed numerous dissections but never saw any suns, moons, continents, universes, and so on. All that we have found within was bones, flesh, fat, and blood." But we cannot really find fault with them. If they had come across a Satguru, and learned the way from him to go in, they would have found that these things are not within the physical body but are located behind the mental veil. Make the mind motionless and then you will see everything.

~

12. The mind is the *satwa guna* essence of the five tattwas,[1] activated by the current of the spirit. Do you follow? It is superior to the tattwas but inferior to the conscious current. It represents the intermediate state (between the tattwas and the soul).

The whole world worships the mind. Very few—some rare mahatmas who can go in—know their true God. In eating, drinking, contacting friends, entering into relationships, in fact in whatever they do, they are ruled by the mind. Rishis, munis, yogis, yogishwars, mahatmas, prophets—all owe allegiance to the mind. When one contacts a Master and by going in gets rid of the three covers (material, astral, and causal), the twenty-five *prakritis*, mind and maya, and reaches Par Brahm, then he realises that he is pure soul. There its effulgence is equal to the light of twelve suns; but here, in this world, man cannot face even one sun. There he is neither fat nor lean, white nor black, and he has no body. All the prevailing religions and cults are within the boundary of the mind. As the soul has forgotten its original home, so the mind

---

1. *Satwa guna* essence: the attribute of harmony and light.

also has forgotten its original home. As our soul comes from Sach Khand, so the mind is derived from Brahm and has come from Trikuti. Great yogis and yogishwars have been tossed hither and thither, and have been ruled by the mind. You may read the Hindu Puranas and satisfy yourself on this point.

When you say that maybe the negative power assumes the form of Christ and thus misleads them, that is not correct. It is not the negative power. It is the impression of one's own mind.

~

13.   Now what do we find here? Just scold somebody a little and he gets up and leaves. Even if one is turned out a hundred times, still he should not leave the door of the Guru. Even if he is insulted a hundred times, he should not leave. The cowardly mind is like a goat: when faced with pleasures and enjoyments it is happy and cooperative; but when the Guru remonstrates with it, then it becomes stubborn and revolts. See the contrast between the actions or the attitude of a cowardly person and a brave person when faced with pleasures and enjoyments. It is only a really brave person who can refuse sensual pleasures when they are easily available. The poison to the soul is in his hand, yet he foregoes it.

If there is any form worth contemplating, it is the form of a saint or of a mahatma who has realised God. But when are you able to get this dhyan? When you cross the sun, moon, and so forth. If the nirat is not developed, no real progress can be made, even if you go on hearing the Sound all your life.

Surat and nirat are the two great qualities. If the nirat is not developed, the veil will not be rent, even if you go on listening to the Sound all your life. I say, even if you are not able to put in much labour, try to develop love for a mahatma or for a realised soul. If you really love a saint or mahatma, then—asleep or awake—you always think of him. Where would you go after death? You go to the place of the person on whom your thoughts have been dwelling all along. This is the verdict of our Shastras as well.

～

14.   If faith in the Master or faith in Nam is lacking, there can be no progress. From the time the satsangi is initiated, the Master looks after him from within. Do not ask the Master for something which is improper. Ask only that he should keep you in touch with Nam and God. Saints do not interfere with pralabdh. The ideal of the saints is to accept the will of the Lord. The Master will give those things to the disciple which he thinks proper. Sometimes the disciple craves wealth, honour, sons, daughters; but the Master does not grant his prayer. It is here that the people err. One's son was ill and did not live, so he gives up the Master; another has lost a case and he says, "Give up the Master." As the mother tries to look after the child in every way, the child also has some duty towards the mother. The disciple should try to develop love and devotion towards the Master, and not sit idle. When he gets a Master and receives initiation, it is his duty to do bhajan zealously and reach Sach Khand.

～

15.   When I was in the hospital on account of the fracture of my leg, one day when I was meditating, Baba Ji's form appeared before me. Baba Ji, or rather what seemed to be his form, said: "If, in a case of emergency, meat and drink are used, there is no harm." But when I repeated the five names, he disappeared. Now, because I had seen Baba Ji in real life and could visualize him, I found out this trick. But those

people who concentrate on the old Masters who passed away thousands of years ago are likely to be misled. His (the saint's) eyes cannot be imitated. Hence, you always require a living teacher for the pupil, a living physician for the sick, a living husband for the wife, and a living ruler for the people. I maintain that no one else can help a disciple so much as a living Master. You may have heard the couplet: "Who could be greater than Rama or Krishna; but even they had to accept a Guru. Lords of the three worlds, they stood respectfully with their heads bowed before the Guru."

~

16.   The Lord is within us, and when he sees that one of his servants is sitting in meditation (literally in expectation of his *darshan*), will he be unmindful? Certainly not. But if the veil is not removed, be sure that the mind is not quite pure. First of all, our own mind judges impartially and delivers the verdict: Today you did such and such bad thing. You were subject to *kam, krodh* (lust, anger), and so forth.

~

17.   It is not permitted to talk of things which one sees within. But there are so many things, it is a pity I cannot say everything; however, everything is possible through the help of the Guru. The most impossible achievements can be made possible through the help of the Guru. One day Baba Ji presented me to Guru Nanak Sahib, Kabir Sahib, Tulsi Sahib, and Soami Ji, and said: "He is your child."

~

18.   The bungalow of the Commanding Engineer happened to be just above my bungalow. One day the Colonel was coming out with his daughter to go for a walk. Just then a cart

driver passed near them on the road and a wounded ox was pulling the cart. The Colonel and his daughter were very much touched at the pitiable condition of the ox and said, "Why have they over-loaded this poor wounded creature?" I replied, "That is true. You cannot bear to see the suffering of this poor creature, but what about the beef which you eat?" The point is that, intellectually, man thinks and argues only up to a certain stage; but it is only when he goes in that he has perfect knowledge. Similarly, we attend the satsang and read the books, but we yield to the pleasures of the senses when we are faced with temptation. I have seen learned people, lecturers, leaders of thought, unable to resist the sensual pleasures.

~

19.   To overcome kam and krodh is real bravery. It is not a small achievement. So many rishis and munis of old lost the battle. What is the use if you go on scouring and cleaning a vessel, and put nothing in it? That is, the way to salvation or liberation lies in not only avoiding kam and krodh, but also in devoting yourself to *Nam bhakti*.[1] Man has within himself whole continents, universes, and God himself, but only when he practises Nam devotedly, can he realise this.

~

20.   *Karma:* The Supreme Creator and the individual spirit in the creation are connected together through the sound current. But Kal, also a creation of the Supreme Being, separates the individual from the current by coming in between as mind and forms. Hence, the individual feels disconnected, but not so the Creator.

---

1. *Nam bhakti:* Literally, "devotion to the Name"; i.e., spiritual practice.

There are three minds, and corresponding to these three minds are three kinds of forms:

1. In Trikuti the *nij man* (innermost or causal mind) or Brahm, or the universal mind, cover the spirit. The forms here are made of very pure maya, so much so that a majority of the seekers have failed to see here the spirit apart from maya or mind, and therefore considered Brahm as all-pervading, etc.
2. Lower down, in Sahansdal Kanwal, the forms of Trikuti get another covering of mind and form, both coarser than the above, the astral form here being governed by the *andi man* (astral mind). In this zone there are the hells and heavens and numerous other *lokas* (regions). Here the tendencies of the mind are directed inward and are elevating. This mind behaves like a wise enemy (seeking to keep us here).
3. Further down, in Pind (the region below the eyes), the astral form gets another covering of coarse material, with which we are familiar. The mind that governs this form is called the *pindi man* (physical or lower mind). Its tendencies are outward and diffusive, and it is most difficult to control.

Now, a body actuated by mind and spirit cannot help performing karma, and the karmic law, "As you sow, so shall you reap," continues to work, and the account is complicated with time. The more one works, the greater the entanglement, like a bird struggling in the meshes of a net.

So cunningly has Kal arranged the snare of forms and minds that it is well nigh impossible for man to escape from their influence. No matter how good and godly we may be, that alone will not take us out of these regions. Says Lord

Krishna: "Good actions are as much binding as bad actions. Good actions may be likened to fetters of gold and bad actions to those of iron, and both are equally efficient in keeping us tied." The escape is through the sound current.

Only when the attention catches and follows the current does the mind become dormant and out of action. At all other times, when the attention is off the current, the mind gets the upper hand. Through long and indefinite time, ever since the spirit separated from its ocean and associated itself with the minds and bodies, not only has the upward passage been blocked, but the spirit has been so bewildered, entangled, and enfeebled that it has lost all memory of its home, and is contented to live a wretched life in this wretched material world.

There are two ways of looking at this creation:

1. From the top, looking down—the Creator's point of view;
2. From the bottom, looking up—man's point of view.

From the top it looks as though the Creator is all in all. He is the only doer, and the individual seems like a puppet tossed right and left by the wire-puller. There seems to be no free will in the individual, and therefore no responsibility on his shoulder. It is His play. There is no why or wherefore. All the saints, when they look from the top, describe the creation as His manifestation. They see Him working everywhere.

Looking from below, or the individual viewpoint, we come across variety as opposed to oneness. Everybody appears to be working with a will, and is influenced by and is influencing others with whom he comes in contact. The individual thinks he is the doer and thereby becomes responsible for his actions and their consequences. All the actions are recorded in his mind and memory, and cause likes and dislikes which keep him pinned down to the material, astral, or mental spheres, according to his actions in an earlier life in the cycle of transmigration. The individual in these regions cannot help doing actions and, having done them, cannot escape their influences. The individual acts as the doer and therefore bears the consequences of his actions.

As stated above, the observations differ on account of the difference in the angle of vision. Both are right.

1. The individual, clothed in coarse material form, sees only the external material forms. His sight does not go deeper than that.

2. If he were to rise up to Sahansdal Kanwal, the same individual would see the mind actuating all forms. The form would be only secondary; mind would be the prime mover in all.

3. The same individual, from Daswan Dwar, will see the spirit current working everywhere, and will see how the mind gets power from the spirit.

4. From Sach Khand, the whole creation looks like bubbles forming and disappearing in the spiritual ocean.

An individual is endowed with intelligence and does every action knowingly. It is, therefore, incumbent on him to find a way of escape from this entanglement. To raise his spirit, he must struggle against the mind, for he lives by struggle. And where there is a will, there is a way. He cannot say that this is no part of his duty.

The karmas are also divided into three groups:

1. *Kriyaman* or new actions;

2. *Pralabdh* or fate (the portion of karmas allotted to this life, as a result of our previous actions);
3. *Sinchit* or reserve.

As an example, we take the case of a farmer: He prepares his land for sowing seed. He has the option to sow whatever he likes. Suppose he decides on wheat and sows it. The crop matures and he gathers it. Some of it he keeps for his consumption during the coming year, and the surplus is put in store. Year after year he is living on the previous year's gathering and increasing his reserve in store, to be utilized in time of scarcity or need.

You will see that he is living and hopes to live on what he himself sows and gathers. Similarly, whatever we do in this life becomes fate for our next life; and some of this is kept in reserve by Kal to be given to us if by any chance (of course these chances are practically nil) we run short of karma. Without karma, Kal cannot keep a spirit down in a body; and without a body, no karma can be performed.

It is open to Kal to add from reserve to fate, or deduct from kriyaman for reserve. Like the farmer who is preparing his land for the coming season, and is living on the gatherings from the last season, with a confidence based on his reserve, we are undergoing our fate, in which we have no choice. But we do have the choice to work anew as we please, for our future. And we have a surplus which is our reserve from past lives, of which we have now no knowledge.

We are, therefore, at present doing a dual function:

1. In regard to fate, we are helpless, but—
2. In new actions we have a free hand to sow for the future.

To distinguish between these two types by intelligence alone is not easy for the individual, but a rough rule may be laid down: That which comes in spite of our efforts, and spontaneously, is due to fate. But those whose attention is concentrated and who have access within can read their fate easily. It is an open book to them.

Now, in the physical body, actions are done by the mind from the heart centre. As long as the mind is centred here (in ordinary individuals the heart is the centre of mind action) it will be influenced by emotions. The sensations of joy and sorrow will be felt, as the body is worked by mind from this centre.

When the mind has been elevated to the eye focus by concentration—in other words, when the mind has changed its seat or centre from the heart to the eye centre—then the feelings caused by outward influences working on the physical body will be felt imperceptibly. Joys of the world will not elate such a one, and its sorrows will not depress him.

The fate actions are stored in the eight-petalled lotus in Anda, above the eyes. Their influence is felt forcibly as long as that centre has not been crossed. When that centre is crossed, and the Master's Astral Form is seen (for that Form resides there), the influence of the fate actions will be perceived nominally. The mind has then become strong, and it has the power to bear them without effort. But fate cannot be effaced or altered; it will have to be undergone. An arrow, after leaving the bow, must find its mark.

The reserve actions are stored at the top of Trikuti, and only when a spirit has crossed the third mind or Trikuti it is said to be free from all karma. Below this, the spirit suffers from the ills of karma.

All actions are performed with a motive, and it is the motive that is binding. It is not easy to conceive of an action which is performed without a motive. The mind is consciously or subconsciously active, and it is ridiculous to talk of karma without a counter-karma. There is no escape from counter-karma. By doing actions, however good, there is no escape. Charity, offerings, or pilgrimages must bring their reward, and the soul doing these things must receive the reward in one body or another.

The escape from karma lies in the protection afforded by saints. They are themselves karmaless. Their actions are not binding on them, for their spirits work from Daswan Dwar, a centre above the three spheres of mind and forms, as stated above. The saints show us the way out.

They say: Let new actions be performed in the name of the Master, the individual working in the capacity of an agent only. The new actions, done in this spirit, will not be binding. The fate actions will have been undergone by the time the life comes to an end; the reserve actions saints partly take upon themselves and partly are undergone by the devotee, as the saints think proper.

Saints put the individual spirit in touch with the sound current, and as the spirit catches it and rises up, it throws off the influences of mind and matter, and gets stronger and stronger. The more the individual works on these lines, the easier the path for him. Otherwise the course becomes lengthy; but the saints are pledged to see him through, after they have initiated a soul. The practice of sound current cuts the rest of karma.

The current acts like a magnet on the spirit. It attracts the spirit to itself, and if the spirit were not covered by the rust of mind and matter, it would go up like a shot. The rust of attachments and impressions is removed by repetition (simran). The repetition of thoughts of the journey within replaces our everyday thoughts. Then the mind, instead of wandering outside, begins to take rest and peace within; and when it goes in, the spirit also goes with it; and when the spirit is in, the current in its turn pulls it up. Once Trikuti has been crossed (this will only be when all karmic accounts are settled), the soul never goes back into transmigration. It will go up to merge in its origin.

~

21. I should like to point out that I have the same degree of love and affection for each and every member of the brotherhood, like a father towards his children; secondly, according to the teachings of the saints, the sins and shortcomings of a soul are viewed by the Master in the same light as a washerman regards the dirt on a cloth. He cares for the cloth and not the least for the dirt. His aim is to cleanse the cloth by some means or other; whether by the gentle method of applying soap or by the rough and ready method of beating the cloth against a slab of stone. It depends upon his will.

In the same way the Master aims at reforming his disciples and curing them of their bad habits and wicked deeds so that the spirit may shine in its purity. He determines as to life's procedure. At first he points out our mistakes in gentleness and with love. If this fails, then he adopts a less gentle course and if even that does not serve its purpose, then he applies drastic remedies. In short, he is bent on reforming.

To explain the matter more fully, the Master at first tries to purify us by his discourses. If this fails, then he applies the soap of poverty, adversity, and disease. If these do not answer the purpose, then he gives another birth to the disciple. He does not rest until he has taken the spirit of his disciple to its source. Even if the pupil deserts him, becomes hostile towards him, or wishes to injure him, he does not slacken his efforts.

I have gone through the report of X. They are not offended with you. They wished that you and others, like themselves, should give up animal food and eggs entirely. They
did not take your words in any ill light nor should you, for if
we are in error and another explains it to us we have no right
to be angry. In that case our only course is to admit our mistake and say that habit compels us to repeat it. It is not proper
to be in the wrong and to be impatient. They should have
been more gentle and affectionate. But they are not to blame
for that. They give more time to exercises than you do and
avoid animal food, and stand on a higher mental plane. Under these circumstances a devotee naturally becomes bold and
forward. This is not pride though it is looked upon as such
by others.

Such a devotee wishes that every one should do as he
does. But this is not the stage of perfection. As the soul
progresses it becomes gentler and calmer. Consequently,
when they go higher, they will become calmer and more patient. What they did was right in a sense, and moreover, I do
not think you are much to blame in the matter as you are far
from our congregation, are ignorant of the rules of the Brotherhood, have read no more than the "Discourses," and are
unaware of the purity of the Society. When you gain knowledge and develop spiritual practice you will not mind even
twenty Xs denouncing you. A heart filled with love cannot
contain anger. Your heart has not yet been filled with love. So
try to devote a little more time each day to the spiritual exercises; gradually the Master will grant you all.

You write that Y is of the same opinion. Her complaint is
the same as yours. She also uses an egg occasionally, as you
do. It was as disagreeable to her as to you. This error is in all
of you. It is proper that you should correct your errors. I think
Z is to blame in this matter. He fell from his principles. You

only followed his example. If he had acted up to his principles, you could have gained by his example. Let bygones be
bygones.

But I must point out that animal food, even if a single
particle is eaten, is detrimental to spiritual progress. What of
eating, those who help in killing are also guilty. You say that
eating an egg is not so bad as breaking a heart. Both are bad.
But a broken heart can be set right by love; however, an animal that is killed cannot be revived.

X told you that repetition of holy names should not be
undertaken for accomplishing worldly objects. This does not
mean what you understood. It means that spiritual progress
is the highest object and all our efforts should be directed to
that end. If we sacrifice all the world for it, it is not too much.
Therefore, to divert our energy from this highest object and
apply it to worldly objects is not proper. When we ask for
worldly things from the Lord we would get them, but then
our spiritual advancement would be hindered. Had we applied our energy to spiritual progress, we would have reaped
greater benefit. The saints of the highest degree never ask for
anything that is perishable. They ask for the Lord from the
Lord. As Guru Nanak says:

What should I ask of Thee?
Nothing is permanent.
Everything is passing away
Even as I behold.

This means that everything is perishable except the Lord,
and that he (Nanak) was not going to ask for perishable
things. He needed the Lord and nothing else. He said: "If the
wealth of all the worlds were put on one side and the love of
the Lord on the other, then those who love the Lord would

only ask for the Lord and would not care for the wealth. He who is filled with the love of the Lord is followed by all the world."

The other reason is that gain and loss in this world depend upon our karma. Many of our efforts are bound to fail on account of our karma, as they are not destined to accomplish their purposes. If we apply repetition of the names and spiritual exercise to gain these purposes, and fail, then our faith in the Lord will decrease because he did not grant us our wishes. That would lead to hindrance in our spiritual progress and love. Our duty lies in doing our best in worldly business and being content with the result as the will of the Master.

There are many on the path who have not penetrated into their interior and who have not beheld the Master in their internal vision, nor have they crossed the stages of anger and lust. They do everything as dictated by the lower mind, and excuse their misdeeds by saying that the Master activates them or that the Creator causes them. Now this is the trick played upon them by the lower self.

The bad deed is due to our low desires, and we hold the Master or the Lord responsible for it. Until our soul goes up and beholds the Master inside, and can talk to him there, we should ascribe every blame to the dictates of the lower mind and not to the Master.

When we have had the vision of the Master inside and we have reached a very high spiritual plane, only then we can say that whatever is done is done by him. In that state there is no sin as sin lies in us and not in the Master. Therefore, a spiritual devotee should be careful against being deceived by the lower self. He should be gentle and forgiving.

If you had the real spirit of practice in you, you would have laughed over what X said to you and would not have given way to anger. Not even twenty Xs would have been able to ruffle your spirit which would have been powerful and patient. Then I would have said that the sound current has produced effect in you. But instead of that you not only lost self-control but also your companions became perturbed, which was not proper.

I would advise that all of you should clean your minds of mutual accusation and remonstrance, and increase love and affection for each other. Each one should admit his or her mistake, ask pardon of the other, and grow in love and faith.

But I do not mean that repetition should be given up. Repetition must be done in the mind so that none should hear it. It is intended to still the mind and not to show off. The important point is that the mind should be brought under control. It plays subtle tricks and has tricked many before you—even the prophets and incarnations. I have seen many whom the mind has made dance to any tune or act upon its dictates, while the people think that they are visited by holy Spirit or that they have taken their soul to a high plane. The evil tendencies lie in the mind while it ascribes them to others.

The path of the saints is the true path, therefore it is a great sin to mislead people by external show. The company of such people should be avoided.

It is probable that my words may be unpleasant to you. But it is my duty. Just think, human life is very precious and is due to past good karma. It was not granted to us for rearing children, or for enjoying ourselves. All these functions are performed even by the lowest animals. The only difference between man and lower creation is that man's life here was meant for seeing the Lord and reaching the highest spiritual plane, in this life. Every minute of it is worth millions of dollars.

We have to give up this physical body, the astral frame and also the causal body. When this is the case, then what is the worth of the world, its relationships and its pleasures? The world should be looked upon as an inn, and our relatives as fellow travellers. Our chief aim should be to unite with our Creator and avoid lust, anger, avarice, attachment, and pride so far as we can, as they are our enemies. At all times our hearts should be full of love for the Master and our own mind should be so fearless that it should not be ruffled if it were given the kingdom of the world nor if the kingdom of the world were taken from it. When the mind has become like that, the Master penetrates it with his real Light.

Whatever I have written is with a view to your benefit and purification, and not with a view to dominate or show off. It is the outcome of my love for you. I do not know whether or not the etiquette and manners of your country would accept it in such a light.

∾

22. The best way of preparing the ground for spiritual instructions is to cleanse one's mind, to give up meat and liquors, to avoid lust and anger, to love the Almighty, and to inculcate a desire to reach the true home of the spirit, from which it came in the beginning.

The reach of Theosophy is very much limited as compared with Sant Mat (the teachings of the saints). The former has for its final goal the first stage of Sant Mat and has subdivided that into many degrees. The result is that travelling along Theosophical lines, one cannot go beyond the first stage of Sant Mat. The method of the latter is very simple, and in modern times, none other can compare with it. The saints method aims at crossing Brahm and gaining Par Brahm (beyond Brahm), thence reaching Sat Lok (the true region, the pure spiritual region).

The region of Pind does not extend above the eye focus, while the region of Brahmand corresponds with the frontal part of the brain. But full details will be given to you by the person who will initiate you.

According to Sant Mat, mind is not the creator of the world. It is the Word which is the Creator. There is no doubt that all the world, so far as the mind and the intellect go, is governed by the mind; but the latter is itself inanimate. It is dependent on the spirit and the Word (holy Sound). There are three minds:

1. The physical or *pindi* mind, which governs the physical frame and the senses
2. The universal mind (*brahmandi man*), which rules the subtle worlds such as heaven, hell, and so forth.
3. The causal mind (*karan man*), which rules the causal region and extends to the top of Brahm.

So long as the soul is within the range of any of these three minds, it is neither pure nor unfettered. The soul cannot know itself until it has crossed Brahm and reached Par Brahm. And until the soul has known itself, it cannot know the Creator of all.

~

23. I am glad to read that you are so earnest about your spiritual progress and devote time to achieve it. You say, "Spiritual progress seems at a snail's pace." The withdrawal of the attention from the body to the eye centre is a slow affair. Mind has made deep attachment with matter and now finds it difficult to detach itself from it.

Repetition of the five holy names at the eye centre is the safest and easiest way, and with faith and perseverance one succeeds. No attention should be paid to the pain in the heart region and the tightness in the throat. They are felt because

the attention does not stick to the eye centre when repeating
the names. It leaves the eye centre and comes down to the
throat and heart centres. The attention should be kept up in
the eye centre. That is a necessary part of the repetition.

Again, breathing should go on normally and no strain or
pressure put on it. As a matter of fact, when doing repetition
one should be unconscious of his breathing, just as one is
unconscious of breathing when he does his daily routine
work. When you will keep your attention in the eye centre
and increase the time in repetition, your concentration will
improve and the pain will disappear automatically. The whole
body is to be vacated, including the heart and throat centres.

In discussing Sant Mat with non-initiates, one is free to
discuss it as any other science or philosophy, but one should
not give out his own personal inner experiences nor what he
learns at the time of initiation—names, positions, and the
distinguishing sounds and lights of different regions, and so on.
One may discuss the principle of repetition, the need for a
living Master, the sound current, or the basic principle of the
human body as the laboratory, the head as the repository of
all secrets, and man as the highest form of creation because
he is endowed with capacity to make contact with his Creator,
thereby solving the eternal mystery while living and the like.

To distinguish a true seeker from a curiosity seeker, one
should apply one's own judgment. Quite often a curiosity
seeker in the beginning changes to a true seeker after hearing
about the subject. Much depends on the way one leads his
life and presents his views on the subject. If one is himself
shaky and unconvinced, not much impression would be
made on the listeners. A true seeker does not enter into discussion; "a word to the wise" rule applies in this case.

"Loving service to my Master is the goal of my life." The
best service that one can render to the Master is to withdraw

one's attention from the body to the eye centre, cross the stars, the sun, and the moon, and meet the Radiant Form of the Master within. This service replaces "I-ness" with "Thou-ness" and completes the duty of the disciple. The disciple has placed himself in the hands of the Master and it is now for the Master to lead him to the spiritual home.

One should take good care of the body, like a rational being, follow the laws of health, take doctor's advice when necessary, and try to keep the body in a fit and healthy condition. There is no need to endure that which can be cured. Tonsils and adenoids are not necessary for spiritual progress, and if these are in a diseased condition and the doctor advises their removal, they may be removed.

"Incidentally, on this path one learns the use of the best herbal medicines, exercises, the proper use of foods, breathing and all means of curing for the body" (quotation from *Mat Prakash*). This may be ignored. Observance of ordinary rules of health and doctor's advice, whenever necessary, are good enough. Emphasis, however, should be laid on contacting the Master within and catching the bell sound.

The soul leaves the physical, astral, and causal bodies in succession as it progresses towards Daswan Dwar. During devotional practice, as the concentration improves, mind and soul vacate the body and pass through the eye centre, then cross the starry sky, the sun, and the moon, and meet the Radiant Form of the Master. From there onwards the Master's Form acts as guide, and the journey is made in the company of the Master.

～

24.　Every item of old karmic debt has to be paid. Kal demands his pound of flesh. I give you an instance of my Master, Baba Jaimal Singh Ji:

At the request of a satsangi, he went to Ambala to hold satsang for a few days. When two days had passed, the satsangi recommended an intelligent, influential person of the place for initiation. Baba Ji asked the satsangi not to recommend him, but to recommend another dozen instead, if he liked. The satsangi insisted and the Master yielded on one condition—that after the initiation he would leave the place at once, and no one should insist on his staying there. The conveyance to leave the place was arranged for, and the man recommended was called in and initiated. Master returned to the Dera at Beas and for ten days suffered so much from dysentery and fever that nobody had any hope that he would survive. I happened to see him then. I had come on short leave. On enquiry, I was informed that he could not refuse the request of the devoted satsangi. (Saints are very tender-hearted and merciful.)

The man initiated had an enormous amount of ugly karmic debt to pay off. The karmic debt was paid through suffering by himself (Baba Jaimal Singh Ji). All cases are not so bad. But no initiation is possible without payment of karmic debt. People may be thinking that saints lead a life of ease. They have crowds of followers, and so forth and so on. But the saint's duty is most difficult. He carries a heavier responsibility than a captain of a ship in a storm. This sea has a bottom and shores, but compare it with the sea of existence through which saints guide the soul and make it one with the One! The more your soul is elevated, the better your service. There is no doubt that pretenders, in the garb of saints, have done enormous harm, but such is the case in other walks of life as well. This cannot be helped.

Nam and *kam* are two of the vernacular terms used in our literature. *Nam* means "Word" or "sound current," and *kam* ordinarily means lust or passion or indulgence in the sensual desires as opposed to self-control, but in its wide sense, it means all outward tendencies of the mind. Nam and kam are, therefore, opposed to one another. The tendency of Nam is towards the inlet pipe to a reservoir and kam leads to the outlet pipe. The reservoir may be filled if the inlet pipe is large and the outlet pipe is small. But it cannot remain filled if the outlet is wide open or even leaking. And the sooner the outlet is stopped, the faster the reservoir will be filled.

Now, take Pind or the physical body as the reservoir. So long as the attention is at the eye focus, it is filling, but when the attention is running below the eye focus, it is leaking. And the lower the attention below the focus, the faster it is leaking. The sensual centre is located very low; therefore, playing of the attention on this centre causes an enormous leakage, and there is a considerable amount of dissipation of energy. Nobody feels happier after the act of dissipation. That act is a happy act if it leaves you happier. Kabir compares Nam and kam to day and night, respectively. Day and night do not go together. If there is day, then there is no night; and if there is night, then there is no day. If attention is given to Nam, there is no kam, and if it is given to kam, there is no Nam. The same idea of reservoir and inlet and outlet pipes may be extended to Anda and Brahmand.

The world is the design of Kal and maya, the negative forces. To keep the soul down, they based the structure of the world on couples, man and woman. If both man and woman were to catch the sound of Nam and rise up, both would be free. Here, one holds down the other. And because we have not seen the other side of the whole picture, we take our present existence and our surroundings as the normal affair. Strictly speaking, we are living an abnormal life. Soul combined with mind and matter is an abnormality. Soul, the queen of royal blood, enjoying the company of servants and sweepers, is an abnormality.

By holding the attention at the eye focus, we are to fill the Pind reservoir. By holding it at Trikuti, we are to fill the Anda reservoir. And by holding it at Sach Khand, we are to fill the Brahmand reservoir. If leakage, wide or narrow, is permitted then the filling is delayed or perhaps may never even be up to the Pind level.

The law admits of no exceptions. The longing for Nam means turning your back on kam. Turning your face to one means turning your back to the other. Saints find human nature weak. They make it strong, step by step. They attach the individual to Nam and, slowly and slowly, as longing for Nam develops, the tendencies toward kam diminish.

Those who indulge in kam for the sake of indulgence are doing no good to themselves. To hide their ignorance or weakness, they call this indulgence a physiological necessity and have gone to the extent of advocating the use of contraceptives, etc. All that is due to the weakness of human nature. Those who indulge for the sake of children should try to control themselves when they have the required number of children. Now what fun is there in having big families which they cannot support? The rest of life is spent as a family donkey, carrying its load. Again, to indulge after conception, and so long as the child is dependent upon the mother, is something inhuman. Here, again, to defend our weakness, we may propound any code; but weakness is weakness, and no amount of defence will convert it into strength.

To rise up is a slow process, but to fall from a height is sudden. Kam is a sudden fall of attention. Saints emphasize the grandeur of Nam and bring it again and again to the attention of those who come in their contact. They advocate looking up, while the world looks down. Whenever Nam will become tasteful, kam will disappear. There is no other way of controlling kam. Raising the focus of attention automatically subdues kam.

Saints have to deal with human nature. If they ask a person to leave kam all at once, before initiation, we know he cannot do so. They attach him to Nam. There is something for him to look up to now. He has heard of the magnificence of Nam from the saints. A tiny spark is kindled in him. He gives it some attention. The days are passing. Partly through receiving knocks (sickness, death in the family, demands on purse, shocks to pride, etc.), partly through age, partly through satsang, partly because he has passed through some of his pralabdh karma (fate), and partly through devotion to Nam, his attention is slowly contracting. So, by the time he reaches the end of his days, he is almost ready to go up and grasp Nam.

Now, if during his lifetime he had made Nam the main object of his study, and had treated the world and worldly affairs as secondary, there is no reason why he should not have gone inside the eye focus and risen up. Saints come across all sorts of cases. Souls that go inside the focus and rise up during their lifetime are naturally few. The majority are of the type described above. But those who are of the world, through and through, have no faith in saints and do not come near them. Please understand this carefully. The law and its use by the saints is the practical uplift of the soul.

Dr Johnson said, after his initiation, that he considered the day, 21st March, the greatest day of his life. When a soul (child) comes in the world we say he is born. In reality the soul has been entombed in the grave of the physical frame, so it is more appropriate to say that it has died. When it comes in contact with the saints and gets initiation, it is attached to

Nam and is getting out of the grave of the physical frame. So it is appropriate to say that it is born, or reborn. The day of initiation is the birthday.

Socrates was familiar with the sound current but gives hints only in his writings. The ancient philosophers gave only hints. The same is the case of the Persian saints and Indian saints (of old). It is only in modern times that saints have spoken out about the current in some detail.

Our shortcomings and lack of love keep us out.

~

25.   Your "elder brother" is within you, occupying the bright right half of the eight-petalled lotus in Anda. (The dark left half is occupied by Kal.) He is there to receive you and awaits your arrival there to lead you onward. So long as the devotee has not reached that far and has not seen him, his faith in the Elder Brother, Friend, Guide, Master, or Guru—no matter by which name he is called—is shaky. The faith matures only after seeing this Form of the Master. By the time the devotee reaches this stage, he too has shaken off the growth of material bonds and sensual, low desires from his mind.

The same mind, which worked through the physical organs of senses with worldly objects, now finds itself in a different world (Anda)—far more attractive and stable— looking at which, the mind begins to discard what it had held dear before. When it grasps the inner Form of the Master and finds that He is the Master of the inner realms, and sees face to face what He does for the disciple, his faith becomes firm. Whatever hymns and songs of praise and devotion that the disciple may compose to express his love and yearning for that Form, he fails to express himself as he would like to. There is nothing in this world to which that Form could be compared or likened. Like the bride returning from her husband, when questioned by her sister companion as to the pleasure of meeting the beloved, the disciple expresses himself in silence and a smile. That is his greatest eloquence.

This inner Form of the Master has a magnetic influence which holds the mind and soul of the disciple there. Before that, the process of concentration is a struggle. You bring in the attention and the mind is running out again. Sometimes you may succeed and sometimes, oftener, the mind succeeds. Therefore, patiently and determinedly enter the arena daily and stick to the focus. As the scattered attention collects in the focus, the mind narrows down its sphere of run, calms down, and begins to be withdrawn from the extremities of the body. As the practice advances, one becomes unconscious of the extremities—feet, calves, thighs, and upwards. On discontinuing the practice, one feels the attention slowly returning to the extremities. It is a slow process. The whole attention is to be taken within the focal centre. When the attention is in the focus, we are unconscious of the body, but we are conscious of the focus and what there is inside of the focus.

When the struggle has been carried on for some time and you feel the change from repetition necessary, then sit in the position for hearing the sound current, but still stick to the focus and do not go after the Sound. We catch it from the ear because we have the habit of hearing through the ear. (But the Sound that we are after does not come from the ear, nor is our ear the organ to hear it.) It comes from above the focus. The attention (surat) hears it.

There are ten different sounds here. We are to catch the bell sound. If the bell is not heard, catch the shrill whistle; and, failing that, catch the sort of noise like that of a railway train passing on a bridge. As the attention goes inside the focus, the different sounds become distinct and the bell will be audible.

Do not go after the Sound. If one goes after the Sound, the attention scatters in trying to catch it. Here again, you will find that there is a struggle. Part of the attention is catching the Sound, while that which is still in the physical body is sometimes narrowing towards the focus, causing strain or pain in the calves or some point in the spinal cord where it is held, and sometimes causes disturbances by communicating outward sensations.

The strain or pain that has been mentioned above should be borne. This is the equilibrium of outward and inward tendencies of the mind. It is not the type of strain or pain that will leave any ill effects on the body. The best way to succeed in this state of equilibrium is to look into the focus and not to let the attention slip down. It is the attention that feels the strain or pain; and if, instead of giving attention to this part of the body, one ignores it and engages the attention in the focus, the strain or pain will disappear and the residual attention will have been pulled up a step. If you do not stick to the focus but let the attention slip down, the strain or pain will disappear also, but the attention is now outward and the game is lost.

However, by daily practice, we are to elevate this point of equilibrium. This point determines how far we have succeeded in withdrawing our attention from the body. So long as the whole attention does not go within, it will not stay within. When it has established connection with the Master within, it is completely within. Below this state it hears the sounds, but these sounds do not pull it up—or, in other words, the scattering tendencies of the attention do not allow it to catch the Sound fully.

The bell sound that pulls or attracts like a magnet commences from the eight-petalled lotus. The tables are turned now. The attention that had found it so difficult to go within, now finds it difficult to stay out. To talk of the joys of staying within is the privilege of a different set of people. Only he can appreciate this state who has gone within—in the eye focus. This Form of the Master is unique. There is nothing in this world with which to compare it.

In my last letter I described the connection between Pind, Anda, Brahmand, and the pure spiritual region, Sach Khand, and stated that the six centres of Brahmand are reflected in the six centres of Pind. The five stages revealed at the time of initiation are the most important stages or stations of the journey.

The light from the spiritual region, Sach Khand, downward, steadily decreases toward Sahansdal Kanwal. If you examine a flame with a slight tendency to give soot or smoke, you will notice that just below the point of smoke there is some redness, and down below this redness is the luminously bright zone; and lower down, the light increases in brightness. Now, imagine that from Sach Khand down to Sahansdal is an inverted flame. Sahansdal is the smoke, Trikuti is the redness from which smoke has been eliminated, Daswan Dwar is the brightness from which redness has been removed, Bhanwar Gupha is glowing brightness, and the light of Sach Khand is beyond comprehension. Although, by analogy, Sahansdal has been called smoke, yet its thousand-petalled lotus with a thousand little candles and a big central candle flame is the final stage of many a prevalent faith. I hope you will understand why Trikuti with its red sun is located below the bright, full moon of Daswan Dwar. The light increases and the sound becomes continuous, finer, and sweeter toward Sach Khand.

The sounds of the Current at the various regions have been mentioned as resembling the sounds of material instruments like the bell, guitar, and so forth, but in reality there is no comparison. To give you an idea in the best way that it can be given, one has to resort to that with which you are already familiar. The unknown is explained in terms of the known. Guitar and so forth are the nearest approaches of sounds known to us here in this world, to give some idea of the sounds of the Current heard at the different regions within. These lights and sounds are the characteristics of those regions, and any soul that goes within must see and hear the lights and sounds characteristic of the regions through which it is passing. The Current is continuous from Sach Khand downward, but it produces different sounds in different regions, just as if you strike your stick against a wall, wood, stone, or metal, it produces different kinds of sounds.

The Current is within us always. We could not live without the Current. The Current is Life. The Sound is going on within, without any interruptions, and so is the Light within. Why do we not see the Light and hear the Sound? The reason is that our mind is shaking. Our attention wanders. One does not see the reflection of his face in agitated water. The moment the water is still, the face becomes visible. If the water is muddy, the mud brings in an additional disturbing factor. So, purity of mind and calmness are the prerequisites to see what lies inside the focus.

When sitting for the exercise, throw out all other ideas from the mind. Just as Pind, Anda and Brahmand are not the abode of soul (Sach Khand is its abode), Pind and Anda are not the abodes of mind as well. Mind is derived from Trikuti. Soul and mind are both misfits here on the physical plane. They are never at rest. How could anybody be at peace in someone else's home? Both are in search of their home and have carried on this search, nobody can say since when—ever since they left their respective homes.

Soul is misguided by mind, and mind by senses, and senses by objects of sense. Objects control the senses, senses control the mind, and mind controls the soul. The whole order is thus reversed. With proper guidance, mind should control the senses and the soul should control the mind. What a shame that soul, the child of Sat Nam in Sach Khand, is subservient to senses, and senses are hopelessly attached to material objects.

Let us now reverse the order. With Master's help and guidance let us commence the journey back. Make the mind and soul, or attention, occupy the focus at the eye centre and leave the senses helplessly behind, dissolve the individual mind in the universal mind in Trikuti, and take the soul, freed from mind and matter, to regions of peace and bliss—its original home.

You have read my letter to X where I discussed kam and Nam. That should give you the basis to understand the sex question in all its phases. If there be any phase of this question which you wish to discuss more fully, I shall be glad to do so.

"How far may I use my own judgment in telling inquirers about the Sant Mat philosophy, about you and my connection with you, and the work generally?" One real seeker for truth is better than hundreds of those who inquire from sheer curiosity, or the mere theorists and intellectual gymnasts. You need not waste your time with the latter class. With this type, the less said, the better. With a real inquirer, you may discuss the subject as best you can without bringing your own personality in and without revealing what you got from Y at the time of initiation.

If there is any point arising out of your discussion of the subject which you think is not very clear to you, you may please refer it to me. Your comprehension of the subject will increase as your practical knowledge increases. There is no need to establish a new sect, for there are plenty of them already. Nor is this work to be judged by the large numbers initiated who do not attempt to go within. As I have said already, one real seeker is better than a crowd that has no deeper insight than an idle curiosity. Sant Mat is pure, unalloyed spiritual work, holds no promise to cure the sick and the blind, nor to improve one's worldly position. Initiates are to follow their normal vocations in life, earn their livelihood as honourably and as best they can, and utilize the means that are within their reach to keep themselves fit. Sant Mat aims at pure spiritual uplift.

Just as a cow, even if let loose, will not go very far away from her calf, similarly our minds do not go very far away from the worldly objects to which they are attached. Our first business is to detach the mind and bring it inside the focus. The whole attention is to be brought in. Although the current is audible even before this happens, it does not attract nor pull up very much, just as a magnet will not attract with any force a dirty, rusty piece of iron.

With attention in the focus, listen to the Sound, but do not go after it. The Sound will come to you of itself. Out of all the sounds—there are ten of them at the eye focus—catch the bell sound, and when the bell is caught, leave the others. When all of the attention will be inside the focus, light will come automatically. Light is there even now, but your attention is shaky and out of the focus. Both the powers—the power of hearing and the power of seeing—should be used: the power of hearing, to hear the current, and the power of seeing, to see even the darkness in the absence of light. I will write to you some other time on the different powers of yoga.

Regarding the time limit to reach the first stage, no time limit can be fixed for an individual, nor is there an average. It is entirely a path of love. I have known cases where, at the very time of initiation, people have conversed with the Master within. And there are cases as well where, even after thirty years, the attention is still wandering out. This much is certain, that after initiation, there is no going down the scale of evolution below human life. The rise up is bound with the past record of karmas.

You may please write to me as often as you like. My reply may be late, but the reply will be given. I am glad that you are working with zeal and faith.

~

26.   Spiritual progress primarily depends on the training of the mind. In ordinary man, the soul is under the control of the mind, and the mind is controlled by the senses, and the senses are led away by the objects of senses (material objects). The attention thus remains wandering from object to object.

The right way should be that the senses do not run after the objects, the mind is not led away by senses, and the soul has the grip on the mind and uses it as its tool to serve its purposes. The soul is to re-establish its supremacy over the mind instead of remaining its slave.

Why did the soul lose its supremacy? Because it lost touch with the Word and associated with the mind. Therefore, there is only one effective method of regaining its supremacy and that is to bring the soul in touch with the Word again. The Word is audible within us, in the eye centre. So we are to bring back our scattered attention, into the eye centre, to catch the Word.

For bringing the attention back into the eye centre, the simplest method is the repetition of the five names, thereby keeping the attention engaged in repetition at the eye centre. It is a slow affair, and slow and steady wins the race. So with faith and perseverance, continue this work.

27.   I am glad to learn that you are taking seriously to the practice of the lesson imparted to you. The more time you devote to it, the better shall be the result. It is a good idea of yours to hold the questions in abeyance till you have been on the path for some time. After some time, you will feel that most of them need not be put at all. But if there are some which demand replies, I shall be only too glad to answer them.

As regards the Shabd being stronger in the left ear, you should take your finger off the left ear whenever it is stronger in the left ear, while keeping the finger in the right ear. This will prove quite helpful in keeping the Shabd in the right ear, which is the proper way of hearing the Shabd. After some time the Sound shall appear as coming from the middle and not from any side. That would be the right way of hearing the Shabd. In case the strength of the Shabd in the left ear persists, you should relax your concentration and bring your mind out in order to subdue the left ear Shabd, which is to be eschewed as being the sound of the negative power, while we have to follow that of the positive power, which is either from the right side or in the middle.

~

28.   You have expressed your inner feelings so clearly. You ask, "Why did you ever accept such an individual?" Dear soul, the Master makes no mistakes in selecting persons for initiation. Only they receive the initiation whom their Maker wishes to bring back to him. He reveals the secret of the sound current to his chosen few.

The number one sign of His being merciful to anyone is that He creates in him dissatisfaction with the worldly routine and a longing to seek the truth. The second sign is that He brings him in touch with a Master. The third sign is that the

Master imparts to him the secret of the sound current. The fourth sign is that the initiate works diligently and faithfully on the sound current and starts his spiritual journey. In the presence of these signs, where is the room for feeling self-disgusted?

The world is a thick forest, thickly populated, where all have lost their way and are ceaselessly and aimlessly running about, life after life, harassed by the great dacoits: lust, greed, anger, attachment, and pride. The remarkable thing about these dacoits is that people associate with them joyfully and, knowing that the result of their association is suffering, have not the courage to dissociate themselves from them. They eat the poison, cry, and eat the poison again. Lucky is he who begins to understand the game of these dacoits; luckier is he who tries to dissociate himself from them; and luckiest is he who meets a master-guide and is put by him on the path of the sound current that leads him out of this wilderness to his eternal home of peace and bliss in Sach Khand.

By and by, with the increase of time in simran and the hearing of the sound current, the scattered attention will vacate the body and come in concentration in the eye centre. There will come a time when these dacoits will be met with inwardly in the form of young, handsome boys. No attention is to be paid to them. Their presence is to be ignored and the attention is to be kept in repetition or the sound current. The boys will go out from the body one by one and, when leaving, will give notice that the owner of the house is now awake and alert and the sound current fills the house, so there is no room for them now. Describing this state of development, Guru Nanak says: "I am lucky to escape from these dacoits and they are lucky to escape from me"—meaning thereby, "In the beginning they were strong and had the upper hand, and when they left me I considered myself lucky. Now that I am stronger and more powerful, they consider themselves lucky to have escaped from me in time."

So with love and faith, continue your practices; and watch that, when in practice, the mind stays inside and does not run out, and if it runs out, put it back in simran or the sound current as the case may be. Everything will turn out all right. When you notice the coming of anger, begin the repetition of the names. As your meditation will improve, the anger and ego will also disappear.

You are right when you say that the intellectual side of the science is far less important than the meditation. The whole secret—the knowledge, the substance and the cherished treasure—lies inside, and without going inside it cannot be had, and the eye that is to see it is also inside.

Reading of scriptures, discussion of philosophies, and recitation of prayers is like churning of water from which nothing but foam comes out. Going within and rising on the sound current is the churning of milk from which butter comes out. The primary effort of man, therefore, should be to vacate the body below the eyes and sit inside, in the eye centre, and dig up the hidden treasure.

The Master, from the time of initiation, is within you and watches you and gives necessary guidance, all of which you do not see. When you will go with him and cross the stars, the sun, and the moon, and meet the Radiant Form of the Master, he will talk to you as we talk to each other outside, and he will be with you always and answer all your enquiries.

"Should we attempt to meditate when ill?" Poor health interferes in meditation but it does not mean that we are to give up effort. The sound current does not stop during illness. It is the soul that has to meditate and hear the sound current, and the soul never gets ill. It is the body that suffers. In fact, during illness the blessing of the Supreme Father is extraordinary. The sound current becomes clearer. During illness, if sitting in posture is not possible, meditate while lying down. In no case is meditation to be neglected. If Kal interferes, you ignore him. Let him do what he likes; you do your duty.

I am glad that you meditate for about an hour in the posture. When adopting the posture to hear the sound current, you can put some cushion under your buttocks in the beginning. After a month or so this necessity will disappear. The meditation will improve gradually. Have patience. I am very pleased with you. The light will gradually become stationary. The light does not disappear. It is the mind that shakes. With the increase in concentration, the sound will leave the right ear and appear at the forehead, where you listen to it eventually.

While taking a bath there is slight concentration, and so immediately after it the sound becomes clearer.

The repetition of the five names by the mind in the eye centre brings in concentration, the contemplation on the Radiant Form of the Master inside gives the power to stay there, and the sound current lifts upward. Therefore, give more time to repetition so long as the Radiant Form of the Master has not been contacted. When the Form appears, then give up repetition and concentrate on the Form, and then the sound current will lead you upward, the Radiant Form acting as the guide.

"Must concentration become complete before we can reach the first region?" Yes. The attention should vacate the body and go inside. Then it will look as if the body is not yours. It is a corpse of someone else and you are separate from it. The same attention which was previously working within the physical body, below the eyes, now works inside on the astral plane. Without going into the astral plane, one cannot see what lies therein.

The duty of the parents towards their children ceases when they become self-supporting. The parents should help them to become independent.

Hindu society does not countenance divorce or separation. Sant Mat does not interfere with social customs. The relation of a Master with his disciples is spiritual.

The fate karma undoubtedly is strong. It has to be borne, and there is no escape from it. But, through meditation, the will power becomes so strong that a person does not feel or mind either its favourable or adverse effects. If meditation has taken us above the point from where the fate karma works on us, we become indifferent to its effect. Therefore, meditation is the antidote to karma.

Illness, consultation of doctors, and getting their treatment is also a part of karma. It is the way the debt of the doctor and of the druggist is cleared. Again, when a patient is getting treatment, his relations and friends cease making remarks and criticizing or bothering the patient, and the patient also has the satisfaction of having taken medicine.

The disciple's material welfare and his success or failure in business ventures is a matter of karma. Before he was born, his life course was all chalked out. The number of breaths he is to take, the steps he is to move, the morsels of food he is to eat, his pain and pleasures, his poverty and riches, his success and failure, were determined beforehand. He himself was the maker of his fate. What he had sown he is reaping now, and what he will sow now he will reap hereafter. If he remains worldly now, he will come back to this world, but if he changes over to the Master and the Word, he will go where the Master goes and where the Word comes from.

Only these two—the Master and the Word—are our real companions who go with us here as well as hereafter. All others associate with us with selfish motives, and their association brings us back in this world. How could such a benefactor as the Master, therefore, be a silent observer of what is happening with his disciple in life? He is giving necessary guidance and help as he thinks proper. If a child suffers from a boil, the mother herself takes the child to a doctor to have the boil opened. The child cries, but the mother sees to the benefit of the child and not to its cries, and has the boil opened and dressed. Hence, what ordinarily is called a misfortune is a blessing in disguise. It is a way of clearing an old account. It lightens the karmic load, and the Master is not unaware of it. The Master is playing his part, and, if the disciple plays his part well, the work of both is smoothened.

Please do not think of coming to India in the near future. We are having a lot of unrest at present. You may come over when times are better.

~

29. Yes, you have at last come on the right path, leading to your home from where you came in the beginning, ages ago. The first object is to make the mind motionless, so that mind and soul are collected in their centre behind the eyes. Till that happens, they do not begin to work inside.

Any posture that you can stay in for long, comfortably, would do. You can get such chairs made on which, on each side, you can rest your arms, and while sitting or squatting in the chair, can close your ears and eyes with your hands. The object of shutting the ears and eyes is to shut out external noises and external sights. This is only for some time in the beginning. When the mind and soul have become accustomed to sit motionless in their centre, then the hands need not be used, as the whole body becomes senseless. It is not a question of time. It depends on love, faith, and eagerness as well.

I could wish that before coming to India you might have made some little progress on the path. Progress must be slow as the mind has been accustomed to wander out for ages, and it is not easy to make it sit still and give up its old habit.

~

30. I am glad that you are anxious for spiritual progress. You should go on gradually increasing the meditation time. The longer your meditation the greater will be your control of the mind. Then you will begin to derive pleasure from meditation, and the inner path will be opened out to you.

If you find that meditation before retiring to bed gives you disturbed sleep, you can discontinue it.

If you work hard on the path, you need not come to India. The Radiant Form of the Master will appear before you inwardly, talk to you, and answer all your questions.

It is true that personal contact is beneficial, but the Master is within every one of the disciples, and those far off should try to work hard on the path while remaining at home. Their going in depends upon the intensity of their love and faith and the amount of work they put in. The Master is near you and in you, and not far off.

Regarding your question, whether to quit when you begin to feel jittery, it is really the mind which is the source of all disturbance. You should try to continue to hold on a little longer every time, so that you may feel stronger and able to fight these obstacles. In the beginning one has to fight the mind and overcome the uneasiness, and persist in holding the centre. By so doing, the mind gives up its restlessness and becomes calm.

~

31.   The more time you devote to meditation, the more distinctly you will hear the sound current, which makes for peace of mind or, as you put it, helps us in chaining the monkey. I am glad to read that your meditation is improving. For ages the mind has been developing an intense longing for the things of this world which ostensibly satisfy it for some time but cease to do so after a while. The best way to divert the mind from the mundane baubles is to give it a taste of the inner bliss which far transcends any earthly joy. This inner bliss can be attained by going in and listening to the inner Sound constantly or at least for as long as is possible every day. This is how the monkey can be effectively chained.

I am glad that you consider meditation the most important business in life. You should increase your time for meditation. It should not be for less than two and a half hours at a stretch, whether the mind takes interest in meditation or not. Sometimes the mind avoids it on petty excuses. When it behaves like this it should be punished by increasing the time that day by another half-hour. With the increase in time, the concentration will be complete, the attention will go in, and the sound current will be your constant companion, giving you joy and peace.

~

32.   I wish that all of you who have received initiation may go inside the eye centre, become the dwellers of the beautiful mansions your Creator has made for you, and be masters of these in your own right. In a way it is not difficult. One is only to look inside one's own self instead of looking out. Yet it is difficult in a way, on account of our having so little hold over our mind. With patience and skilful handling, man has trained wild animals, even lions. By repetition of the names and by hearing the sound current, and all this in its own interest, the mind can be trained to sit inside the eye centre and enjoy that sweetness and bliss which it has not tasted before.

Mind needs vigilance of a higher order than is given by parents in bringing up their children. It is a very wayward child. So long as it is not trained, it is our worst enemy; but when trained, it is the most faithful companion. And the point is that one has to train it to get the best out of it and to realise his spiritual origin. This can only be done in the human life. We are lucky that we are human beings and have the opportunity to go in now, in this life. Why leave it to uncertain future? So with love and faith in the Master, keep on with your repetition and listening to the sound current, and all will be well.

My advice to you is that there should be no break in your daily meditation. If sometime there is not enough time, the meditation may be reduced that day but not neglected. There is a proverb here: "If you are going fox hunting, go with the preparation of a lion hunter." The same applies to mind hunting. Every day one should be on the job with renewed determination.

good gist

~

33. Your desire to come closer to the Master and render service to him is natural and laudable. The best service to the Master is to do devotional practice with love and faith as instructed; for, by doing so, you do Master's work. You help him in performing his duty of taking you to Sach Khand. Realise the Master within you. He is very near, in the third eye.

Man is the highest form of creation. The lower forms of life—beasts, birds, insects, and the vegetable kingdom—have not the capacity to cast off their coverings of mind and matter and to be one with the Creator. The angels (life in paradise, in the astral plane) are simply enjoying the fruits of the good actions that they performed in human life, and when that period is over, they too will be reborn as men, and their further course will be determined by the sort of actions they will perform then.

The point is, the angels have not the capacity to unite with the Creator. This capacity is given to man, and man alone, and therein lies his greatness. All his life he has worked against his own interest. If he fails to utilize this unique opportunity of achieving the real object of human life, he will be the greatest loser. Parents, children, food and drink are available to all forms of life, but not Nam—the sound current. Man has the capacity to grasp it. It is within him, behind the focus of the eyes, and is ringing all the twenty-four hours, as if calling him back.

While doing his normal duty—living with his family, earning his daily bread, serving his community and country—he should find time to make contact with this current by first withdrawing his attention from the nine portals of the body and holding it in the tenth portal—the eye focus. It does not cost him anything. The attention, which is running out uncontrolled, has to be held in the focus of the eyes by making the attention do some work at this focus. That work is the repetition of the five holy names.

The result that inevitably follows from this practice is that the attention will cease to run wild, will come within the body, and then from the body, will withdraw to the eye focus. First the feet and then the legs and arms will go numb. Then the attention will come up along the spinal cord, and, when it is all inside the focus, it will appear that this body is not mine, that I am separate from it and will not like to enter into it again. The covering of the coarse matter will be cast off. The attention will then be uninfluenced by worldly happenings, because it has detached itself from the material world, and will then be able to catch the current without interruption. In time, it will rise up and be on its way home.

There are no failures in Sant Mat. Sooner or later, the soul that is keeping its contact with the sound current will reach its home. When the way to the home is known, and one keeps the way, where is the room for doubt that home will be reached? Let the other brothers and sisters read this.

~

34.   I am glad to learn that the sound current interests you and you devote your spare time to hearing it. The sound current is a wave of the ocean of spirituality, of which the soul is a drop. The ocean, wave, and the drop are alike in nature. All three are one. If the soul catches the current and follows it, it can reach its destination, the ocean—and, by merging itself in the ocean, can itself become the ocean.

Every human being has this current in him, but is disconnected from it by the mind, which has placed itself between the soul and the current to keep them apart. Ever since the creation started and the soul separated from the current, it has not gone back to its spiritual home. The simple reason why we find ourselves here in this material world now is that the curtain of the mind keeps the soul ignorant of the current and keeps it attached to the material of this world, which is changeable. Our hopes and desires are confined to this changeable world, and, for their fulfilment, we take birth here again and again, and thereby ever remain dissatisfied and in unrest.

Mind is fond of sweet taste. It does not find lasting taste in the changing environments; therefore, it runs from object to object, and continues wandering. If it can get a lasting thing and a sweet thing, it will certainly attach itself to that and cease its wandering. The current is the only lasting thing;

all else is changeable. Therefore, when mind attaches itself to the current, and cultivates it, it receives what it has been longing for, for so long. On getting it, the mind becomes tranquil, the curtain is lifted, and the soul unites with the waves and the ocean.

With love and faith, continue your practices. Bring the scattered mind into the eye focus and vacate the body below the eyes, so that you go nearer the current and come under its full influence, to get full advantage of it. This is the sole aim of human life....

Everyone uses his intellectual powers for earning his livelihood. Spiritual powers, however, should not be wasted on material things. They should be conserved for making further spiritual progress.

~

35. I am glad to read in your letter that you are a seeker after truth for the sake of truth. Truth is valuable indeed. It is the only thing we should run after. It is not the property of any country, religion, or person; but everyone, irrespective of caste, creed, or country, is entitled to it. It is within everybody. Just as water is present under all soils, and those who toil and dig for it get their lands irrigated and succeed in raising crops, similar is the case with seekers after truth. They will surely get it if they toil for it. They have only to seek it within themselves. In case there is any point you are not clear about, please write to me.

~

36. Concentration of mind is the key to spiritual truth. In this world it is not difficult to be a king or to have sons and daughters, wealth and luxury, but it is difficult to get at the spiritual truth. Again, a heart that loves the truth is rare. You are on the way to it. Sound current is the road and Master is the guide. The greater the interest you will take in it and value it, the sooner your soul will benefit and be purified.

When I address you as "Dear Daughter," it is from the spiritual viewpoint. Our worldly relations, like husband and wife, son and father or brother, are temporary—at best till death, when we part not only from them but even from our own bodies. The soul is separate from the three bodies (material, mental, and causal); also from Pind and maya. Only Satguru remains with the soul and takes it to Sach Khand, the place of perpetual bliss. What better name than son or daughter can be given to a soul that accompanies so far?

Study your books and grasp the truth they contain, and make that truth the part and parcel of your life, but remember that if that truth is not grasped by practising inwardly, the books have been studied in vain. The knowledge is within you and it is from within yourself that you are to find it. Books give the description and induce you to go within, but do not give the experience and knowledge. Description of a thing is not the thing.

Concentration of mind is the first and foremost thing here. Mind also does not like to be imprisoned because it has been free from time immemorial—ever since we separated from the abode of bliss. You should therefore concentrate your mind and soul within you, in the focus of the eyes, and understand that as long as the current of the whole body has not centred in the eyes, and the body has not been rendered feelingless (you would be conscious within but not conscious of the body), the mind has not been imprisoned.

In this process, when you find your hands and feet or other parts of the body becoming unconscious, do not be afraid of this condition. These have to be rendered numb, for as long as they are conscious, the mind has not been concentrated. And with a wandering mind, the path inside is not seen. When your mind is collected in the focus of the eyes, you will see light and stars within, and when you see one single, large white star, fix your attention on it and try to catch the bell sound within.

When you see any form inside, then repeat the five names. And write to me the details of the form and of the tone with it, if any, but do not speak of these inner visions to anyone else. Again, do not accept anything offered by a spirit within.

∽

37. You say you prefer to be alone, for when alone you feel the presence of a host of disembodied individuals and this fills you with joy and peace. It is good to be alone, provided the mind is well under control, has an inward tendency and takes pleasure in the spiritual exercises. When you feel the presence of the disembodied spirits, repeat the five names revealed to you. Evil spirits do not stay when those five names are repeated and thus they would not be able to deceive you. Only good spirits stay, and the spirit that stays when these names are used is worthy of your trust. Converse freely with it.

If you continue your efforts and concentrate in the eye focus, your attention will be drawn inward and, rising a little higher, you will come across the Astral Form of the Master which will stay when the five names are repeated. This Form will be coming and going in the beginning, but if you will increase your love for it, then it will stay and converse with you and will reply to your enquiries, and will guide you and take you upward towards Sahansdal Kanwal (thousand-petalled lotus). But the effort should be done with love and not simply as a matter of routine. Do it with a longing to see the Master.

You say the progress is at a snail's pace. That which is acquired slowly and after effort is permanent, and that which is acquired quickly and without effort is transitory and subject to loss. Slow and steady wins the race.

Ever since we separated from the primal source, our mind and soul have been wandering outwardly so much that we have forgotten what our source was, and have so wretchedly attached ourselves to things of this world—though knowing that we are to leave them one day, yet our attachment with them is so deep that we always think about them and never about the primal Source. This acquired habit will go, but by and by; and as the attention will be withdrawn from outward things, it will go inward.... To help the initiate is the mission of my life.

〜

38.   When you sit in the exercises, then see that the mind is at rest and does not go out and unnecessarily think about other things. When, by repetition of the names with attention fixed in the eye focus, you have become unconscious of the body below the eyes, then your attention will catch the sound current.

Select the sound resembling the church bell and discard all other sounds. Then slowly your soul will leave the body and collect in the eyes and become strong. Then fix your attention in the biggest star, so much that you forget everything else except the Sound and the star. Then this star will burst and you will see what is within it and beyond.

After crossing the star you will have to cross the sun and the moon. Then you will see the Form of the Master. When that Form becomes steady it will reply. This Form will reply to all of your enquiries and guide you to higher stages. I do not wish you to stop at the appearance of the stars but wish to take you higher up. These stars are of the first sky only, and Hindu philosophers have spoken of seven skies. You will also see other skies.

It is necessary to give up and forget about the things of childhood. You should look ahead instead of looking back.

You have expressed a wish to see the Master so that you could visualize him when your thoughts are turned to him. After crossing the star, the sun, and the moon you will see that Form which will never leave you, not even for a moment.

~

39. The patience with which you have borne the pain is admirable, particularly when you say that despite the pain you were able to withdraw the attention to the eye focus. The karmic law is supreme and inevitable, and the sooner we reconcile ourselves with it the better. Nothing happens which has not been ordained. As far as possible, no requests for physical needs should be made, for whatever you are destined to get you will get without fail. From the Master, ask for the Master, for when he grants you that, you will get everything with him. Why ask charity from a giver instead of the giver himself?

Listen to the Sound while sitting in the eye focus with attention on the light. Do not go after the Sound. If you leave the focus, the attention is scattered. When hearing the low sound, you should hear the finest sound within the low sound at the eye focus. The power that is to uplift you will come automatically.

When any evil spirit appears, repeat the names. It will disappear. With the exception of the Master, you are not to salute or bow down to anyone within, for by so doing there would be loss of spiritual power.

~

40. Just as in spite of physical hindrance you have forged ahead, similarly we are to go ahead inwardly with the spirit current in spite of the mental distractions which come in our way. As the karmic debt grows lighter, the inward progress increases. Karmas are performed by the body and the mind; as long as the spirit current is working with the mind in the mental sphere, the mind is active and is doing mental actions. When the current is withdrawn from both, then there is no karma.

The devotee beholds stars, sun, and moon within. It is the wavering of the mind which produces eclipses or casts shadows. To assist people directly when they suffer from evil spirits or, as a matter of fact, from any cause, means consumption of energy. Psychic power is only the concentration of the mind. This does not decrease when one follows Sant Mat, for the saints' teaching is based on the concentration of mind. But progress cannot continue if the concentrated energy is utilized for purposes other than further inward progress. The utilization of spiritual power for controlling spirits, etc., is therefore to be avoided.

$\sim$

41. When you sit for the exercises, assume an easy position. When one begins to feel tired, that is the time of struggle with the mind, and there should be no surrendering here. One should keep on the struggle a bit longer every day.

Frequent changes of posture mean undoing of concentration. The first stage will have been completed when the scattered mind has been collected in the eye focus and takes pleasure in sitting there. One will be superconscious within. Then the Form of the Master will appear. To distinguish this Form from the forms assumed by the negative power, you have been given the method already. The first stage is a bit difficult, for it is crossed with struggle. The journey beyond is pleasant. The karma and the struggle are interdependent. When the karmic debt becomes light, the progress will be rapid. A soul that is free from the body and the mind can perform no binding karma.

∼

42.   The appearance of stars and suns at hit-and-miss times is due to lack of concentration. Sometimes in sleep, when the mind is quiet, the soul rises up of itself and sees what lies within, but cannot remain there long on account of its newness to those regions, nor does it possess the necessary energy to stay there. On these occasions the sound current is absent. Only when the soul rises with the current will it be superconscious.

You say you heard music within which surpassed all that you had heard before. This music is of a very elementary nature, and is not the music of the pure spirit realm. It arises from the vibrations of the astral plane. Maulana Rum, a great Persian saint, says: "If He were to give out a bit of that divine music, the dead would rise from their tombs."

Fasting is not a necessary element to meeting the Lord. Whenever there is heaviness in the stomach, fasting will remove it. It plays no part in the training of the mind and should not be practised. There is nothing like normality.

∼

43.   The genuine anxiety for missing the exercises for one reason or another is a sort of spiritual exercise by itself. The mind remains directed inwardly. But attempt should be made to find time for the exercises. Social service is good. It partly purifies the mind, but it does not lift up the mind nor the soul. The uplift will be done by the current only. Hence, the time reserved for the exercises should not be spent in doing service to others. I like your charitable disposition, but would

advise you not to miss the exercise. Every moment spent in the exercises counts. The benefit is in proportion to the time spent.

≈

44.   I am glad to read that you have grasped the significance of service to sound current and of justice to yourself. Guru Nanak, a great saint of the sixteenth century and the first of the Sikh Gurus, says: "If one can concentrate his attention in the third eye, then he has done all the pilgrimages, devotions, kindnesses, and charities." The soul is hungry. Its food is the current. It finds no rest without it. Its wanderings will continue as long as it has not merged itself in the current.

≈

45.   I was glad to read that you saved the child through your careful handling when the doctors had failed with their medicines. The change in diet and the surroundings had their effect. Children imbibe influences imperceptibly but most surely. Serenity and tranquility are positive virtues, and a serene and calm mind has much more power than a turbulent, vindictive mind. Temper influences temper. That is why so great an emphasis is laid on good company. Even wild beasts calm down when they come across a serene mind. Goodness is its own reward.

When the attention goes in newly and sees the light, it cannot behold it long. It is not used to it, and cannot stand the glare, so to say. By and by, as it will grow powerful, it will have the capacity to face the light and then pierce it.

I also note with pleasure that you have no desire left now to consult the astrologers or mediums. They can foretell but not alter events.

≈

46. Will you please state in your next letter how far in the body you succeed in the withdrawal of the current from the extremities of the body. The current is in very intimate contact with the matter of the body. The separation from matter is a slow process which requires constancy and determination. It is only a question of time. There is no room for disappointment.

When love begins to run smooth, the charm is gone and life becomes a monotony and a routine. Some shock is necessary to break the monotony. A period of disappointment intervenes often in the life of the devotee. This is desirable. It has a purpose. It gives the shock. After a time spent in disappointment, the intensity of love for spiritual uplift increases. A temporary obstruction in the path of determination gives it momentum to proceed ahead.

~

47. You appear a bit concerned about your slow progress. The power—Guru—is within you and is ever busy in making matters easy for you. That power is far more eager to meet you than you can possibly think of. The karmic debt of many an intricate nature is to be paid, and it is proper that it should be paid while in the physical frame, so that there is no stop on the way within.

Your duty is to sit within and knock at the door, and the door will open. The power within does not err. It will open the door when it finds that the time has come. Increase your love and devotion, and entrust yourself entirely to its care. The power within is not ignorant of what you are doing. It is with you and constantly watches you and guides you. When your love for that power exceeds your love for yourself and the "I-ness" has been replaced by "Thou-ness," the Form of the Guru will make its appearance visible within.

48.   In your letter you gave a detailed account of your condition as the spirit current is withdrawn to the eye focus. You
make mention of the pain in the limbs which you experienced
in the beginning but which has now disappeared. At the
fourth ganglion you are troubled with gas, and later on with
the constriction of the muscles of the throat; and then with
the smothering of saliva; and at times up to the fifth ganglion
there is absolutely no sensation. Later on you see the interplay of light and darkness and the dim stars. With time and
practice, the process will become practically instantaneous,
just as you say that withdrawal from the limbs is instantaneous and without pain.

The spirit has lived in bodies for ages, and its connection
with the body has become so perfect that the withdrawal
looks almost abnormal. But that is through ignorance. It
falsely believes the body to be its home, and when the spirit
learns that its home is not in matter but that it is imprisoned
by it, and that now in the human form there is the chance to
break this connection, it wakes up, and the longing to ascend
is aroused. It gains strength slowly. Rising and falling and
struggling against mind and matter, it makes headway up
with the help of the saints. The rise and fall are natural and
so is the struggle. For that which is achieved after struggle
gives strength, self-reliance, and incentive to go ahead.
Achievement thus obtained is lasting and can be reproduced
at will.

Before you had taken to these spiritual exercises, your
spirit went up occasionally without your having any control
over it. It had a glance at the stars and so forth, and often
returned with knowledge of what was to happen in the future. But you could not create this condition at will. Now you
go to the fifth ganglion. Only one step further and you will
have withdrawn the current to within the eye focus, and all

that lies within will be an open book to you. It takes time, and slow progress is better.

The troubles of gas and constriction of the muscles and flow of saliva will not interfere if you keep your attention in the eyes instead of attending to gas or saliva or the breathing. When we talk with our friends we do not give any attention to breathing and the like. Similarly, in exercises (repetition) we are talking with somebody at the eye focus and not below it. The idea of breathing or gas or saliva arises only when the attention falls below the eyes, and the moment it goes up again the idea of breathing and so forth must disappear.

In the beginning, when the current leaves any centre there is pain at that centre. And at the heart centre it appears as if one is going to die. But with practice, the passage through these centres becomes smooth and painless. Two hours at a time are enough.... Coming to the eye focus is dying while living.

~

49.   I am glad you have located the star. You may now fix your attention in it and when this is fixed and gets steady, the star will burst and you will cross through it....

Pain and pleasure of the devotee are in the hands of the Master. He arranges them as he sees fit. The devotee should take delight in pain, for that is also a gift from him.... A real devotee makes no distinction in pain and delight; his business is devotion.

~

50.   The cluster of stars does not disappear. It is the shaky mind that wavers and loses sight of them.... The spirit goes within and returns. The sky and stars that you see, and the voices that you hear now, are on the way to the gate within.

Within, you will hear much sweet music, hearing which the spirit will waken up and the mind will sleep. The music that we hear in the world outside dulls the spirit but awakens the passions of the mind. On hearing this inner music, a spirit would not covet the throne of a monarch.... Anger, passion, attachment, greed, and pride come under control; but that point is not yet reached ... but when you see the Astral Form of the Master and when your spirit will stay in that Form, the state will be reached.... That music will spontaneously attract you and pull you up.

The stage of the inward journey that you are crossing now takes rather a long time. This is the transitional stage. Spirit is accustomed to stay out and you are forcing it within. The spirit permeates every part of the body. It takes time to collect it. When this stage is crossed, the path beyond is easy. Purified spirit is attracted by the magnetic music within....

There is only one way to destroy karma, and that is through the practice of the sound current. When saints initiate a soul, they advise it to avoid evil deeds and do good actions, but without any desire for their reward.

This much for the present actions (kriyaman karma). The store karma (sinchit) is sometimes taken over by the saints. And as to the fate karma (pralabdh), that which remains to be undergone is paid up slowly during the lifetime. The severity of the fate karma is not felt so much by a devoted satsangi.

As the spirit gets strong, the will power increases, and the power to bear the karmas is strengthened. By following the advice of the Master, the disciple becomes karma-free and is fit to reach his abode.

When you will have crossed this sky, you will meet the Master's Astral Form. This appears to be coming and going, but in reality it does not. It is the mind that shakes. When this Form will stay, fix your attention on his face so much that you forget whether he is you or you are he. When there is that much concentration, he will talk to you, answer all your questions, and shall always be with you and will guide you onward to the next step, showing innumerable scenes of the astral plane on the way.

On reaching Sahansdal Kanwal (thousand-petalled lotus) the five vices of passion, anger, attachment, greed, and pride will disappear forever. In the forms of small boys they will inform you they are going away now, for the place is too hot for them to stay. These negative powers will no longer be able to give shock to the spirit.

After crossing the flames of Sahansdal Kanwal and going through considerable spiritual journey, you will reach the second sky with its stars and moons and suns, which lies below Trikuti. Crossing this sky, you will enter a crooked tunnel ... then you enter the Brahm stage, which is so strange and wonderful!

~

51. Genuine grief (over separation from the Lord) gives impetus to further progress.... Saint Paul is perfectly right when he says: "I die daily." He who goes within the eye focus daily, dies daily, and for him death holds no fear.

... The Sound is in both ears. On the right side the sound is from the positive power, and on the left side it is from the negative power, Kal. The sound on the left side is never to be attended to. The sound on the right side is to be grasped. Really, this sound is not associated with the ear. It comes from above. Because we have the habit of hearing sounds in the ear, we imagine that this sound is in the ear. While keeping the attention fixed in the middle of the two eyebrows, try to catch the sound current on the right, but do not go to the ear to catch the current. If you go to the ear to catch the current, you have left the eye focus. If you stick to the focus, you will soon find the sound leaving the ear and coming from above. It will have no connection with the ear, neither with the right nor the left. The sound that one hears outside the focus is not the pure sound and therefore has little attracting power. The bell sound is the sound that pulls up. The bell sound will not allow the mind to run away. It will hold the mind, or rather, the mind will stick to it like a piece of iron to a magnet.

~

52.   You know by experience the difference in this concentration and your previous idea of concentration. So long as the attention has not left the external objects and the body below the eyes, and does not sit calmly in the third eye; or, in other words, if it has not made the third eye its home, the concentration is incomplete. In the incomplete state the attention may catch the current for a short time but will lose touch with it again. This make and break is the transitional state. In course of time it will require effort to bring the attention out from the focus to carry on the functions in this world.

We are out to conquer the mind—the mind that governs the world.... Study the intelligent man. Is he at peace? Does he know rest? Nobody is happy. We are fighting a powerful enemy.

In America you do not come across the various ways people have followed to attain spirituality. In Europe and America, in their pursuit of "science," the pioneers and their followers have made untold sacrifices. So in India particularly (and elsewhere also) there is any amount of effort in a variety of ways in spiritual science. Compared with these practices that of the Word is easy.

If for one reason or another sufficient progress has not been made by the satsangi while alive, then the practices can be done by the astral body. If the physical, astral, and causal planes have been crossed while alive, then on he goes after death. The continuity of progress is not broken.

~

53.   Other minor troubles will disappear.... The Sound will come. There is a combination of ten sounds here at the eye focus. Out of these catch the bell sound. Please keep to yourself whatever you may see within. If somebody offers anything within, please do not accept it. The negative powers frequently mislead. Avoid pride and do not be flattered. Humility is the armour of the saints and their devotees.

~

54.   You say that X refuses to accept initiation on account of family opposition. You are perfectly right in not urging her, but let her feel free to do as she likes. Nam is not so cheap that it should be broadcast. It is a rare article.

Anybody who spends his spiritual powers for fulfilment of wishes connected with this world, cannot have access to high spiritual worlds. Mental and spiritual powers should be conserved to secure access to higher planes of spirituality. Worldly desires pull the attention down and bring it outward. If one spends here what he earns, then there is nothing left for the day of reckoning. Anybody who wishes to go high, will have to keep his attention detached from the world and its affairs.

The names by themselves carry no value. It is their practice in the proper way that brings benefit. The names, if repeated at the centre of attention, will bring the attention in concentration. No more, no less. That is the limit of the course of simran. To go up, the sound current is necessary. Without sound current, there is no way to Sach Khand.

Merely to know the names, and to take them as the secret of Sant Mat, is ignorance. Sound current *is* Sant Mat, and the sound current that pulls one up is met at Sahansdal Kanwal; and to reach that far, you know from experience what effort is needed.

So long as one has not freed his attention from matter (his body), and come inside the eye focus, nor made contact with the Astral Form of the Master and thereby cast off his "I-ness," one is not accepted by the sound current. So long as one is encased in the body (the attention working in the nine portals of the body), he is worldly and of this world; and so long as one is encased in "I-ness," he is not of the Master.

The "I-ness" is the curtain between him and the Master's Astral Form. When he has realised the Master within or, in other words, the Master within has accepted him, he is fit to catch the current uninterruptedly. Then the attention remains absorbed in it. An about-turn has taken place. The attention that was finding it so difficult to get in, now does not like to come out.

Let people say what they like. To talk of philosophy is one thing—anybody can talk about it—but to be a philosopher is another. There is a proverb here which may be expressed as, "If a dog walks through a cotton field, he does not come out dressed in a suit."

There is nothing in Sant Mat which needs to be concealed. Everyone is carrying it within himself already and can have it by searching within himself. The only difficulty is that it is not easy to go inside; and if one goes in, he does not talk about it lightly.

"Y writes that he has found out that it is not necessary for any one of us to go to India just for the initiation but that we can receive equal benefit or substantially equal benefit by remaining here at home."

As far as the Master is concerned, time and space make no difference to him, for the Master is not confined to physical form. The Master takes on this form for man's guidance— to talk to him, to sympathize with him, to make friends with him, to develop confidence and faith in him, to induce him to seek peace and happiness within himself, to show him the way to it, to teach him by becoming an example, to develop in him godlike attributes, and to pull him up out of his physical form to his astral form.

And, so long as the disciple has not contacted the Astral Form of the Master, in other words, has not become independent of his own physical form, he is a limited being. Thus he is subject to influences of his environments and the ups and downs of life, which confound his intellect, put him in doubt, and often throw him off the right track. To remove his doubts and seek support for keeping on the track, the disciple will have to approach the Master; and if he is far off, he will stand in need of some sort of means of keeping in touch with the Master—an intermediary to carry verbal messages, post, telegraph, telephone, or even wireless. The case will be something like a patient receiving treatment from a physician at a distant place instead of receiving treatment by entering the physician's hospital, or like a student receiving tuition through correspondence instead of studying in a school, sitting at the feet of his teacher. However, there is something in the personal contact with the physician and the teacher which does not come in the prescription or in the lesson received through correspondence. The same holds good with the Master. There is thus a lot of difference in being near the Master and in being at a distance from him.

... The view that one must see something at the time of initiation or he would never be able to see anything later is wrong. Experience also does not support it. Everyone is running his own course of life, which is different from all others. No two persons are alike in habit, form, and thought. All are at different stages of development. At initiation, they cannot be expected to behave alike. Only few see anything then. The majority take time—some weeks, some months, and some years. All are not equally keen.

A lamp which contains all the parts and is charged with oil and wick, and is adjusted properly, needs only a touch of flame to kindle it. A lamp containing all its parts along with oil and wick, but not in adjustment, needs some effort to kindle it. But a lamp that is leaking and has run short of oil or in which the wick or some essential part is missing, needs some time to put it in order before it will be fit to kindle into flame.

I am happy with the efforts you are putting in your bhajan. Bhajan is our first duty. All other pursuits of life should be taken as a means to attain this end.

I also wish that you should rise up internally and make contact with the Master within you. Please put in a little more effort and make the whole body senseless so that the attention goes right out of it and remains centred in the focus.

… Enclosed is a translation from a poem from the Sikh scriptures which brings out the importance of Name in comparison with other practices.

A HYMN FROM THE ADI GRANTH
RAG SORATH OF ARJUN DEV, FIFTH GURU—ASHT PADIAN

I read the sacred books (as a daily religious duty), and studied the Vedas minutely, and performed the yoga practices, like *newli karma*,[1] and controlling the

---

1. *Newli karma*: To sit erect by lowering the shoulders and flattening the back and, by the force of the breath, to move the abdomen right and left, as well as up and down, as curds are churned in the churning vessel.

kundalini;[1] but I did not get rid of the "five ones."[2] On the contrary, the spirit of egotism got a stronger hold of my mind.

O Dear Friend! That is not the way to union (with God). I performed such actions of various kinds. Having been disappointed, I have resigned myself at the Supreme Lord's door, and pray to him to endow me with the power of discrimination. I observed silence. I used the palms of my hands as utensils, roamed about naked in forests, visited places of pilgrimage all over the world, but was not able to shake off illusion.

With faith in my mind, I took up my abode at holy places and observed austerities as a means of salvation,[3] but millions of such efforts cannot purify the mind.

By giving away in charity—gold, one's wife, horses, and elephants—in many ceremonious ways, and by making over lots of grain, clothes, and land (for charitable purposes), one cannot attain access to the gate of the Supreme Being.

One who is always engaged in performing various types of worships or in performing the six actions enjoined on the Brahmans,[4] with egoistic frame of mind, does not get the way of union with the Divine Being.

---

1. *Kundalini* is the coiled energy (above the *mul chakra*) which on unwinding, becomes connected with the spinal cord and gives the practitioner miraculous powers.
2. The "five ones": The five deadly enemies; namely, *kam* (lust), *krodh* (anger), *lobh* (greed), *moh* (worldly attachment), and *ahankar* (egoism).
3. There is a saw (called *karvat*) at Benares. The priests in charge of the saw claimed that anyone who had his head cut off by it would go to heaven. Many wealthy people and rajas sacrificed their lives in this way to attain heaven, and left their wealth to the priests. This practice has since been stopped.
4. The six actions: Acquiring knowledge and imparting it to others; the giving and receiving of charities; the performance of *yajnas* (rituals), and causing them to be performed by others.

Then I tried unsuccessfully the practice of hatha yoga, the eighty-four postures of yogis and *siddhas*.[1] These prolonged life, but did not stop repeated births, and did not take me nearer to God.

The revelries of kings, their pomp and show, their undisputed authority, the sensual pleasures and luxuries enjoyed by them—these open the door to the infernal hell.

Listening to the divine music inside, and being in the company of saints, are the foremost of all acts of piety. Nanak says these fall to the lot of that person who is pre-destined to obtain them. O God! Thy servant is intoxicated with this wine (of divine love). By the grace of the remover of the distress of humble beings, this mind is absorbed in the divine music.

SUMMARY

One cannot attain salvation by external rites, leading a life of outward piety, and by performing religious deeds like under-taking pilgrimages, keeping fasts, bathing in sacred pools or rivers, engaging in yoga practices, or other similar acts. No one can be really happy by enjoying sensual pleasures. True happiness or bliss and salvation are attainable only by the company of saints and the practice of Surat Shabd Yoga.

∼

55.   Some points are intended for and are appreciated only by high-level devotees. The code of lovers is different from the code of intellectuals.

"If one here in America, by means of diligent efforts, should rise up within, would that not prove the possibility of doing so to the other American disciples?" To rise up within

---

1. Those who developed the highest miraculous powers.

by diligent efforts, under the guidance of a Master far off from America, is not only possible but is practicable by all. If it were not practicable, initiation would not be given at all. The comparison, however, is between two disciples, both putting in diligent efforts, one at a distance from the Master and other close to the Master. The second one is distinctly at an advantage.

Withdrawal of the attention or vital current from the nine portals of the body and holding or concentrating it in the tenth (eye focus) is done by the standard "simran, bhajan, and dhyan" method. It is a slow affair and takes time. The current begins to withdraw from the extremities. First, hands and feet go numb, and as practice advances from legs up to the knees and then thighs, slowly the whole body, further up along the spinal cord, should go feelingless while the *man* (mind) is conscious within the eye centre.

Sant Mat, or the system of the sound current, is all-inclusive. All other systems end in its first two regions, most of them in the first. You may gladly discuss the theory of Freemasonry in the light of Sant Mat. Of course, the greater your actual inner experience of Sant Mat, the more convincing will be your talks. And when you have contacted the Master internally, you will be a different man. You will have traversed Pind and part of Anda, and will be in a position to get directly as much help from the Master as you desire. As a matter of fact, it will then be the Master speaking through you or for you. I would therefore suggest that you make your internal rise as your primary goal and give it your first consideration, and giving others the benefit of your experience as a secondary object only.

All kinds of food are not suitable for all purposes. The food of a wrestler does not suit a man engaged in office work or literary pursuits. Each kind of food has its particular effect on the system, and thereby on the mind. Dull, loaded souls do not feel this effect. Meat and eggs (fertile or infertile), and highly concentrated foods and intoxicants do not suit those who wish to subdue animal nature in them and who wish to still their mind and gain access to subtle planes. This is not mere theory; it is based on practical experience. Even followers of systems that concentrate their attention on centres below the eyes, and who usually do not object to the use of meat, give up its use of their own accord and scrupulously abstain from it when the attention rises above the eye focus.

I do not remember allowing the use of eggs—fertile or infertile—to anyone, and if it was done, it should be taken as a special case. On the point that infertile eggs do not contain the germ of life hence their use should be permitted, then it would be but a short step for the weak minds to take, from infertile to fertile eggs. It is safer to keep them out from the dietary of an *abhyasi* (spiritual practitioner).

"Bowing to internal powers." When a person bows to another, he accepts him as his superior and subordinates his mind to him, and goes in a receptive mood, ready to accept and absorb the influence of the person bowed to. If the person is some form of representation of the negative power, then bowing to him will leave a negative effect which is not desirable. Devotees are therefore instructed not to bow to any personage internally on the path, except to the Master. All forms, except the Master, will disappear when the five names are repeated. Hence, when inside on the path, bowing to Master alone is justified.

This principle can be applied in practice when dealing with persons in daily life or in a ceremony. The devotee has his Master with him in his eye focus. At the time of initiation, the Master placed himself there in his Astral Form. So when in his dealings in this world, a devotee has formally or otherwise to bow to another, the proper course for him is that he should think of the Master in his eye centre and bow to him. This will not interfere with any ceremony. He will have bowed to his Master and thereby avoided the influence of others, while others will see from his movements that his conduct towards society and ceremony is correct. Outwardly he deals with the world as he did before, but internally he is bowing to his Master.

Kal, Niranjan, and the negative power are one and the same.

~

56.   She asks if she gathers karma in her professional work, and if she should discontinue giving massage. Strictly speaking, we gather karma every minute; but many of these karmas are neutralized, as it were, and rendered ineffective and inoperative by karmas of an opposite character. And, finally, all karmas are destroyed by Shabd. This final destruction, of course, takes place only at Trikuti, but the regular daily practice of listening to the internal Sound is also very helpful. An impersonal attitude, doing things for the sake of duty and not as a matter of personal inclination or personal gratification, incurs no karma.

Sant Mat does not bar real and earnest seekers, but we are not out for collecting mere numbers. We want men who will follow the path, and be a credit to the satsang. There is no "royal road" anywhere in the world in the sense that you should gain something without having made any effort, but it is a royal road in the sense that it leads you straight and unmistakably to the mansions of the Most High and with the minimum of trouble.

Saints are liberal and broad-minded, and do not attach much importance to the outer husk of forms and formalities. What they want is that people should go in, whether as Hindus, Muslims, or Christians. That is their sole mission and sole interest—to make people go in, and, with the help of Shabd— the true Word—reach their original spiritual home whence they had originally come.

Yes, the principles of Sant Mat are eternal and immutable, and all saints, from times immemorial, whether in this or in any other land, have preached the same doctrine of Shabd as the only means of true salvation, and initiated their pupils into the mysteries of the five shabds. So did Soami Ji, and he has moreover left incontestable proofs in his writings, in which he has emphasized the importance of the five shabds over and over again. Our teachings have not been changed in any way. They are the same as they were and are in perfect accord with the teachings of Soami Ji—nay, they *are* Soami Ji's teachings.

~

57.   If X dissuaded you from taking part in healing work it was for your own good. You have been initiated. What was the object of initiation?

The souls in this world have been wandering in millions of births and deaths from the time of the creation, and they are subject to pain and pleasure in their various bodies. No one can tell when these souls separated from their source in the pure spiritual region—Sat Lok—and descended into this world. No one can tell how many bodies each soul has had to adopt up to this time. Sometimes it was in the vegetable king- dom, sometimes in the insect world, sometimes it assumed the form of a bird, sometimes of a beast, sometimes of a man, angel, god, devil, and so on.

In every form the soul had to pass through pain and plea- sure, and at the end of every life, it had to appear before the divine accountant (Dharam Rai) to render accounts of its actions before him, and was again sent to this world in a form appropriate to its karma.

God made man in His own image. Man is the top of creation. It is only in human form that man is endowed with superior faculties and is better off than the lower creation; yet, in this human form also, no one can claim that he is perfectly happy. When this is the case with the top of the creation, what can be said of the lower forms? Their life is simply miserable; and, being devoid of sense, they cannot liberate themselves from birth and death.

It is only man—and not even gods and angels—who has been endowed by the Almighty with faculties, by developing which he can attain the highest spiritual region, provided he is initiated by a perfect Master and works hard to elevate his soul to the higher regions. Without a perfect Master, however hard one may try, he cannot make much progress in the spiritual world.

The sole object of initiation by the perfect Masters is to help the disciple to free himself from the bondage of transmigration by taking his soul, in his lifetime, to the higher regions. If he fails to do this, then he cannot be certain of what may happen to him after death.

If the soul gives up this highest ideal and wanders into bypaths actuated by false ideas of service to humanity, or spends his spiritual powers not in elevating his soul but in foolish pursuits as curing the sick, and so forth, then he resembles a man whose own house is on fire, but instead of trying to extinguish the fire of his own house, he goes off watching the houses of others, to prevent them from catching fire.

The initiation that has been granted to you is like a wealthy man giving a quantity of seed to a poor farmer, so that by sowing the seeds into his lands he might raise good crops, and after harvesting them not only make himself rich but also help others to acquire riches. If the farmer, instead of sowing the seeds into his lands, distributes them to starving neighbours, then he may claim to have fed them for one or two days at the utmost; but when his seed is finished by such foolish distribution, then all shall starve, including the distributor himself.

The initiation given you is a seed to enable you, with your hard labour, to accumulate spiritual wealth and, after freeing your soul from the covers of mind and matter, to obtain everlasting life for yourself. And then you can do immense good to others.

What is real service to humanity? To free the soul—which has been for ages subject to transmigration—from the cycle of births, and to raise it to the pure spiritual region from where it will never be sent back to undergo births and deaths. All other forms of service are merely temporary.

If a person succeeds in healing the sick, still he cannot save them from death or give them everlasting bodies. After their death, they will have to assume lower forms, according to their karma; but the man who tried to heal them by using his spiritual powers and thus abused them, will die spiritually destitute.

～

58. As for vicarious atonement, such doctrines you can leave alone. Nobody wants you to believe them. When you go into higher regions, you will see the working of the law of karma.

The Master does not expect anyone to idolize him. A boy, reading in primary classes, cannot judge the attainments of a B.A. or M.A. The Master only wants you to look upon him as your elder brother or friend, to follow his directions, as those of a benefactor, and work hard to go into the higher planes within you. When you go there, you will see for yourself the position and dignity of the Master in those regions.

It is suggested that you give up this false notion of service. Serve yourself first of all, then think of serving others. A prisoner cannot liberate another.

~

59. By the way, I have only one business, and that is to look after souls hungry for spiritual food and for release from birth and death, which is more than enough for me.

The four lives may be on the earth plane or elsewhere, just as the Master thinks fit. Saints, as a rule, try to send up loving, eager devotees much sooner.

Your ideas about the Master merging in the Deity and the disciples merging in the Master, and through him in the Deity, are correct.

The term "vicarious atonement" was not liked because it is a definite church dogma, though the idea is substantially correct. The Master, however, does not take all the unassigned sinchit karmas on himself, but only as many as he thinks necessary. You have no idea of this immense reserve which has gone on accumulating. They are finally destroyed in Trikuti, when the soul reaches there by the help of Shabd.

Thank you for your solicitude for my health. Please do not worry on that account. We have about a hundred thousand satsangis, and their spiritual needs have to be attended to, which means no small strain. Masters come in the world for the good and benefit of mankind, and think more of mankind's health, moral and spiritual, than of their own.

~

60.   You may please explain to them that the mind is no mean power and its control is not an easy walkover. If we carefully examine its working, we will find that it governs all creation, not only on the physical plane, but on the astral and causal planes as well. The angels in heavens, the learned, the pundits and commentators, the hermits and the family men, rich and poor, beasts, birds, insects, all do its bidding.

Under the powerful influence of mind, men act, and the acts become binding on them and become the cause of life hereafter. As we sow, so shall we reap. Whatever we are reaping now, we ourselves have sown before. Therefore, we are the makers of our own fate. The framework of our present life, which cannot be altered, was constructed by us before we appeared on this plane. We are also the makers of our future. What we sow now, we will reap hereafter.

So long as mind is our master, it will keep us on the wheel of birth and death. When we are its master, it will be our most faithful ally. Therefore, its control is imperative, and the object of human life is to control it and thereby get off the wheel of life and death.

The only power that can control the mind is the Word or Nam. To catch the Word, one has to enter the eye centre. The simplest method for reaching the eye centre is repetition of the names. So, while performing worldly duties with full efforts, diligently and conscientiously, find time for the spiritual practice. The Master sits in the eye centre, and from there gives necessary help and guidance. With faith and love and perseverance, the mind will be conquered in time.

~

61.   As for X, she says that it is like bidding goodbye to the closest and dearest friend "I ever had" and going to a stranger. By "friend" she means Jesus Christ. Christ never visited

America, and died many centuries ago. She claims to have seen him in visions, yet she has no proof that it is really Jesus Christ whom she saw. Had she seen him in physical form on this earth, then she could have identified him and would know whether it was really Christ whom she saw inside. Perhaps she is not aware that internal planes are full of vicious and evil spirits who can assume any form, and can mislead. Even followers of a living Master are sometimes led astray by Kal, who, assuming the form of the living Master, appears to entrap them.

The sure test is that at the time when Christ appears before her in visions, she should talk to him and inquire from him the way to higher internal regions, and request him to take her up to those regions. If he can do so, then she has no need of getting a new master and giving up Christ. If he does not take her up, and she is desirous of traversing the higher regions, then she will have to attach herself to a living Master who is able to take the soul upward.

～

62.   I am glad to learn that you devote one hour daily in the prescribed posture in your meditation. The primary thing is to bring about concentration of the mind, and that can be done by repetition of the five holy names, carefully, while keeping the attention fixed on the eye focus.

As you advance in concentration, you will begin to get light and sound, both. While repeating the names, you need not try to catch the Sound which is the result of concentration. Please give three-fourths of the time to repetition and one-fourth to hearing the Sound; but while hearing the Sound, do not try to repeat. Yet, all the time keep your attention fixed on the eye focus. You need not try to visualize anything during repetition. Do not expect hasty results, please.

My advice is that you should give more time to meditation
and try to go in.

~

63. You should get some work—small business occupation—to earn sufficiently to keep you going. You may do anything you think proper and profitable to earn a living. Where
there is a will there is a way.

I am glad to find that initiation has changed your outlook on life and has given you an aim in life. Our aim is twofold: primarily to work hard in meditation, go in, and lift our
souls up; the secondary object is to maintain our bodily
health and earn sufficient income by rightful means in order
to lead a comfortable life.

~

64. The audible life stream which we call Shabd is the everlasting form of the Lord and is always within everyone of us. At
the eye focus it assumes the Astral Form of the Master and in
this physical world it assumes the physical form of the Master.

The function of Shabd is to lift the soul up; but it cannot
perform this function until the mind and soul concentrate at
the focus of the eyes and, having vacated the physical frame,
cross the solar system—that is, the stars, the sun, and the moon.

The soul and mind permeate every pore of the physical
body, therefore Shabd cannot pull them up. It is by means of
repetition of the five holy names—while keeping the attention between the eyes—that the currents of the soul gradually
leave the body and collect behind the eyes. When the concentration is complete and the entire body has become numb,
then it is easy for the sound current to pull up the soul.

Therefore, please work hard upon your repetition and bring
about complete concentration. No external circumstances

can obstruct the progress of the soul. It is the lower tendencies of the mind that obstruct the soul's progress. Keep your thoughts pure. It is lust and anger that make the mind impure and prevent spiritual development.

One should never be contented with one's spiritual progress. One should always hunger for the repetition and hearing the sound current.

Yes, what happens with you is happening with all. Sometimes the mind and the soul get easily concentrated and sometimes they are very difficult to concentrate. It is not the same every day. The reason is that when the mind is scattered for any cause, it becomes difficult to bring about concentration. And when the mind is not so scattered, concentration becomes easier and more pleasant.

When you cross the solar system and go beyond, you will find the Master in his Astral Form, waiting for you and ready to take you up to higher regions. It is up to the disciple to reach that point, and after that it is the Master's duty to take the soul up.

You need not take the trouble of coming over to India. The time is not opportune and, moreover, I do not stay at one place but am always moving about. It is not necessary for your spiritual progress. Wait for a year.

Regarding the use of contraceptives, if you want good spiritual progress, let there be pure unselfish love between you and your husband, without any admixture of sex. It will keep up your health and give you spiritual advancement without any fear of unwanted children. If you waste your energies in sex enjoyment, you cannot progress spiritually. Yet I do not want to interfere in your relations with your husband. You are free to do as you like.

The best service that you can render me is to work hard for your spiritual uplift.

65. I am sorry to learn that you find little time for your spiritual meditation on account of your various worldly engagements. You should try to give some time to it daily. Your distress is due to want of meditation.

Your husband should know that if he gives up spiritual practice, it is he who will be the loser. He should not give it up in despair of results, as it takes years to make the mind motionless. And one should continue working on this path up to the end of his life, even if he does not get results to his own satisfaction. It is the only thing that goes with us after death. If he gives this up, he will go empty-handed in the end. Your relationship with him is of this world. If he gives up meditation, you should not do so as everyone has to account for his own self at death, and get the reward of his own meditation and practice in the other world.

The Master is waiting inside for his pupils to come in and partake of his grace and love. It is our fault that we do not reach his "feet" in the astral plane, above the eyes.[1]

~

66. You can always refer your difficulties and problems to me without hesitation, and I shall try to the best of my abilities to assist you.

The law of the karmas is very complicated and intricate. Circumstances in which we are to work are created for us according to our karmas of the past births, and we should try to work under them so far as those circumstances permit.

Yes, the Master is with his disciples, in his Astral Form. You will be able to see and talk to him when you will go in the astral plane.

---

1. Reaching the Master's "feet" is a way of expressing the initial contact and experience of the Master's spiritual presence. It is another way of referring to his Astral Form.

Neither X nor Y are aware of the sound current, and without it nobody can go into the higher spiritual planes. Therefore, their preaching and teaching cannot be complete. They possess no knowledge of the holy names or our way of meditation. The result is that your taking part in their work will do no good either to them or to you; instead of that you can study the books by Dr Johnson and other Sant Mat literature.

I also could wish that there was a teacher of Sant Mat in your country. You have not given me the full name of Z, so I cannot know who he is and how far he will be able to hold a satsang. After initiation one has generally no need to join any religious or spiritual association. It is a mere waste of time, which can be more usefully devoted to meditation. But there can be no harm in joining a society aiming at social uplift, etc., if it does not absorb too much time or if it provides a means of livelihood. Only so much time should be devoted to worldly or other work as is necessary to keep us going.

~

67. In this world it is difficult to find a happy person. One thing or the other is always going wrong, and man finds himself miserable and careworn. Only he who has taken his attention in and hears the clear bell sound is free from worries and cares of this world. Man takes birth here and his destiny comes with him. This destiny cannot be changed. Man has to undergo it. The destiny is of his own making. What he had sown before, he reaps now. Therefore, the wise undergo their destiny with patience and fortitude, while the unwise undergo it all the same, but are dissatisfied and worried.

Lasting peace and happiness are within us. Peace and happiness derived from worldly objects and companions are transitory, because they are not lasting. They change and in time vanish. Their attachment leaves behind scars which disfigure life. Therefore, while working for a decent, comfortable life, one should not lose sight of the aim of life—permanent peace. By the very nature of things, this is not obtainable in the matter and mind regions, because these are themselves changeable. As one is going in and up, one is getting independent of the changeables, and finds peace in spiritual regions. Peace is excellent, but is obtained through effort.

~

68.   Man is a wonderful creation. He not only carries his past history with him; but the whole creation, visible and invisible, and the Creator of all are within him, and he has been gifted with the capacity to see all that lies in him and to be one with his Creator.

The search is to be made within one's self and it costs nothing. The whole thing lies behind the veil of the mind. When the mind has been made motionless, that which lies behind the veil becomes visible. The mind, which wanders outward and seldom sticks to its headquarters in the eye centre—whether we are awake or asleep—has to be trained to stick to the headquarters and, instead of running out, is to look inside the eye centre. This is not an easy task. But just as other habits are created by practice and perseverance, the mind also is to be put in the new channel by love and faith and perseverance. It is a practical course. It is a fight against the mind. "Slow and steady wins the race."

Regarding your questions about the past life, as I have stated above, you will have firsthand knowledge of it when you will be able to go within yourself. Suffice it to say that the present life is based on the past life. Unfulfilled hopes and desires of one life become the basis of new life and form the framework of the new life. Therefore, the main run of the present life was determined before birth. This cannot be changed and has to be borne, whether we do it patiently or restlessly. But we are free to cast our future.

Sant Mat teaches us how to end this cycle of birth and death and go back to our eternal home. The teaching of Sant Mat is the Word which is present in all. We need the help of somebody who himself practises the Word, and it becomes our duty to catch it and trace it inward. The teacher is there, outside and inside, to give guidance. Therefore, with high aim and faith and perseverance, seek the Word within you and be master of your own house within, instead of wandering out. The richest gold mine is within you. The Word is dearer than all the gold, rubies, and diamonds, finding which the mind gives up hankering after the things of this or other worlds.

~

69. I appreciate your eagerness to take to simran and bhajan as much as possible, and I hope you will progressively devote more and more time to them. Your inability to concentrate properly is due to your worldly desires, which must be brought under control till you reach the point when love of God becomes an all-consuming passion, and you consider it the be-all and end-all of your existence.

You know fully well that nothing is really yours in the world, in the sense that nothing will go with you after death, except Nam. It alone will take you to the feet of the Almighty, under the guidance of the Master who is always with his votaries at the time of death and keeps them company throughout the spiritual journey.

He is always with you even now, though you may not see him with physical eyes. By constant devotion to bhajan, time may come when you can see within yourself the Radiant Form of the Master, and once you get it, you will be fully planted on the way that leads to God and eternal salvation.

70. Your karma is all right. It is not to blame for your supposed want of spiritual progress. It is due to the effect of your sudden bereavement and breaking of family tie. The consequent sorrow and anxiety have weighed down upon your mind and soul. The remedy is to give up all sadness and anxiety, and work hard upon your repetition. You should give three-fourths of your daily time to repetition and only one-fourth to hearing the Sound. Take care, please, that during repetition the mind does not wander out. It will not begin to work inside unless it is still. To make the mind perfectly motionless requires years of hard labour; therefore, do not expect results in a hurry. When you labour on the path, you will succeed. No one has yet gone disappointed from that door.

Following are the answers to your questions:

1. You should consult the doctors. Usually the soul becomes active in the embryo after three months.

2. When a baby is born into this world, the number of breaths he is to breathe, till his death, is already fixed, and nobody can increase or decrease it.

3. Suffering and poverty are also pre-ordained for everyone before his birth, according to the karma of his past birth. They have to be undergone, yet a Master's disciple who raises his soul becomes indifferent to external surroundings.

4. Material help should not be sought from the Master. It is perishable. Ask for permanent and everlasting objects from him, such as spiritual uplift, freedom from the cycle of births, and the like.

~

71. The Master is always present with his disciples, in his Astral Form. In order to get more firmly rooted in your spiritual practice you should work hard. The bluish constellations and stars are at the threshold of the inner world. Try to penetrate within.

1. Progress does continue even though one's Master may have left the earth plane forever. This is based on experience. My Master initiated a lady, and departed from this life. Several years after that, the lady's soul went inside very far.

2. No one can go into the spiritual planes without initiation; therefore, you cannot expect to see your relatives who were not initiated, in the other world. If they have gone into the spiritual planes, then you will meet them and talk to them; but not those who have been reborn in this world in some physical form. After death the astral and causal bodies retain the features of the physical body, but there is a vast difference in the materials of the bodies.

3. If one has to be reborn into the world, the soul will have to go into the mother's womb and take natural time to come out.

~

72. People on other planes are not much interested in the physical plane. They have their hands full there, in their own doings. The karmic law is supreme on the material and the mind planes, and nothing happens of its own accord, spontaneously, so to say. The law governs the planes; therefore, no haphazard happening of events takes place anywhere, whether the events are of microscopic or astronomical dimensions. In peace and in cataclysms or catastrophes, only they suffer who are destined to suffer.

All that has been created is bound to change and decay. There is dissolution of earth, planets, sun, and stars, but at very long intervals—too long for human conception. Who can say when this present planetary system was created?

Prophets, yogis, and astronomers give their estimates, and the latter revise their estimates with every new discovery, but who can say how often this dissolution has been repeated? Only He who creates, knows it. Suffice it to say that for human beings sitting outside the eye centre, the time is infinitely long since the creation came into being and when it will disappear again.

So there is nothing to worry about the next war or the atom bomb; this very kind of loose, vague talk was indulged in during and at the end of the Great War I,[1] and is also indulged in after floods, earthquakes, famines and plagues. The worry should be about the entry into the eye centre and meeting the Radiant Form of the Master, so that the Master is made a companion on whom reliance can be placed here and hereafter. He who has been connected with the Word cannot go amiss in catastrophe or peace. He has a place to go to and goes there, and is not lost.

~

73.   I am glad you have received initiation. Now it is for you to work your way inward, within you. With love and faith devote time regularly in repeating the names in the eye centre, and see that while doing repetition the mind does not run out to do something else; and if it does, bring it back again to the eye centre and continue the repetition. By and by the mind will go inward and sit in the eye centre, the attention will begin to be withdrawn from the limbs, and in time the whole body will be vacated. Light will appear and the spiritual journey will commence. It is a slow affair in the beginning.

The spiritual power developed by repetition and concentration of the mind in the eye centre should not be wasted in spiritual healing. This power should be reserved for making

---

1. World War I.

further progress inward. If it is used in healing, there is nothing left with the person except a sense of depletion and exhaustion. It is a bad bargain. The spiritual healer takes the karmic load of the patient and thereby himself goes under, and never makes much headway in the journey inward. He lives from hand to mouth, spending what he earns.

Youth is wayward. But proper guidance through example and precept goes a long way in keeping it on the right path. You may point out to your daughter the advantages of leading a good healthy life with spiritual uplift and ultimate salvation as its goal; for human life is a rare gift of God. In the whole creation, man alone has the privilege of meeting his Creator. And the sound current, which is present and audible in everybody, is the way to rise up, go back to our spiritual home, and meet our Lord.

~

74. I was pained to learn that your husband did not appreciate your love, fidelity, and solicitude for him. My advice to you, given at the time of your marriage, was from the point of view of a Hindu wife. Among Hindus, marriage is regarded as a sacrament and a permanent union. I am glad to learn that you have done your best to follow that advice. If he cannot pull on with you, then you can do whatever you think proper. You have done your duty towards him. I am satisfied with your behaviour in this matter. You have my full permission to do as you like under the circumstances.

I sympathize with you in your wish to have a small home of your own, where you can enjoy privacy and solitude, and make progress on the path. Try to gain your livelihood by some profession or employment which would leave time for your spiritual practice, yet bring you sufficient income to live comfortably.

Do not try to strain your neck or shoulder muscles during spiritual meditation, nor put any kind of pressure on your brain, eyes, and so forth. I think nobody told you at the time of initiation to strain your nerves. Spiritual concentration does not depend on putting pressure on any part of the body.

The aim of spiritual practice is firstly and primarily to make the mind still and motionless so that no thought of any kind may disturb it while it is listening to the Sound. As the vibrations of the mind are made quiet, the sound current will of itself become clearer and clearer, without any need of putting pressure on the eyes, ears or brain.

And for stilling the vibrations of the mind, all that is necessary is to repeat the five holy names with care and attention, so that the mind does not wander. If it wanders during repetition, then a second link should be applied to it by concentrating on the form of the Guru. But there is no need of putting any strain on the body.

Any posture in which you can remain for long would do for concentration. Frequent changes of position interfere with concentration.

If we concentrate our soul in this lifetime, then we pass our days happily in this world, and at death the Master appears and takes our soul with him to higher worlds, to our unbounded joy and happiness. Therefore, try to achieve spiritual progress in your lifetime so that you may rise above worldly circumstances. The spiritual advance you make in this life will go with you.

Thank you, I am enjoying good health and wish that you labour in the path and lift the veil within so as to take your soul to higher regions. Do your day's work, but let your attention remain fixed on Master's Form or repetition or hearing the Sound. If you go on working with patience and perseverance, you will get everything.

75. I am glad to learn of your progress in your spiritual practices. If you continue to put in time regularly in your practices, you will have more experiences of higher realms in your spiritual flights. Men do not see them for want of inversion of all of their outgoing faculties. Shabd is all-powerful and is resounding in all directions.

The time factor is necessary for the achievement of the goal before you. You need not be disheartened at your slow progress in the spiritual way. If a satsangi has not been able to give full time to his practices and has progressed very little during his lifetime, but he is imbued with the love of the Master and has no attachment for the world and its desires, the Master is so gracious that the satsangi is not given any rebirth. He is placed, after death, in a suitable place inside, in the first or second region, where he completes the deficiency before going further up.

As regards the young child with the beautiful purple aura you saw in your practice, you should pay no heed to him. He is one of the five evils personified—lust, anger, greed, attachment, and pride. They leave the satsangi, one by one, as he progresses on his way up.

Each man is enveloped with an aura bearing colours according to the quality of inner waves of thoughts surging in him; sensual appetites create the impression of a dark red radiance. The clear cut conception of a logical thinker is experienced as a yellowish figure with a sharply defined outline. Blue colour represents love. White colour speaks for spirituality, and so forth.

In your practices you should not put any strain or pressure on your eyes. Repeat the names mentally. When concentration will be developed, the soul will of itself withdraw inside, back of the pineal gland. No attempt should be made to locate the gland or the nerves leading to it. The seeker who devotes time regularly in his spiritual practices need not despair. Why lose heart and entertain weak thoughts? Have a strong desire that you have to attain the goal in this very birth. If you go up even one plane in this birth, you will not come back into the physical frame again. Rebirth is only for those who have worldly desires.

~

76. ... and am glad to learn that you have deep love for Sant Mat and work upon the path. Although you are separated from my physical body, yet you are not away from my mind. The Satguru in his Sound Form is taking proper care of you and is within you. When, by means of concentration, you have closed the nine portals of the body and have crossed the solar system, the Master in his Radiant Form will reveal himself to you. He will talk to you in the same manner as you talk to people in this world, will answer all your questions, and will be with you all your life.

You should not be sorry for being alone. We are born alone and leave this world alone. None go with us. Even this body has to be left behind. It is the Master and the sound current that keep us company at death and after.

The internal spiritual journey is very sweet and interesting, and so also the study of books relating to the path. When you go up high enough, you will see much finer and more interesting scenes.

What you have said about seeing the Radiant Form of Master Jesus is quite true. You will meet him again when you go in, but you are to go much higher up. You should die daily, as you died on the day you saw the vision of Christ. You should devote much time to your spiritual practice so that you may see those things daily. Those visions and scenes are still within you, and when you go within you will see them.

Please keep your mind and attention present during meditation and work hard.

Let not the thought of karma discourage you. When you work with a firm resolve, you will overcome all obstacles. Do not despair, but go on working hard. It is not a path of despair. Always keep a firm resolve of going in. You have ceased to see those visions and scenes only because your attention came outward and the concentration scattered. If you now work hard, you can go still further inside, because the path which has been indicated to you is much higher. When you work, you will see with your own eyes and will not need to ask others.

∽

77.   As for your nose trouble, it must be due to something wrong with your stomach and bronchial tubes. You might get it treated by some physician. It is due to past karma, yet it does not imply that you should not take steps to get rid of this nuisance.

So long as you are suffering, you can go on repeating the five holy names while sitting in an easy chair, while lying or in any comfortable posture, and even when walking. This continuous repetition will bring about concentration of the mind and make your will power strong.

Do not lose courage. The Master who has given you initiation is bound to take you to the highest region. If, owing to illness, you cannot complete your course, he will give you another birth with far better circumstances favourable to spiritual advancement. He is not going to leave you in the lurch.

If you cannot sit in the prescribed posture, you can sit ... with both hands joined in your lap. The object is to bring about concentration of the mind and make it motionless.

This will not cause pain in your arms and hands. Do not strain your body. And do not try to make spiritual progress in a hurry. Do it calmly and quietly.

Whatever you again want to ask, you may do so without hesitation, and a reply will be sent to you.

~

78.   Had you continued to keep your mother at your house and served her till the end, you would have discharged a filial duty, for she had nursed you in your helpless infancy. But perhaps she was too exacting and too difficult to please. You did not mean any harm to her, and had every good intention when you sent her to be looked after by a private lady. Let her remain where she is. She has to undergo her own karma, which is called pralabdh.

The total number of breaths which one is to take till death, the morsels which one is to eat, and the steps which one is to walk are all preordained at birth, and no one can alter, decrease, or increase them. There is no harm in praying to the Lord that she may be relieved of her pain and suffering. The Master helps the relatives of his pupils when they depart from this life. You should go on doing your meditation and repetition so that it may do her some good after this life.

~

79.   If the meditation is performed in a reclining position, such as in bed, it takes longer time to bring about concentration, and very often sleep interrupts the meditation.

If husband and wife are agreed as to their religious belief, it is conducive to their happiness. If husband and wife are filled with the same desire for making spiritual progress, they are helpful to one another. If at a time one is slack, the keenness of the other makes him work up. Thus both of them, being travellers on the same path, are helpful to one another, their destination being the same. But each has his own karma to undergo. The karma of each partner is different. Yet if a couple meditates together, they also become companions in the spiritual journey.

~

80.   I am sorry to learn of the demise of your mother. One feels grieved when a dear one goes away forever, and this grief is natural so long as the attention is attached to the body, relations, and friends, and has not entered the eye centre.

At such times the mind is in tension and raises questions of life and death, and experiences strange dreams. Sometimes in dream the attention gets directed towards the eye centre and, from a distance, catches flashes of what goes on in or near the eye centre, in the astral plane. The flashes are usually blurred and seldom clear. A clear flash turns out to be correct. Again, in this tension, one may experience a little pull towards the eye centre and its painful effect on the body—a dying sensation—because one is not accustomed to withdraw the vital current from the body at will. But dreams are dreams, and it is good that no importance is attached to them and they are thrown out from memory. Reliance should be placed on experiences gained by going inside consciously.

The world is an inn where travellers assemble from different directions for the night and by morning take to their respective destinations. In the family one comes as father, the other as mother, and still others as sons and daughters. All are directed by their respective karma and leave the family in their time. In every birth—in the insect, the bird, the animal, or the human form—one gets a mother and a father. The number of mothers, fathers, and near relations one has had are countless. For whom then should one worry? Our worry does not help them. The worry should be to reach the eye centre and make it one's home, and meet the Radiant Form of the Master and the Shabd that pulls up, so that there is no birth hereafter, and no worries.

Your mother had not received initiation, so her future course is guided by her karma. The best you can do for her is to complete your own course of repetition and thereby complete your concentration. Your mother will get some benefit from your efforts in this line.

At death the suffering is acute, and one should learn to die daily to withstand this pain. Withdrawal of the scattered attention from the body into the eye centre is death—leaving the physical plane and entering the astral plane.

The dream of the semi-conscious state, as said before, is not to be relied upon. If the attention were catching the true Shabd, there could not be a dream or an unconscious state. Shabd brings in superconscious state.

Physical defects do not stand in the way of rising from one region to another. The mind and soul are to go up; the physical body is left behind at the eye centre. The vital portion of the reproductive area is vital for production but not for concentration and rising up.

So long as there is sex desire, there is no real love for the Master and the Shabd that will free one from sex desire and pull him up. Superficial love does not count for much. There is antagonism in Shabd and sex desire. Shabd pulls up the attention towards the eye centre, and sex desire throws the attention down to the lowest centre—the reproductive organs. Physical contact pulls the attention down. There is no question of a lift of one or the other through contacts.

The use of liquor is bad. It unsettles the mind, and an unsettled mind brings in its train all the evils which one in a normal state avoids.

81.   I went through your loving letter with the care it de-
served. I was pleased to read it, as its contents indicated the
good-heartedness of the writer.

When you sit for bhajan, you should enter into an agree-
ment with your mind, considering it as an entity different
from you, that it should not bother you for the period of two
hours. You can tell it that if it misbehaves, you will sit for
even more than two hours, for as long as it does not feel the
ecstasy of internal bliss! This is how the human mind is to be
controlled. As a matter of fact, our mind is like the proverbial
serpent guarding the spiritual treasure, which cannot be obtained till the menace of the serpent is surmounted. Never
mind the past. Look to the present and the future in the spirit
of a true devotee.

Do not mind if your limbs begin to ache after sitting for
long in meditation. After some practice they will cease to be
troublesome and will, as it were, go to sleep; as by means of
bhajan, the soul and mind are drawn up to the centre above
the two eyes, where you have to focus your undivided attention at the time of bhajan.

When, by this means, your mind begins to accept control
and discipline and becomes motionless, you will see within
yourself the effulgence of the spiritual world which will lead
you to the stars, sun, and moon—all within you—and after
them, to the feet of the Master, which you so eagerly wish to
reach. When you reach that stage, the Master will speak to
you just as you converse with the people around you in this
physical world. Just think! All around you is perishable, and
after death none can befriend you or guide you except the
Master and Nam.

Why should Dr Johnson's book frighten anyone? It is
no use shutting one's eyes to the law of transmigration, which
is far more real and inexorable than some people, in their

shortsightedness, feel inclined to admit. The saints show the path that leads out of this vicious circle of creation on this earth. It is only by means of bhajan that a person can travel a path that leads out of it and takes one to the sacred feet of the Great Almighty.

When a loving devotee dies, the Master takes care of the soul. He guides it and instructs it even after death. In this respect the death of a devotee is totally different from that of a man of the world. But it behooves all disciples to give as much time and attention to the development of the spiritual side of their being as possible. It is only thus that the soul can be freed from the bondage of body and mind, from the downward pull of the senses, and can work its way up to the great ocean of which it is a drop.

If you really think that the purchase of property at —— or elsewhere will be a sound business proposition, you may go in for it. The war cannot last forever! It is, of course, open to you and your husband to make an honest living in any way you like, compatible with your means and aptitude.

⁓

82. I am glad to learn that you have received initiation. Now it is for you to concentrate your scattered attention and withdraw it from the limbs and the body into the eye centre, and sit there, within yourself. When the eye centre becomes the headquarters of your attention, then the sound current will be able to pull the attention upward.

The method of concentration (repetition of the names) is a natural process. Everyone is busy in repeating words, audibly or mentally, concerning his work in life. Here, words connected with the spiritual journey have been substituted in place of the words used in daily routine life. The withdrawal of the attention from the limbs and the body, into the eye centre, is not new either. Everybody, when he goes to sleep, brings his attention—intentionally or unintentionally—into the eye centre, but lets it fall down to the throat and navel centres instead of holding it in the eye centre. The only difference in the process of concentration is that we are to hold the attention in the eye centre and not let it drop down.

The sound current is present in everybody already, only its presence has been explained at the time of initiation. Therefore, the whole process is perfectly natural. There is no artificiality in it. It is safe, does not cost anything, has no outward symbols. No other person can interfere in it; it can be practised by all, and does not clash with any religion.

With love and faith, devote time to this work regularly. As has been said above, the achievement of results will depend on your effort. There should be no hurry here. A calm, peaceful mind, working slowly but steadily, will attain success sooner.

It is only when we sit in meditation that we begin to discover the power, the waywardness, and the obstinacy of the mind. The mind that has been running wild ever since we came into the wheel of life and death will take time to yield. You are just beginning the fight against it. It is a lifelong fight; and the reward is, if one conquers his mind (makes it motionless in the eye centre) he wins the world.

You say you feel lonely. The whole creation and the Creator are within you. If you take your attention inside of you and attach it to the sound current, you will be at peace with yourself and with the world. The lasting peace lies inside of us. It is not to be had outside, in worldly objects and worldly companions.

If you find yourself under a mental depression and feel physically exhausted and cannot bring yourself up to meditate by sitting in proper posture, then do it while lying down. But there is the danger that this may become a habit. Defeat is not so bad as the admission of defeat. Under all circumstances, the fight against the mind should be continued. Mind is our enemy. It tries to throw us off by all sorts of things, on one pretence or another.

Thank you for your good wishes at my birthday. All that I wish is that the initiates reach their spiritual home in Sach Khand as quickly as they can.

≈

83.   I am glad you have received the instruction. Now it is for you to work up. The help of the Master is always there. The Master is not far off from you. He is within you, in your eye centre.

Man and the world are so constituted that there is always one thing or the other cropping up and demanding our attention. Such things should be attended to, but one should find time daily for the spiritual work. It should not be ignored. If full time cannot be given, give as much as you can. Even five minutes would do. The spiritual work alone goes with us to our credit after death. All other will be left behind. The day that is gone will not come back again. So with love and faith and perseverance, go ahead.

≈

84.   I am sorry you are so much upset by the shortcomings of the initiates. People accept the teaching gladly because it appears to them so simple and natural. In their first zeal they accept the restrictions on their diet, but when it comes to live by them, they begin to falter. The mind plays its cunning part and deceives them, and in many subtle ways they try to get around these restrictions, even not sparing the Master. It is

characteristic of the mind that it does not take the blame on itself but throws it on someone else and, if need be, on the Master as well.

This is their weakness. The Master, out or in, would never relax these restrictions. Have you come across a mother who would give poison to her children? Meats, eggs, and alcohol are poisons, and he who uses them will suffer. There is no escape from it. Go in and see with your own eyes what tortures the users of these have to bear, whether initiates or non-initiates.

Those who indulge in these are disciples of senses and not of the Master. Their attention works on the sense plane. All their talk about the Master, in or out, or about their spiritual progress is sham. "Quick little petition to the inner Master" is a huge deception. The inner Master is not so soft and easy to reach! It is true he is merciful, but it does not mean that the wrongdoers and the wayward would escape punishment.

The saints do not hand over their initiates to Kal, but the initiates have to suffer for their misdeeds. Suffering purifies, and only the pure enter the eye centre. Anybody who breaks marriage vows and deserts children for sense indulgence is a slave to lust. Lust is his master. The same applies to other indulgences. Mind is our enemy, and he who follows his mind is playing in the hands of his enemy and has no chance of escape.

To reach the eye centre and cross the starry sky, the sun, and the moon, and come face to face with the Radiant Form of the Master, is the duty of the disciple, whether he does it in this life or the next. It is his work and he is to do it. So why not do it now and why postpone it?

Sant Mat does not advocate compulsion. Human nature is weak. This is Kalyuga. The initiates come under the influence of the worldly people. They lack satsang; therefore, they fall. Let us have patience with them. By and by they will be able to stand on their feet. Let us judge them kindly.

The Master has many forms—physical on the physical plane, Radiant on the astral, and Shabd Form on the top of Trikuti, and then another in Sach Khand. The Radiant Form resembles the physical form, and from this resemblance one distinguishes him inside, from others. Same is the case with the disciple. The physical form he leaves behind at the eye centre; with his astral form he travels the first region, and with his causal form the second region. The Radiant Form of the Master enters into conversation as we converse in dreams. Dream is the nearest analogy, but we are dealing with the superconscious state.

When you have made contact with that Form, you will find the Master present everywhere, and your mind will be so strong that it will be almost impossible for you to blame them when you look at the shortcomings of others. Your happiness will be independent of your surroundings. You will not be shaken by the ups and downs of the world.

It should be the effort of every initiate to work up as best he can, to reach the eye centre and meet the Radiant Form, so that he stands as a pillar of strength, unmoved by the winds and storms of passions.

～

85. The law of karma (results of past actions) and the doctrine of predestination and preordination are true and inexorable. We reap what we sow! Our actions in past lives bring about our fate in this life, on which our bodies are fashioned. The fate is to regulate and govern our present being; but being itself the offspring of past actions, it always behooves us to lay the foundations of a better fate by doing good and noble

acts. So there is always a place for endeavour and effort toward a true understanding of the operation of the law of karma.

You are right in thinking that an initiate who is filled with loving devotion to the spiritual path is a blessing for his wife and children. It would have been better if your consort had been initiated; but, in any case, it is good for her that you are an initiate. The Master tries to take care of souls that are ultimately connected with his disciples, unless they are absolutely recalcitrant and impervious to his divine spiritual influence.

I would enjoin on you the paramount necessity of regular repetition of the holy words taught to you at the time of initiation, and of constant listening to the sound current. It is this practice, regularly performed with loving devotion, which can give you salvation.

~

86.   Sant Mat is extremely liberal, more liberal than can be conceived. You may use any word or words that you love to associate with the Creator in your morning meditation period, till you have received your initiation. It is the love and faith at the back of what one does, that counts.

The real form of the Master is the Word. It is present everywhere and is the mainstay of all that is visible and invisible. The Word takes on the human form to connect people with Himself, for people would not understand in any other way except through someone like themselves. Saint John, chapter 1, verse 14, says that the Word was made flesh and dwelt among us....

Your Master is within you and watches you. Only the veil of the mind hangs between you and him. Make the mind motionless, and all that lies hidden behind it will be an open book.

Many thanks for your letter and the fine feelings that it gives expression to. It is a reflection of the purity of your heart.

~

87.   I am glad to learn of your spiritual progress—your "hearing of the music all the time; it comes through the brain and not through ears"; of your "seeing the astral light colour always in motion"; of your having "seen yourself in some of your past lives." I congratulate you on that. You are on the right path.

There are ten different sounds audible in the region of the eye centre—drum, whistle, violin, and so forth, including the bell and the conch. Eight of these are local, but the bell and the conch are connected with the higher regions. As the attention is withdrawn from the body and concentration improves, and the eye centre is being approached, these sounds begin to be audible. As the mind becomes steady and sticks to the centre, it begins to distinguish one sound from the other. In the beginning one listens to whatever sound is audible; but with the improvement in concentration, this gives place to some finer sound. Ultimately one picks up the bell and rejects others. The bell will take one as far as the thousand-petalled lotus, and from there one catches the conch.

When doing repetition of names at the allotted time, daily, please see that the mind does not wander about. The attention should be in the light within, and repetition should be continued without any thought of the body. The body is to be completely vacated by the attention. And during the time given to repetition, no attempt should be made to catch the Sound—only repetition of the five names with attention in the light within.

When the concentration is complete, it will appear as if you are separate from the body and the body is a corpse of someone else. The starry sky will appear in time. Fix your attention in the bright star and continue repetition as before. When the star is approached, it will burst, and the attention will penetrate through it. The starry sky has been crossed. In the same manner, the sun and the moon in succession will be reached and crossed by the attention doing repetition all the time. After crossing the moon region the Master's Radiant Form will be visible. Fix your attention in that and hand yourself over to the Master. The repetition takes the attention that far and no further.

When listening to the Sound at the allotted time, hear the Sound only, catching the bell sound if possible and, in its absence, any other sound that is audible. At this portion of the time repetition is not to be done.

During any other time besides the regular time for doing the spiritual practice, keep your attention in the sound current.

This music comes from Sat Lok and reaches us after penetrating all the regions below it. It is superior to angels in the astral plane. They hanker after it and do not get it.

When you have completed your concentration, and the attention has completely vacated the body and gone in and made contact with the Master's Radiant Form, you will hear the sound current all the twenty-four hours—awake or asleep. The body will sleep but the soul will remain conscious within.

Please do not be afraid of the shackles. There is no such thing for the practitioner of the Word. Your attention is not steady. It does not stick to the eye centre but falls down and feels the pressure. Keep your attention up in the eye centre.

The sound current, the Word, the Nam, and the Shabd are synonymous. The five names used in repetition are the words which can be uttered by tongue or can be repeated mentally.

88.   I am glad to learn that, after all, you have come to realise the value of the path of the saints and are trying to go in.

The internal visions and experiences should not be revealed to anyone except the Master. They are liable to disappear if revealed to others. They should be kept a close secret if you wish to continue to enjoy them. These visions and scenes are for personal satisfaction and peace. If they are painted and exhibited to the outside world, whose eyes are not awakened to the visions, they will not be appreciated.

Regarding posture, as it is difficult for Americans and Europeans to sit in the prescribed posture, they are allowed to take any easy and comfortable posture in which they can sit for a fairly long time. The object is to help bring about concentration. In India people can sit for two or three hours at a stretch in the prescribed posture. Yes, you can sit in a chair. The object of keeping the hands over the face and the thumbs in the ears is to keep out external light and external sounds.

One should give at least two hours every day to meditation. The more time you can spare, the more speedy will be your progress.

At present it is not advisable for you to come to India. You should make some progress in concentration before coming here. The Master is within you, in the Sound Form. When your heart is with me, you are not far away.

There is no greater wealth than progress on the spiritual path—a wealth which accompanies us even after death. We accumulate this wealth by perseverance.

∼

89.   You ask for a message. The message is that you develop the power to withdraw your attention, at will, from the outward objects and from the physical body, and concentrate it

in the eye focus. Enter the astral world, make contact with
the Astral Form of the Master, become very intimate with
him, make him your companion, catch the sound current,
cross the mind planes, and reach your eternal spiritual home
in Sach Khand so that your wanderings in the worlds of mind
and matter may end. Do it now, while alive. This is the purpose of human life.

If progress in this line has not been made, life has been
spent in vain. It is not difficult to acquire worldly fame,
wealth, kingdom, and miraculous power, but it is difficult to
turn away one's attention from these and go inside to catch
the sound current. Love, faith, and perseverance make the
path easy and possible to attain the unattainable. I shall be
glad to hear how far you have succeeded in making your attention steady in the eye focus and how far your body becomes unconscious.

90. I am glad to find that you think that my letters have
been helpful to you. Progress on the spiritual path depends
upon purity of conduct and, secondly, upon persevering
labour, to still the activity of the mind by means of repetition. Until the mind is made motionless, it cannot perceive
the light within. But there is no reason to despond. It takes
time to overcome the habits of the mind.

There is no harm in your accepting help from your
brother. I am grateful to you for your offer of contribution to
our charity fund, but I can assure you that we have no desire
to accumulate our fund to more than our daily needs, which
we are able to meet. I should like you to spend what you have
on your own personal comfort and needs so that you might
be able to carry on repetition and spiritual exercises without
anxiety and without interruption.

I have read with interest your account of followers of the Bahai. I have also read some of their books. They aim at external wellbeing of humanity and purity of conduct. Yet their teachings, so far as I know, do not prescribe any mode of spiritual exercises for the uplift of the soul internally.

The method of spiritual exercises prescribed by our Masters is natural. It is not the design of any human brain. It has existed ever since man was created and leads the soul from its seat in the eye focus to the highest regions of pure spirit.

The Masters do not lay down any ritual or ceremony, but prescribe a mode of spiritual advancement which can be practised by any man or woman of any creed or faith, as it is a method of internal concentration and progress, and does not concern itself with outward formulae or social rules.

You should treat your Bahai friends with love and patience, without trying to argue with them, yet without giving up your own spiritual devotion. The Master does not want you to think that your social intercourse with Bahais is meant to be a trial or test.

~

91.   You have complained that in meditation your mind wanders back to past events. That should not be. When you sit in meditation, keep watch over your mind and never allow it to go out. If it goes out, bring it back. Try to forget your past life and past connections or relations. What has passed away will not come again. There is no use raking up old memories. Let bygones be bygones. Obliterate the past from the page of your memory. Devote all your spare time and efforts to concentration, so that you may go in and become happier and more peaceful.

I have read your life history with interest, and you have fought the battle of life bravely under difficult circumstances.

The ways of providence are mysterious and difficult to fathom.... Mind is your enemy and it deceives you by bringing past events in your meditation.

~

92.   I am sorry to hear of your illness and other troubles causing interruptions in spiritual work. This karma was weighing down the soul and I am glad that it has been washed away. This is also an asset in meditation.

We have incurred upon our mind and soul the heavy burden of the karma of numerous past lives. As this burden gets lighter and lighter by suffering and spiritual exercises, spiritual progress goes on. After an amount of illness, interruption takes place in meditation, yet the meditation should not be given up.

Now that you have recovered, begin again. If the body feels numb and sleepy during meditation, it is a sign of spiritual progress. The mind is always seeking pretexts for deferring meditation, but we should not listen to the mind's arguments and pretexts. We should overrule all its argumentation and perform our daily repetition.

You have asked for my instructions to make up for lost time:

1.   When you begin meditation, expel all thoughts from your mind and tell your mind that all anxiety and all kinds of thoughts can wait till the meditation is over.
2.   Do not allow any kind of idea or thought to arise while doing your repetition or listening to the Sound.
3.   When the mind and soul sit quietly within, the spiritual progress will begin.
4.   Clearness and intensity of Sound depend on the degree of concentration. The greater the concentration, the clearer and louder the Sound.

93.   Your view regarding the attitude you should have taken towards your bodily suffering and family trouble is brave, and I greatly appreciate it. It is mainly the reaction to our problems that matters.

The Lord is within us. He wants to wash away our karma, to make us pure and fit to get into his presence. Our only course amidst sufferings of any kind is first to bear them patiently, with courage and fortitude; and secondly, to pray to the Lord for forgiveness. The Lord hears our prayers and showers concessions which we cannot see unless we go in.

... Our main object in this life is to try to make headway on our path inward. No doubt your illness has caused much hindrance and disturbance in your spiritual exercises. Yet if one can perform the repetition of the five names during illness, while lying down or resting in bed, it might give peace of mind during a period of trouble.

~

94.   I was glad to receive your letter intimating your initiation. It is a straight path, though difficult and laborious. The first thing is to make your mind motionless, which is possible only by means of repetition of the five holy names, with care and attention. It takes years of labour to succeed in this. The rest becomes comparatively easy.

Ordinarily, one should devote one tenth of one's daily time, that is, 2.4 hours at least, and then he can increase the time to four hours gradually. It requires patience and perseverance.

~

95.   As for the pressure on the top of the head, that cannot be due to meditation. Yet I shall advise you not to put any strain on your eyes or brain; do not try to go up all at once. See the internal light and hear the chimes calmly and quietly, without hurry and impatience to go up at once. Slow and steady is the best rule in spiritual practice, as it is in mundane affairs.

It all depends on the mind, which does not like to concentrate and go in. It is accustomed from numberless past births to wander about and remain scattered. So it will take time to make the mind motionless and collected. Go in with love and faith. The Master, in his Astral Form, is waiting to receive you in the eye focus and is protecting you so far as is consistent with your karma, which needs to be washed off.

God is one and there is only one way to reach him, and that way is within every human being regardless of caste and creed. The major part of humanity is utterly ignorant of this internal path and wants to find God in external objects or practices.

The internal spiritual path and teaching have nothing to do with world religions and social rules. Just as by attending a school, one becomes master of science, so is the case with spiritual knowledge. This method of spiritual concentration and uplift is natural. It was not designed by any human being. It is the design of the Creator, and none can alter, amend, or add to it. It is as ancient as man. The Creator, when he created man, designed this path in him.

≈

96. You say you are "highly interested in attaining the higher realms of God's spiritual world." We are to seek God's spiritual world and God within us. The spiritual worlds lie behind the mental worlds and the mental worlds are at the back of the physical world. Our attention is, at present, held by the physical world through the nine portals of the body— eyes, ears, nose, and so forth—whereas access to the mental and the spiritual worlds is through the tenth portal, located

in the eye centre. So long, therefore, as our attention does not develop the capacity to detach itself from the world, vacate the nine portals of the body, and collect in the eye centre, we have not even come to the starting point of the path to the mental and spiritual world. From this point—the eye centre—the attention sticks to the sound current and follows it right through the mental worlds to the spiritual worlds and God. The Master, who is familiar with the path, acts throughout as a guide.

The method, as was explained to you at the time of initiation, is the simplest when compared with other methods. This has been followed and recommended by the past Masters. It is natural, within all, designed by God, and as old as the creation itself.

Because our attention in the long, long past lost touch with the sound current and got attached to the mind and the physical world, adopting forms of life according to the actions performed, it has become materialized, in a way, and now finds it difficult to detach itself from the material world, vacate the nine portals of the body and concentrate in the eye centre, thereby dematerializing itself and becoming fit to make contact with the sound current again and enter the mental plane.

The simplest way to dematerialize the attention is simran—the repetition of the five names by the attention in the eye centre. When the attention is engaged in the eye centre in this repetition, it begins to withdraw itself from the world and from the extremities of the body, leaving them numb. As the practice increases, leaving the whole body numb, the attention concentrates in the eye centre and enters a new world.

This method is natural with us, as everyone in this world is engaged in repeating words—a farmer is mentally making use of words connected with his work when he thinks of his fields and bullocks and plans agricultural operation; a house-wife thinks in words connected with what is in stock in the house and what is to be purchased for the table; a lawyer thinks in words connected with his cases. In this method of concentration, by repeating words in the eye centre, there is no change in our daily habit; only new words have been substituted, thereby changing the subject matter but not the habit. The words we use in concentration refer to nothing in the external material world but refer to our spiritual journey within us.

Therefore, let there be no doubt about the simplicity and the efficacy of the method. If followed with faith, love, and perseverance, it is bound to give results. Strong effort is needed in making every venture a success. I am glad to read in your letter: "Nothing else in life is as important to me as drawing ever closer to my Father's home." This is the aim of human life, for it is given to man alone and to no other form of life, to reach his Father's home.

When sitting in meditation and repeating the names, there should be no attempt to look for light. So long as the attention is wandering outside and has not collected in the eye centre, who is there to see light? The faculty that is to see light within is yet outside. The attempt should be to keep the attention engaged in the eye centre in mere repetition of names and doing nothing else. When hands and fingers get tired, pay no attention to these but keep the attention busy in the eye centre. Light is not to come from the outside. Light is there inside already, only we are out. When we will go in, we will see the light.

There is no power on earth or heaven greater than the power of sound current. It is the primary power. All other powers are derived or secondary. So anybody who is connected with the sound current, and practises, must accept once for all that he cannot be adversely affected by hypnotists, spiritualists, mediums, or any of their clique. Even the angel of death dare not come near one who is connected with the sound current. Sound current is the cure for all weaknesses that flesh is heir to. Please throw off the ideas from your mind that you are under the influence of a spiritualist. Nothing of this sort.

Another fact of equal importance is that we have to undergo our fate karma. Before a child comes out of its mother's womb, its fate is recorded on its forehead, hands, and feet. It is the result of our own actions done in our past life. Whatever we had sown then, we are to reap now. There is no change in that. The wise put up with that patiently, even willingly, and the unwise cry but undergo it all the same. But if one concentrates his attention and catches the sound current, his will power becomes strong; thereby his capacity to go through his fate karma increases, and the ups and downs of life leave no scars on him.

So, in whatever walk or circumstances of life we find ourselves placed, we should endeavour our best to earn our living honestly; discharge our duties faithfully; live a healthy, normal, moral life; willingly put up with our fate; and devote ourselves to the practice of the sound current, so that our past account is settled and our future is along the path of the sound current, which leads to our spiritual home.

You may adopt any course in which you think you will be able to live a healthy, normal life leading to your spiritual home. The choice is yours.

～

97.   X cannot cause you any harm if you perform your meditation and hear the sound current with love and faith. Do not entertain any sort of apprehension from X but go on

doing your meditation. Master is within you and always watching over you.

Regarding your marriage, I have already expressed my thoughts in my previous letter. If Y loves you, you can marry him. But if he is addicted to animal food and liquor, it is possible that he may induce you to take the same. In that case your spiritual progress will be hindered. Yet, if you can prevail upon him to give up the use of these articles, then you will be able to pull on well with him and both of you will live happily together.

You can do whatever you like for earning your livelihood, but continue carrying on your meditation so that your spiritual progress may also continue.

~

98. You complain of your mind wandering out during repetition. When you sit for the purpose, you should warn your mind not to generate any thought of any kind during the time, and to throw out any idea that crops up. Keep a guard over your mind and do not allow it to go out during repetition. In this way you will be able, by and by, to still the mind.

The direction (one meal a day) in *Sar Bachan* is meant for those who have given up the world and its work, and who have resolved to do nothing else but meditate in their lives. Those who live in the world and have to earn their own living or look after a household should take as many meals as will keep up their health.

You cannot see or hear with my eyes or ears. In order to see the light or hear the sound, it is necessary that your mind should acquire the power of concentration, for which you should work hard on your repetition while keeping the mind present. As you get concentration, you will get light and sound.

99.   Man is a limited being although he has the ability of becoming limitless. The degree to which this ability has been developed by anyone changes his outlook about nature. Therefore, there are different ways of looking at the same thing and interpreting the same phenomenon.

Take the instance of man: He is the product of his own activity in the past—his karma—which expresses itself as his hopes and desires, under whose influence he works now in this life. Nature has impressed the same karmic activity on his hands, feet, forehead, and so on. The palmist reads his destiny from the markings on the hands. Some read him from the markings on his feet or forehead, or from the eyes. A phrenologist judges him from the structure of his head. An astrologer casts his life from the position of planets at the time of his birth. Yet others, who have controlled their own minds, see him as the impression of his mind in matter, and read him directly from his mind. All are right in their respective spheres.

The same applies to what controls weather. The Weather Bureau forecasts it from the observations of the atmospheric conditions. An astronomer sees it as the effect of planetary motions and the cosmic forces. An astrologer casts it from the position of planets and stars.

As all nature is one, the natural phenomena and the living forms are interrelated, and weather plays a very important part in the life of man and beast. When things go beyond the grasp of the intellect, man tries in faith to propitiate nature by singing hymns, performing *yags* (sacrifices), and so forth.

Saints see God in action throughout nature, and abide by His will. To them cosmic forces, karmic law, planetary motions, nature, weather, forms of life and their activity are outward expressions of God in action. They see harmony in them. In our ignorance, we see a little part of nature and think, "Nature is cruel." If we go within, we develop a wider outlook and begin to see harmony in nature, in place of discord.

～

100. There can be no harm in rearing cattle for sale to feeders who do not slaughter cattle. It may be that by this restriction you may be losing a part of your profits in trade; yet, for the sake of principle, I hope you would not mind the sacrifice. If you think that the cattle business would bring you good income and that it would be easier for you on account of past experience, it would *not* be worthwhile not to take it up or give it up during the present war conditions. While earning, make enough money to lead a life of ease and comfort after the war is over.

I am glad to find that you are determined to go ahead, both spiritually and physically. A firm resolve and the determination to carry on in the face of all obstacles go a long way in bringing about success.

The prescribed posture results in concentration in shorter time than any other posture. Keep up your courage and determination. Sooner or later you will be successful.

～

101. You have nothing whatever to do with X or with any other disciple. No doubt X took part in your initiation, but that was merely as my messenger, and he can exercise no sort of control or authority over you, whether spiritual, mental or physical. You are in direct contact and connection, spiritually, with me alone, though I do not say that you should not associate with any other disciple whom you like.

At initiation you were given the names of the lords of the five planes as well as the names of the planes themselves. You are to repeat only the names of the five lords and no other name. They are to be repeated seriatim, from the lord of lowest plane to the lord of the highest plane. You are not to repeat any name that may have been revealed to you by anyone before your initiation.

This repetition is meant to bring about concentration of the mind and soul; and, as a result of the concentration, the extremities of the body should feel benumbed during meditation. As you advance in your concentration, gradually the whole of the body will feel benumbed. You will see light within, as you concentrate.

Remember, please, that any disciple of the Master who carries on meditation in the way revealed to you at initiation is free from the effect of every kind of magic. His soul cannot be under the control of any other soul, provided he works with love and faith, abstains from animal food and drink, and keeps his mind pure. If you keep your mind and conduct pure, you cannot come under the influence of anyone. No one can stop your spiritual progress.

Do not be anxious. Work upon your meditation and write to me about your progress from time to time, and you will be given good advice.

102.   Everybody in this world has to undergo a heavy burden of karma, accumulated during numerous past births; and anybody who takes upon himself the duty of initiation, without my authority, has to bear a part of the karma of the one whom he initiates without my authority. Until a soul has reached the third stage and has cast off the three coverings, he cannot bear the burden of other's karmas, and not even his own, which have to be washed off before the soul is allowed to leave the second stage for the third. A person so

interfering in initiations not only delays his own progress but has to carry additional burden.

Master does not want to raise an army or to collect subscriptions. He only wants to do good to true seekers after God. His motive is pure, selfless. He does not expect any kind of reward or fees from them.... You need not try to dissipate your mental and spiritual powers in winning people over to your point of view. Master is present with everyone, and it is his work to attract people towards himself. You should work hard on your meditation, keeping your mind free from sexual thoughts.

You are doing right in keeping your attention inside; and if you work hard, you will have clear vision of objects and persons and scenes. You will also see the form of the Master clearly. The parents of a devoted disciple are always helped by the Master, even if they died long ago.

$\sim$

103.   Thanks, I appreciate frankness but this seems to be a case of misunderstanding. My letters are, of course, drafted by secretaries, according to verbal instructions, but there was absolutely no idea, nor can there be any, of parading anybody's personal problems or letting down anybody as it were. On the other hand, it has always been our principle to treat personal problems as confidential ... I am sorry to find you so perturbed, but I can assure you that there was nothing personal about it, and this should put you at ease. You should take a charitable view, as becomes a student of Sant Mat.

Now, as to the various questions asked and points raised in your letters:

1.   *Yes-mentality, knowledge, and belief.* You say that you are not a yes-man. Well and good. We too do not want this

mentality. Sant Mat is based upon real knowledge, the knowledge that promotes honest inquiry.

It is a liberal system and does not stifle opinion or insist on blind belief. To start with, it asks you to accept some fundamental concepts, only by way of a working hypothesis, even as in Euclid you take a theorem for granted only that you might be able to demonstrate its truth in the end. You must not forget, however, the subtle nature of the subject which cannot be adequately discussed and understood by mere intellectual reasoning. It deals with eternal truths, beyond the reach of mind and *buddhi* (intellect), and can therefore be comprehended properly only when the student goes in and gets some background of personal spiritual experiences. Those who devote sufficient time are verifying these truths for themselves, and these include both Indians as well as foreigners. We do not force conviction upon anybody. We like the conviction to grow from within as a result of one's own personal experience. Let the student devote sufficient time and work as directed. The rest will follow.

Till then, one must have faith, or work would be impossible. If the great explorers and adventurers of the world who widened the horizon of our knowledge had no faith in their enterprises, they would not have been able to go on and suffer many privations and hardships. What distinguished Columbus from his followers? An unshakable faith and an indomitable will.

2.   *Master.* Your conception of the Master is correct. He is in the world for our good and guidance, for without a Master, who will teach us? Man can be taught by man only. The Master is unselfish, without any prejudice, and our true well-wisher and benefactor. He is with us in this world, in spiritual regions, and even in the court of the Most High; but this realisation comes only when the veil of mind has been lifted.

3. Life and its law. Yes, life is change. Nothing is here at a standstill; the direction is the result of the interplay of so many forces, known and unknown, including our own efforts.

The whole universe is subject to laws, but the same laws may not be operative and to the same extent in all places. This is again a point which is best understood when one goes in.

When we talk of universal laws, we mean the laws of this known material universe; and even here our knowledge is far from complete. How little do we know about conditions on Mars or the moon? How can you know, by mere intellectual discussion, the conditions in fine ethereal and spiritual regions? Here you have only to believe; if you want to know, you must gird up your loins and go in.

Life is an immensely complicated affair. Every effect is the result of so many causes, and likewise every cause has so many effects which differ in intensity according to prevailing conditions. If we know all the causes accurately, and their background, we should be able to predict the effect accurately. I do not follow your line of reasoning here and how this is relative to the career of a student of Sant Mat.

4. Initiation. I do not wonder if you are unable to appreciate the value of initiation, because you have not gone in. It is true, one must work and transform himself to reap the fullest advantage, but even to be initiated is a great privilege, and perhaps you will realise it by and by. It is no small thing to be set on the right road and have an unerring guide who is always ready to keep you on the way as soon as you make a start, who makes himself visible as you progress, and stands by you in all circumstances. Think of the thousands who worked hard, denied themselves all pleasures and even comforts, and yet could not reach the goal because they were not initiated by a perfect Master. The posture and the key words have got their significance. They may not appeal to some people, but you doubtless realise that every game must be played according to rules. The fact is that the overcritical often waste their opportunities while the simple-minded win the day.

5.   *Initiation by a perfect Master.* Man is the image of God. As you say, man has great potentialities; but till these potentialities are realised and actualized, they are of no use. In this phenomenal world, man the master appears as man the slave; (for) as long as he is the slave of his appetites, he cannot know real happiness. He must first learn to control himself and be his own master before he can be master of the world.

This can be done only by realisation within, and for that, contacting a perfect Master is the first step. We must learn to rise above the senses. This is expressed in our terminology by saying that we must rise above this house of nine doors and knock at the tenth gate. We have been turned out of the royal palace, as it were, and the door banged on us. Someone must remind us of our rights and teach us how, by turning our back on the delights and pleasures of this world, we must boldly knock at the tenth door and seek admittance. That someone is the Master.

Meeting the Master is a condition necessary and precedent to the working of his grace, and does not imply any limitation of opportunity as you seem to think. The opportunities are offered to those only who have some chance of profiting by them. We do not complain that the rain comes through the clouds only and does not fall straight out of the blue void. We are convinced that this is the law. Similarly, this law operates with regard to spiritual matters. We must know whence and how we came down and must return by the same route. The key is in the hands of the Master.

An imperfect Master would not be able to lead the initiate to the highest goal. Please remember we are talking of the highest ultimate goal, and for that the perfect Master is absolutely necessary. One may make progress, as it is ordinarily understood, even without such initiation and, if ardent enough, may reach the region of the stars, the sun, and the moon, but he will not be able to go beyond that.

Sant Mat's ideal is very high. It aims only at the highest and the absolute good. That is why it does not think much of so-called spiritual healing, etc. The comparative value of such work is inferior to what Sant Mat offers. Why should you be contented with a cent when you can earn a dollar?

Your reference to a person cast on an island is not quite clear. If such a person is initiated, he has nothing to fear, and may even do a little better because there will be few distractions in his case. The Moghul emperor, Akbar the Great, wanted to ascertain what would happen to children if nobody talked to them, and if they would develop any natural language. He had some newborn babes transferred to a building called the Dumb Palace, where they were looked after by dumb attendants. They all grew up to be dumb and uttered sounds like animals.

6. *Healing, social service, etc.* We do not inculcate isolationism or selfishness, but advocate the highest ideal of service. Service is indeed the backbone of our organization; and most of our workers, from men and women working in the kitchens to secretaries and superintendents of departments, are honourary. The highest service to yourself, to others, and to the Master is going inside.

Healing is not bad but we aim at the best, as has been said before. These other services, rest assured, will not be neglected. There are plenty of others to carry out the services of the type you mention. To keep our eyes fixed on the highest ideal and work for it day and night cannot be called niggardliness. Is the chemist who carries on his research in his laboratory and denies himself the usual social pleasures a selfish man, or an isolationist? There is another point, too. Your power of good now is very limited. It is not bad to send good thoughts, but these thoughts bind you to lower planes. Golden fetters are also fetters.

If you charge your patients, this is not much of social service, and if you do not, you will have to come down again to reap the fruit of your good actions. Doing good will certainly bring its reward, but it will not bring about the release from birth and death. Perhaps you do not appreciate this point of view.

Again, let us suppose that a philanthropist visits a jail and donates a sum of money for giving the prisoners a treat, or induces the authorities to improve their conditions of living; or, again, the Red Cross Society sends parcels of sweets, clothing, and other things to these prisoners. They have all improved the prisoners' lot and momentarily made them happy. But they are still in the jail. Then comes an unostentatious-looking figure who holds the key to the jail. He opens the door and tells them that they are free henceforth, and even arranges for their passage home. Who has rendered the greatest service? That is the way of saints.

X was under certain conditions allowed to continue the healing which was her profession, and I am glad to hear you say that she has rigidly and conscientiously adhered to those conditions. But the general rule remains the same and Y was right in pointing out the general rule. He had no authority to relax the conditions. The fact still remains that her progress has not been as rapid and satisfactory as it would have been if it had been possible for her to devote all her time to her spiritual practices. This is no disparagement of X but a plain fact and the natural result of the law which operates without regard to persons.

7. *Four lives.* Your reference to the maximum of four lives is rather amusing. There is absolutely no compulsion to finish your pilgrimage here in the compass of four lives only. In fact, nobody can go up as long as he has desires on the earth plane. They will surely drag him down. The Master can show the way and help you along the path, but does not force you. Please note that it is a privilege and not an obligation.

For souls with intense longing, one life may be enough, but the saints generally try to finish up the karmas of the initiates within a maximum of four lives. You may look upon it as something queer, but once you begin to go in and taste the joys of spiritual life, your point of view will change.

8. *The Master.* The Masters are very broadminded and do not care at all what you think about them. You may certainly look upon the Master as a friend if you find that helpful, and he is certainly the best and the truest friend. I will again say, go in and see for yourself.

You may come here and study things for yourself whenever it is possible and convenient, but you will have to wait till the end of the war at least. In the end I would add that Sant Mat teaches true humility, forbearance, and charity, and it is this spirit that ought to permeate our thoughts as well as our actions.

≈

104. I am glad you read my letter in the spirit in which it was written. You already had taken such a generous view, as your letter revealed. I am also glad that you keep an open mind and conscientiously try to get other viewpoints.

"Having been raised in Christendom, to me the life of Jesus the Christ—has been, and still is, a height of perfection still unattained by the majority of us—which being the case, he has held the place, not of an idol, but of an ideal—a model, if you will, for real life." Almost similar opinion is held by the followers of other religions regarding the lives of the founders of their religions. There is some justification for that, as the founders appeared on the scene at different times and in different countries with different political, economic, and social backgrounds. No two lives are therefore strictiy comparable. General inferences may be drawn.

When the spirit of the religion disappears, religion deteriorates, and priesthood appears. And "priests of all religions are the same," and so are their followers. Whereas every founder practised and preached morality, brotherhood of man and oneness of God and, above all (this is their mission), invited people to accompany them to the Kingdom of their Lord in Heaven; the followers, in fact, are slaves of their senses, thereby selfish, and have no use for the Kingdom of their Lord in Heaven.

Some read scriptures and feel virtuous, some do little charitable acts and feel over-virtuous and—on the strength of the founders whom they never met and therefore could not possibly accept—claim heaven to themselves and deny it to others. How simple a device to bypass Satan and attain salvation!

In my last letter it was stated that to live the life of Christ, one must develop the latent powers in himself which Christ had developed. Man is an inexhaustible store of powers. The whole creation is within him along with the Creator. The drop is in the ocean and the ocean is in the drop. Creation is in the Creator, and the Creator is in all creation. In the absence of the tapping of that power from within, it is impossible to grasp the significance even of the moral teaching of Christ— what to say of the Kingdom of his Father in Heaven.

So long as our attention is attached to the sense organs, we are slaves of the senses. Whichever sense pleases, pulls the attention over to itself. The attention of the eye is irresistibly pulled out when it sees a beautiful object. The attention of the ear is pulled out when it hears a sweet voice. When we came out of the mother's womb and opened our eyes, we saw the world; when we opened our ears, we heard the voices of the world; when we opened our tongue, we replied to what we heard; and thereby we established our connection with the world and became of this world. We practised this in mother's arms, at the feet of the teachers in schools, and do the same in daily life. This is our life—confined to this world, the material plane.

Before we came into this world, our attention worked on a different plane—the mental plane. Coming out into this material plane we forgot all about the mental plane. If now we can close our eyes, ears, and tongue—do not allow our attention to run out through the eyes, ears, and tongue— we disconnect ourselves from this material plane and reconnect ourselves with the mental plane. Our mental powers will be developed. On the strength of these powers, we would be living on the material plane, but would not be of matter— would not be slaves of the senses and the objects of the senses. We would be the masters of our senses, for our attention would not run foolishly through the senses, and we would use our senses when we would wish to use them. Then lust, anger, greed, attachment, and pride will have been replaced by continence, forgiveness, contentment, discrimination, and humility.

When well established in the mental plane, marvellous powers will develop. One could heal the sick, give sight to the blind, cast out devils, feed hundred thousands from one loaf of bread, walk on water, and fly in the air. But it must be stated that the use of these powers is dangerous—is playing into the hands of the negative power. The condition is like that of an engine running wild, to its own destruction, without a governor.[1]

Sant Mat does not permit their use. They draw out the attention from the sound current—the positive power—and stop the attention from rising above the mental plane and entering into the pure spiritual planes. Sant Mat invites its votaries to go within themselves and verify all this. And here is the rub. If going within were so simple, priests would not have taken to the study of scriptures. They would study themselves—God's book—instead of man-made books, and would have found God, instead of indulging in talk about God. If a priest is asked to commit to memory fifty pages of a book by the evening, he does so; but if asked to put his mind out of action for five minutes, he throws up his arms in despair. This is the reason why there is so much talk about religion and so little of it in practice.

Then there are the moralists who seek salvation through morality. When the attention uses the senses at will, which means when the attention has established itself in the eye centre, there is morality in practice. But the Kingdom of Heaven is far away yet. Morality is a means and not an end.

Then there is a group which believes in salvation after death through service to mankind. And what is this service? It is charity, in one form or another—all kinds of charitable deeds including mental healings intended to give relief from suffering. They are very good acts, no doubt, resulting in good rewards, but bonds on the attention all the same, for to get their reward there will be rebirth. Such acts do not break the continuity of birth after birth.

And reliance on salvation after death is the finest form of self-deception man practises on himself. If there is no

1. A governor was an apparatus installed in a car to keep it from going at very high speeds.

salvation while alive, it will not come after death. He who is illiterate when alive cannot be a scholar after death.

The sum total of these observations is that there is one power and one only—the sound current—which leads us from the eye centre to our spiritual home. All other powers (without exception) keep us confined to the material and mental planes, giving us forms according to our actions. If, during lifetime, entry has been made into the eye centre and the sound current (bell sound) has been grasped, life has been usefully spent. If this has not been done, even though all else has been done—and most successfully—then life has been wasted. This done, all is done; this not done, all else done is as if nothing is done. Such is the finding of Sant Mat and it is a fact. It is not an arbitrary mandate.

Only the other day I was in the foothills of the Himalayas for satsang. Some twelve hundred were initiated. The hill folk are usually simple and pure-minded. At the very time of initiation there were many who saw light within themselves, and some heard the bell sound. On account of their scattered minds, it is difficult for the educated to concentrate. But with faith and perseverance it becomes easy.

When this is the only way, and we are to go this way, then why not go now? You have received initiation (first step). You know where to go—Sach Khand. You know the way—through the eyes, and the five stages whose distinctive marks have been given. You know the method—simran—to reach the eye centre, and—sound current—from this centre upward. It is now for you to take the next step—reach the eye centre. You may depend on your Friend for assistance. When the child begins to stand on his legs, the father gives his supporting hand.

"The idea that all efforts should be given over to personal advancement, while universal service should receive scant attention." The position is that we should not attempt rendering a service in which we are not qualified. He who has learnt swimming just to keep his head above water must not go in deep waters to save a person in trouble there. Instead he can shout for help, throw in a rope, push in a log of wood, or do some such things. It is better to have only one tragedy in place of a double tragedy. If he is an expert swimmer, it would be criminal on his part if he did not go to the rescue.

Universal service as the aim of brotherhood is an excellent idea. But universal service and individual are contradictory terms. So long as an individual has not made himself universal, he is incapable of rendering universal service. And the individual is an individual so long as his attention is confined to the nine portals of his body. As such he functions very imperfectly even on the material plane. The mental and the spiritual planes are inaccessible to him. He does not even know what lies on the other side of the wall, and little knows what is wrong with himself.

He has to cure himself from the disease of individuality before he thinks of brotherhood and universal service. When he has concentrated himself in the eye centre, he will have cast off the matter from him, and matter will be no hindrance to him. He will know what lies on the other side of the wall. He will be partially cured. When he has thrown off his mind after penetrating through the mental planes, and has entered into the spiritual plane, he is pure soul. Matter and mind have been cast off. From an individual confined to the material plane, he is now capable of functioning at will and unhindered on the material, mental, and spiritual planes. He has become universal and completely cured. The whole world benefits from such a one.

Defining a thing to a person means expressing it in terms which the person understands—in other words, of which he has the experience. Saint John, in chapter 1, verses 1–5, has tried to explain the Word, bringing the definition down to our experience, step by step. He describes the Word as (a) identical with God, (b) maker of all things, (c) the life, (d) the light of men. At the other end the Word is God, and at this end it is our life and light, which in our darkness we do not comprehend. He who has comprehended the Word as light, life, maker of all things, and as God, bestows upon as many as approach him the power to become the sons of God. So God, the Word, and the Son of God form the Trinity—three aspects of the One.

All saints are Sons of God; their mission is to make others the sons of God; their method is the Word—sound current. There is no other method. The difference lies in the extent to which this Word has been traced by its votaries. The Word is light. It resounds throughout the whole creation—material, mental, and spiritual—within us and outside us. It is light and sound both. Sant Mat connects with it as sound. The lights and sounds at the different stages of the journey are already known to you. The significance of the Word will grow step by step with experience.

Many thanks for sending me love and a little portion of universal blessing....

A potter considers his own pots the best till he sees others of better make. So do the followers of a particular religion, till they experience something better. It is true and very true that Christ lived a pure, sublime life. His Sermon on the Mount gives his moral teaching and is the beacon of light for the guidance of humanity. The strength to live up to this teaching he derived from the practice of the Word, the sound current. And the higher the rise on this current, the greater the strength. There are many who excel others in this field and go beyond their reach. You can realise the truth of this statement if you work your way up.

The physical, astral, and causal bodies are the cages, one inside the other, to keep the soul from escaping and flying to its home. It is a parrot in a triple cage. When the cages are cut off, it comes into its own and is free to fly. This is freedom of man, to be attained in human form while alive.

I doubt if light and sound vibrations could be fitted in a mathematical equation. But this is a fact: the Word gives out both light and sound. At this end, in the physical plane, the light and sound are lost in gross matter. On the finer planes—astral, causal, and spiritual—sound is audible and light is visible. At the upper end, the sound is the finest music unheard by human ears—and the light is of millions of suns and moons in one ray. Some idea, just an idea of the beauty and grandeur, has been given to you in terms of sounds and lights of this world. The reality is beyond description, and our mathematics is too poor to solve even our problems of the physical plane.

～

105. Jesus says, "Call no one Master save 'Christ'." Every saint has said the same. Correctly speaking, man, as he is (not what he is capable of)—that is, so long as his attention is working in the nine portals of the body and has not entered through the eye centre into the astral plane and seen the Astral Form of the Master and his working on that plane—is incapable of making a distinction between one who is "christened" and one who is not "christened," for he does not see inwards, and his will is weak and is easily swayed away by senses and objects of senses. It is not given to the blind to catch one with eyes. One who has eyes may, if he likes, associate with the blind, of his choice. However, the blind (whose attention is working from the eye centre in an outward direction and does not see within) can work diligently on repetition of the names and the Word, and thereby experience the withdrawal of their current from the extremities of the body towards the eye centre. Step by step, they can develop in themselves the capacity to see the latent "Christ" and the Master, for he is in tune with the Word and responds in an active manner by clearing their way to the eye centre.

A schoolmaster goes out of his way to help his shining students. Saints go a step further. So long as they are in the human form they do not call themselves Masters and do not wish to be called Masters. They call themselves his humble servants. If we ask them who is the Master, then their answer is "the Almighty or the Word."

The Word is the latent "Christ" in all. People are in darkness and do not comprehend that they are the Word in and out—flesh, light, and life. If they could comprehend the Word in themselves, they would be in light and alive and in the Kingdom of God in Heaven. Jesus was Christ on account of his comprehension of the Word in him, and thereby he had risen above the weakness of the flesh and was capable of lifting others to his level. The Word is universal law, the Word is God. Therefore, living in the Word is living in harmony with God and universal law, not otherwise.

Unfortunately, the span of life in this Kal Yuga is too short and the struggle for existence too keen. There is little time for leisure and search for truth. But we have to work in these environments to develop the latent "Christ" in us. It cannot be ignored or postponed if the full benefit of the human form is to be derived. I am glad this work receives your attention.

... Your Friend or Master is within you, nearer than anything else, and watches you. Whenever your attention is directed towards the eye centre, He hears you and responds, but his response is missed by you because your attention wavers and runs outwards. If you could hear inside, you would be in tune. I wish you may come up to him and see him inside, face to face, instead of merely sensing his presence.

"There are many who like to discuss philosophy in the abstract but care little for placing that same philosophy into practice." This is human nature expressing both its strength and weakness. The strength lies in the fact that man, although in practice finds himself weak and incapable of executing what he wills, yet perseveres in seeking that "something," the attainment of which will make him strong and happy. He is an eternal seeker and in all his wanderings in transmigration, has been in search of what he lacks. His discussion of philosophy is his innate urge to seek light.

The weakness lies in that in his long wandering he has almost lost his capital and is bankrupt now, too weak to stand unaided on his legs. He was soul at one time when he was in intimate touch with the Word. That was long, long ago, when he was in spiritual regions. When the soul lost touch with the Word and associated with the mind in the mental planes, the jewel was thrown away and the imitation grasped. The debased coin could pass as genuine on the mental planes only, but is not acceptable in the spiritual planes. The access to the spiritual planes was thus debarred.

The coin was further debased when mind and soul left the mind planes and associated with gross matter in the physical plane. Here the jewel is no longer traceable, man has no knowledge of soul and very poor knowledge of mind. The coin has become spurious and has no purchasing power in the markets of the mental and spiritual planes. Soul has been materialized, and human nature has become very weak. Therefore, people talk of philosophy and are too weak to put it in practice unaided. They need a living "Christ" not only to rebaptize them with the Word but to help them both by precept and example. His talks are definite and specific instead of vague and general, and he (the living Master) is the living example of what he says. His teaching, the real philosophy, the substance of philosophy, is the Word which can be practised only under the guidance of a living Master or "Christ."

When Masters and "Christs" of old were in the flesh, they came in contact with people and, in their physical form, were in a position to associate with them and help them. When they are not in flesh and are back in the Word, they are helpless to instruct us, for we are out of tune with ourselves and cannot comprehend them. The Word has been, is, and will be, the basic reality. It is imperishable and all-pervading and is present in all beings. If people could derive benefit from this all-pervading Word, or if this all-pervading Word could help people directly, there would have been no need at any time for the Masters or "Christs" to appear in flesh amongst people. If there was need for their appearance at one time, the same need requires their presence now.

A living teacher is needed to school our children, a living doctor to prescribe for our ailments, a living judge to settle our disputes, and a living Master to give us our lost jewel— the Word. The few who try to put their philosophy into practice feel the need for a living Master, for they come across difficulties and, to get over them, need guidance.

In other words there is dualism in man—a strong outward tendency or a centrifugal force (the mind) which prevents him from getting in touch with the Word and keeps him slave of the senses and the objects of senses. Throughout his life, whether in the lap of the mother, by the side of the father, at the feet of the teacher, in company of wife and children, or in his vocation of life, he receives training to develop this outward tendency. The weak, inward tendency— the centripetal force—remains undeveloped. In Masters and "Christs," the outward, centrifugal force has been nullified and the inward, centripetal force has been developed. They have disassociated their souls from the mind and associated them with the Word.

When we associate with Masters, we come under their influence. They talk of our latent strength, of our spiritual origin, of our Kingdom in Heaven, point out the way within us of going back to our eternal spiritual home—not merely point the way and ask us to go alone, but go with us all the way and further, put us under no obligation, and charge no fee. Could there be a better offer?

Masters in the flesh are rare. They are superior beings and have fully developed their latent powers. Their attention, unlike ours, is not confined to the physical plane. At will, their attention has access to the astral, mental, and spiritual planes, and functions on these planes. They are universal although outwardly they appear as individuals like others. When in the flesh they speak to us of other superior worlds and the Creator, and of our aim in life. To strengthen our belief, they place before us the writings of the past Masters as authority, and induce us, in all rational ways, to experiment and investigate.

Man learns of the universal from a man universalized—a Master. The universal power cannot give him guidance except by manifesting itself in a man; in other words, by becoming a Master. The Master would teach man by stages, unfolding himself as the student rises in grade. There is no other way. Man could not learn from the unseen universal Creator. He has been with him all through the long, long past. When the Creator wishes to bring anybody back to Him, He brings him in touch with a Master and, through Him, with the Word. This is how it has worked in the past and how it will work in future.

Dr Johnson: "Living Master is necessary. To follow a Master not alive is fruitless." The Word is the teaching of the

Masters. To follow a Master means practising the Word—catching the sound current from the eye centre and riding on that. Only a living Master can give us the Word. We can neither get it from books nor from Masters not now alive for the simple reason that the Word is not present in books, nor with their help (books) can we catch it from within ourselves, and we do not know how to come in contact with them (Masters). The teaching of the living, or the dead Masters when they were alive, is and was the Word, and if the Word has not been contacted in human form, one's life has been "fruitless."

Living a good moral life, giving charities and doing service to humanity, and such other things—or, let us say, putting into practice the Sermon on the Mount—is not really the teaching of the Masters. This is the sphere of moralists, social reformers, preachers and schoolmasters. It is like the sale of separated milk from which cream has been removed. The Masters give free cream, butter, and clarified fat *(ghee).*

There is one point, however: A dead Master is not dead to his initiates. The disciples on earth have lost the benefit of his physical form, no doubt, and for that they must go to his successor. His Astral Form remains with them, and if they have access to their own eye centre they make contact with that Form and get guidance from it on the inner planes. In case they have not entered the eye centre and their attention is confined to the physical plane, their efforts should be to reach the eye centre while receiving encouragement and guidance from the successor. Dead Masters are not dead for their initiates, but they can not make new initiates. This is done by the living Master.

Suppose you see a form when awake or in dream and it poses as "Christ" and asks you to do this or that and, let us say, foretells events which come out to be correct. How will you know that this form was really Jesus "Christ"? You have not seen him in physical form. The astral plane abounds in negative powers which can assume any form they like, and their aim is to deceive.

If the idea is correct that a dead Master, because he has become universal, is in an advantageous position to teach others—meaning thereby connecting others with the Word—we should be able to find a dozen or half a dozen Christians in the world who have studied the Word to the second or the first stage, or are even familiar with the Word.

Sant Mat is nature's design, not man-made; nor can man make additions, subtractions, or modifications in it. There is no theory about it. It is a hard fact—a substance. It already exists complete in man. Man has only to look within himself to see what lies in him. No imagination is involved.

… If you find my answer requires further elucidation, please write without hesitation. You may please read your Bible with your friends, particularly Saint John, in the light of Sant Mat. Dr Johnson's *The Path of the Masters* clears many passages in the Bible.

⁓

106.   I am glad to receive your loving letter and congratulate you on having such a clear and penetrating reasoning faculty. Here are a few observations on your problem:

Every deep-thinking person tries to form a mental picture of the universe with a view to solve its mystery and reconstruct the picture, giving it a new colour or touch when he has gained more experience and received more light. The mind and the intellect being blind, their range is extremely limited. With these tools the riddle remains unsolved. As a matter of fact, nobody sitting in the Pind part of the body has any clear understanding of the problem. He gropes in darkness.

Sant Mat gives us the Word as the key to the solution of the problem. With every little rise within, there is a new experience and rapid change in the viewpoint. In Anda one begins to see some light; and after crossing Brahmand, all the coverings on the soul are removed, the soul is naked (free) and is capable of knowing its origin in Sach Khand. Reaching there, it experiences that He is infinite, He is the light and life in all—"All is He" or "All is from Him"—and that Almighty God, the Word, and the soul are of the same essence; that the Almighty God is the ocean of consciousness and bliss, the Word (God-in-action or Creator) is a wave of the ocean, and that the soul is a drop thereof.

Only He is infinite, and all that has been created is finite. In this sense the soul, the mind, matter, and the various forms of creation are finite, and work in their respective finite spheres.

The activities of the mind are limited to the three planes—physical, astral, and causal. It has no place above Trikuti. Soul alone goes up to Sach Khand, working independent of the mind. In the three planes mentioned above, the soul works through mind and matter—the mind becoming the active agent. In Brahmand the soul takes on a covering of the finest phase of mind and matter; in Anda it takes on another covering of comparatively coarser form; and in Pind it takes on the third covering, in addition. With each covering the light of the soul is dimmed, and in proportion it is cut off from the Word.

The same applies to the mind. Mind, having been activated by soul, works in the three planes and progressively goes dull with its descent from the top of Trikuti down to the physical plane.

Both the soul and the mind, when confined in the coverings, forget their origins—the soul its Sach Khand and the mind its Trikuti.

One has the option to look at the mind as one mind working in the three planes or that there are three minds or three
aspects or phases of the same mind. It makes no difference.
In its dullest state in the physical plane the mind is synonymous with imagination. Sant Mat does not give the mind any
divinity or infinity. As the moon is bright due to the light of
the sun, so the mind is bright due to the light of the soul—
the brightness depending on the amount of the light received.
The inherent nature of mind is materialistic, outward, and
negative. When it faces inwardly it gets illumination from the
soul, and when it faces outwardly it is associated with matter.

Your reasoning is good. "Man must be eternally perfect."
The Creator is within him and so is his complete creation.
When man has explored himself and seen the creation and
the Creator within himself, he is eternally perfect. But so long
as his investigation is incomplete, he is imperfect. Man alone,
out of the whole creation, has the privilege of "using his faculties as he sees fit," and of going within, right up to the Feet
of his Creator in Sach Khand.

Dream is real when one is dreaming. Only when he awakens or comes into the other (conscious) state and compares
the two states, he calls the conscious the real, and the dream
the unreal or an illusion. When the attention leaves the physical plane, enters the astral, and compares the two, only then
the physical world becomes unreal, and the astral the real.

The finite mind which was working on the physical plane,
on entering the astral, casts off one covering and merges into
the finer phase of the mind, loses its separate existence, and
becomes a subtle mind. It has knowledge of the two planes
and can function on these two.

When it has entered the causal plane by casting off the
astral covering, its range extends to the third plane and it is
higher but still mind. The universe of those who call the mind

universal or infinite, extends to the causal plane, and often only to the astral. They have not penetrated further. Their infinity is finite in the experience and terminology of the saints. Their "God" is the "mind" of Sant Mat.

It is incumbent on man to seek his origin because he is a "thinking" person. He is expected to "supervise his planning department," go inside, and go ahead to get his reward.

I wish that you to go within and see the reality with your own eye and to your satisfaction, and compare it with what your reason has pictured. The substance lies within you.

~

107. I am glad you have received initiation. I would wish that you work your way up and enter within your eye centre and realise what the Creator has placed within you. He is there himself, and through the Word is calling you home. The Word is his voice. So, slowly and steadily, put your mind in repetition and withdraw your attention from the body into the eye centre; thereby completing the concentration so that the attention is capable of grasping the Word.

In the family, the members meet as travellers in an inn, some coming and some going—in their own time. The meeting and parting is determined by the karma of individuals—one comes as father, another as mother, another as son or daughter, and near relatives. Karma determines friends and foes, and karma has cast the mould of life. Everybody is running his own race.

~

108. I very much appreciate the spirit of love and devotion in which the letter is written. You have done well in giving up spiritual healing, which resulted in your taking upon yourself a part of the karma or sins of those whom you wanted to heal.... Having given up supernatural healing of the sick, the most important problem for you is how to earn your living. On that part you must be the best judge. You might take up any honest occupation you deem fit, by which you may be able to live comfortably without overworking yourself.

Solitude is good for spiritual progress.... Social functions, besides wasting one's time, distract one's mind which, therefore, becomes difficult to concentrate. Without concentration, spiritual progress is impossible. Try to devote some part of your morning time, before beginning your household or worldly duties, to concentration and hearing the sound current. That is the best time for the purpose.

The greatest book is man, and every religion has advised us, "Know thyself!" That knowledge of yourself comes only by concentrating and collecting the currents of the mind at the eye focus. By practice, the mind will become habituated to concentrate at that focus, and the sound will become clearer. This is the real way to go within and have knowledge of yourself, which is the great book we came to study on this planet.

≈

109.   I cannot forbid you to marry, as all of us here are married people. You may marry X with pleasure and live wherever you like, but do not let your spiritual practice of meditation and repetition lessen in any way on that account. You can carry on your repetition even while doing your daily household work. If that gentleman also gets initiated, it would be very good for both of you, so that you may both become of the same mind and pass your life comfortably.

If an initiated person takes his soul inside, he does not think of sex. My idea in giving you permission for marriage is that it may become easier for you to live on in this world.

The dreams of which you complain are due to indigestion. Sometimes, when one's impressions during the day are connected with sex matters, one is liable to get such dreams. You should not mind it. As he is not pulling on well with his wife, there is no harm in your marrying him after he gets a divorce. After marriage you will have no need to offer your services for healing purposes, as you would not have to earn your own living.

About Y and her illness, the recovery depends upon her past karma and the will of God. You may keep her with you and look after her.

~

110. Please take care that during your repetition your mind does not wander out. Keep the mind present. The teaching is the highest and most natural philosophy. Purity of mind and character are great aids in the path. This is a labour of years. Please do not expect hasty results, as the mind takes time in becoming motionless and quiet.

~

111. I am very much pleased to learn that you have been working hard at your spiritual meditation and got benefit out of it. If you continue to persevere in your labour, you will be successful one day. When a disciple works at his concentration, he must get internal peace and joy. He becomes pure-minded, and his words will correspond to his deeds; and the rays emanating from his pure mind will affect the minds of his associates and his companions. This is the benefit which is derived by the people around and in contact with a disciple.

Regarding your question as to how you can be of service to the Master, the latter does not accept any worldly presents, all of which are perishable. The best service that a disciple can render to the Master is to follow his instructions, to concentrate and to cross the stars, the sun, and the moon, and contact him on the astral plane within.

You are quite right in not troubling your head with far-off matters. Your only concern should be to control your mind and to go in.

~

112.   It is always spiritually beneficial to consider oneself as the humblest of the Master's disciples. You need not worry if you cannot help your friends for lack of spiritual experiences. They are all grounded in the experiences of the saints. Experiences will come at the proper time, when the weight of karmas is lifted with darshan and satsang of the Master, and through bhajan as directed.

As regards helping your friend's distant relation, the idea is laudable, but Sant Mat does not countenance giving such information by the exercise of spiritual powers. Saints can know of the whereabouts of your relation's missing son, but the exercise of supernatural powers for obtaining such information is not the way of the saints, who are always resigned to the will of the Almighty. Saints have the good of their disciples at heart and they sometimes convey information to their disciples about coming events in their life by hints. Otherwise, they never foretell future events in spite of having full knowledge of past, present, and future.

~

113.   I am glad to learn that you are devoting some time daily to meditation and concentration. There is no harm in discussing the principles of Sant Mat with those who are sincere seekers; but in your own interest, please do not divulge

what you have learnt at the time of initiation. If any person becomes interested in this science and asks for initiation, you may please recommend his case to me, if you consider him suitable. He who imparts this secret takes upon himself the karmic load of others.

I shall be glad to know that you are living happily and in circumstances congenial to your peace of mind, and doing bhajan, for it is bhajan alone that counts in the long run. All other activities, no matter how charitable and good-intentioned, and of service to humanity, bring us back to this physical plane. The Master and the sound current—and they are really one, not two—are our companions here and hereafter. Hence, their companionship should be cultivated even if everything else has to be sacrificed. Best effort should be put forth to go in and develop complete concentration, so that the Master and the sound current become living realities.

If one now wishes to meet a sage who played his part here in the old past, one will have to go within himself and reach the stage where the sage resides. And there is no going within except with the help of a living Master and the practice of the sound current. I wish that you go within now and meet your Lord Jesus, and redeem your "pledged word to the church" to whose allegiance you are sworn for this life.

It is good that you have entrusted your family affairs to the care of the Master and made your mind easy. With love and faith, go within and complete your concentration. With the increase in concentration, the will power will grow strong and you will be able to function without being perturbed by the family and worldly ups and downs. When we sit in bhajan and direct our attention inward, the Creator within marks our presence, hears our prayer, and blesses us.

～

114.   The spiritual journey is like going up a slippery road. One false step, one weak thought, and the attention is down and out. The labour of years is undone in a few moments.

The nature of the mind is fundamentally negative. Although this negation decreases as we rise up, so subtle is its working that great rishis, sufis, and prophets willingly and joyfully gave themselves up into its arms and played to its tunes. All the creation in the physical, astral, and causal planes is held bound—hands and feet—by it. At times it cannot only lose faith and find fault with the Master, but will easily go to the extent of even denying him. This is due to the effect of bad karma. When the period is over, there is an awakening again. Such happenings are not unusual with the devotees. All the travellers in this journey experience such shakes, which are helpful, in a way, in putting them back on the road, the repentance giving a push and becoming instrumental in making them go ahead.

The Master, whether in or out, makes no mistakes. The point is that both forms observe the etiquette of their planes. Both have the interest of the disciple paramount with them. There is no selfish motive with them. They are one, not two. They work in harmony and one knows what the other does. So long as one does not come across the physical form, the inner Radiant Form is not met with.[1] Therefore, the outer form is the means in bringing a devotee in touch with the inner form; hence, priority in importance goes to the outer form.

If any disciple makes a report of his progress and thinks honestly but erroneously that he has gone to this or that stage, the Master will not discourage him by pointing out his error, but would encourage him to go ahead and give necessary instructions to stick to this and avoid that, knowing that when

---

1. This means that so long as one has not been initiated by a living Master (whether in person or by proxy), the inner Radiant Form is not met.

the disciple goes higher up, he will see his mistake for himself. Pointing out the error may discourage him. This is not desirable.

If there is any doubt lurking in your mind, put it to the Master inside, and whatever answer he gives inside, take it as correct. Get hold of him and go with him and remain with him, throwing aside all doubts.

~

115. A boy is fond of play and is averse to going to school, while the parents wish him to sit in school with the teacher and study. The boy does not know the value of studies. Play gives him pleasure, and an occasional shock or knock he does not mind. Parents use threats and inducements. They cooperate with the teacher, and the teacher's task is easy. By and by, the boy learns the value of study, and as he gets disciplined, he does both—study and play—and enjoys both, and in time he is a scholar and an athlete.

In a way, similar is the position of an entrant in the "university of spirit." The Guru wishes him to open and enter the tenth gate and make contact with Nam, but he is fond of play in the nine portals of the body. He gets enjoyment in this play. Setbacks and mishaps in his play he considers as part of the game of life. The value of Nam is not known to him. The Guru induces him to go in by discourses on the grandeur of Nam. His is a difficult task, for he gets no support from parents. The parents (Kal and Maya) do not wish the entrant (soul) to enter the university of spirit (tenth gate or third eye)—what to say about contacting Nam.

The parents (Kal and Maya) allure him with easy temptations and create worries, sickness, and other adversities to confound his intellect. Their function is to keep the soul away from Nam. Slowly the entrant grasps the new position, and slowly the entrant realises the true worth of his parents. Slowly he begins to dissociate from them, and slowly he takes the Guru as his real benefactor; and slowly he leaves the nine portals and makes his approach towards the tenth—to make contact with Nam and work on Nam.

When the wild nature has been disciplined and the entrant has started his studies in the university of spirit, the going-in is easy, and a new kind of play inside the tenth gate starts giving enjoyment, compared with which the worldly enjoyments and allurements are trash.

It is true, therefore, as you say, that in preliminary stages the progress is slow. To give up worldly pleasures, to control the senses, and bring the attention in one centre by controlling the wild runs of the mind while still alive and kicking, is not an easy task. But what is it that with love and faith man cannot accomplish? You strengthen your will power and go ahead. Success is sure. Remember that once the seed of Nam has been planted, it must become a tree and bear fruit. Brahmand may perish, but the seed of Nam will not perish. There is no superior nor more precious thing than Nam. The sweetness of Nam—Shabd Dhun—is incomparable and incomprehensible in both the worlds. Nam is within you, for you, and within your reach—just inside the tenth gate. Saints ask: Can there be a simpler proposition?

You have asked for the fulfilment of some of your wishes. For their fulfilment you need not go very far. They are already with you, inside you. If you take courage and work your way up, you can get all of them. Mind goes after tasty things. It seeks satisfaction in fulfilment of desires, and no desire satisfies it for long. After some time, one discards what he has obtained and runs after new pleasures, and thereby is never satisfied and is always hungry. The remedy lies in taking the mind to Sahansdal Kanwal. The nectar there is now being stolen by maya and kam, krodh, and so forth. When you take your mind there and make him drink it, he will be satisfied forever, for the nectar is the sweetest thing known.

Then all desires will vanish and mind will be at rest. It will then accompany you as a faithful servant, and not as a bad master, as at present. Before you have reached Sahansdal Kanwal—but gone inside the eye focus after full concentration of your attention, and have crossed sun and moon—you will meet the Master. He will always remain with you. You may talk to him whenever you like and you may see him whenever you like. Your room will be barred, but the Master will be with you. When that Form will be with you, then it does not matter much if the outer form is not close by.

As for your cases, you should treat them to the best of your ability, serve them, and otherwise help them if necessary, but leave their recovery to His will. He is just and whatever happens to patients, happens in accordance with their karma. You should not burden your mind with anxieties about them. Keep your mind free. Your treatment and service will help them, but not your worrying about them. Worry weakens your power to be useful to them.

Whatever you have written concerning the attitude of a negative power that comes in your way, I understand. Here again, what is happening is for your benefit, so that your mind renounces and becomes free from all the worldly attachments and establishes a close relation with the Satguru and Nam. For without the Satguru, one cannot make contact with Nam, and without Nam, there is no way to reach our home.

No article of this world, nor friends, nor relations go with us; even our body does not accompany us after death. Then why worry about those who will not accompany us? Your anxieties and worries pull you down. When, with concentration, attention goes up, it sees something and becomes happy; and when it remains low down, the scenes are absent and you are discouraged. Mind your concentration and do not mind the current. When the concentration is complete, the scattered energies have been drawn in, and there will be so much sound current that you will not be able to stand it. The bell is ringing higher up and you are sitting lower down; therefore its sound is not audible. With your approach toward the focus, your faith will develop and become stronger. There is no real and lasting program without good, hard effort. There are many anti-powers. The negative power I have referred to is one of them. You may not worry about it at all.

~

116.   Individual mind is Kal on a small scale. It is Kal's agent, attached to every soul to keep it out from the eye focus and keep it entangled in this world. No individual is at peace with himself and no one is happy. In ignorance, doubt, and fear, men go about. When such is the case of the individual, the case of groups of such individuals and nations cannot be expected to be any better. The world is a plaything of Kal. Both the parties in this war profess to be Christians, and Christians are killing Christians for transitory things of this dirty material world. When art flourishes, luxuries come in its train, and the weak side of human nature takes the upper hand. Forces of evil are let loose and war is the ultimate outward expression. In spite of the development of science, the world is ignorant of the value of human form. It does not know that it is the residence of our Creator. In this form we have the opportunity to meet him and end our woes and wanderings. Then we would wish that we may never come back to this world; let others enjoy it.

I am glad that you give time to bhajan regularly every morning. Please see that at the time of bhajan, the mind stops its running. Tell your mind not to secrete thoughts at this time, and if it does, then throw them out immediately. The secret of success lies in making the mind motionless. The treasure that you are seeking will be yours when the mind is motionless. Brahmand does not lie in the physical part of the body. It lies inside the mind. So long, therefore, as the mind has not been made motionless, Brahmand and the treasure remain hidden and unapproachable. The extent to which you render it motionless, you are nearer to the treasure—Nam. Twelve hours' sitting in bhajan with mind wandering is not so useful as one hour sitting with mind motionless. One round from a rifle held and fired properly will hit the target, and any number of rounds fired improperly will go off the mark.

Grief resulting from failure in bhajan is also a form of bhajan. Grief is a sign of one's helplessness in attaining his wish. It is an admittance of defeat by the mind. One should take advantage of this position and, with strong will, double up his efforts to achieve his wish.

Satsang is to bhajan what a fence is to a crop. Satsang is the water on which bhajan remains fresh and green.

I appreciate your consideration for the feelings of your friend. It does not serve any useful purpose to find fault with any system of philosophy which our friend or companion loves. Experience is the best teacher. A person carries a tin-coated wooden sword which outwardly resembles steel, and the person honestly believes it to be steel. It is no use entering into arguments with him to convince him that it is wood and not steel. The best course is to ask him to try it in action. In one or two strokes it will have shown its worth and real nature. For your information I will say that, compared with Sant Mat, —— is a child's play. All its degrees end in Sahansdal Kanwal. Its practitioners seldom reach that far. Most of them indulge in intellectual and mental hallucination.

Sound goes with concentration. With concentration of the mind, the Sound will become clear. How strange that being so wise you cannot go in. Last month I was touring in the foot hills of the Siwalik Range. People there are very simple-minded. At initiation there were three ladies whose attention went in at once, and it became rather difficult to explain to them the details of the path—light, sound, regions, and so on. Their necks had to be massaged to bring the attention out. They were illiterate. They would be quite justified if they called the worldly-wise ignorant.

When the attention is held in the eye focus by simran, withdrawal of the current from extremities must commence. Pain in limbs and so forth is felt only when the attention does not stay at the focus. If legs and arms do not go numb, it means that mind is not working (doing simran or hearing current) in the focus, but is running about. Make the mind motionless. Your time for bhajan is insufficient, and that too, you give with a heavy heart—full of anxiety. I like your regularity in bhajan, but make the mind motionless. Two hours are sufficient if mind becomes stationary. Otherwise, tire it out by giving more time.

So long as the attention of a disciple has not reached *tisra til*, it does not see the protecting hand of the Master over the disciple's head, nor what the Master does for the disciple. The Master looks after the disciple as a mother looks after her child. One of our disciples, Kehar Singh, had gone to America. Through him, many Americans received initiation. He was informed by an American that there is always with him a man who protects him. My son Bachint Singh had good strong bullocks. Cattle lifters, with the intention of taking away his bullocks, would come every night to find a man standing guard at the house, and were disappointed. Later on the thieves themselves made this statement to Bachint Singh.

Your informer is right when he says that there is light on your head—one has to go inside to realise the value of Nam. Sitting outside the eye focus, in the nine portals of the body, the attention perceives but little the effect of Nam.

You have not correctly grasped the meaning of the statement, "Kam is controlled only when Sahansdal Kanwal is reached." Controlling of negative tendencies of mind is a progressive affair. Understanding intellectually that negative tendencies are harmful is the first step. This is *vivek* (discrimination). If this is accepted, then body and mind should be engaged in other pursuits. The stronger the will power, the greater the success in keeping the mind away from negative tendencies and keeping it on positive tendencies.

By will power, people succeed in this field. With the approach to the eye focus there is almost an aversion to negative tendencies, and the liking for Nam is awakened. In Sahansdal Kanwal the negative tendencies disappear altogether, and complete success over them is attained. Here, the burning fire of kam at the lower centres is extinguished forever, never to kindle again. So if you make up your mind to tackle this negative power with your strong will power, there is every likelihood of success. If one does not think of kam, it does not trouble him. During the most part of my service I lived alone, away from my wife, and there was no trouble due to kam. I kept myself busy in work.

Learn and practise by all means whatever your —— friend teaches so that you have firsthand knowledge of ——, provided he teaches any practice of holding the attention above the eye focus. There is little peace of mind and satisfaction in centres below the eyes. Any attempt to concentrate attention on any centre below the eyes is harmful in so far that it will be equally difficult to leave that centre and bring the attention up again. Attention already has the bad habit of sinking below the eyes. It is easy to fix it below the eyes, but it is a negative process. The object is to rise up. To create a habit of fixing attention below the eyes is a hindrance in its rise. If your friend teaches any practice of holding the attention below the eyes, it should not be followed. The practice of simran, as taught in Sant Mat, pulls up the attention. Breathing exercises may be good for health, but the centre of breathing lies lower than the centre of attention—the eye focus.

If a fact has been stated by some reliable authority (saints) in the past, one can believe it. If some modern authority (Guru) supports it, the belief becomes firmer. When the same fact has become one's personal experience, the element of doubt that always accompanies belief disappears, and what was fact to modern and past authorities is a fact to him also. The value of authority or belief to a believer lies in making an experiment on the lines recommended by authorities and testing this belief. If the result comes out to be as expected, the belief becomes a fact to the experimenter. The belief in reincarnation should be tested by experiment made on lines laid down by its expounder. One begins to know something about it when the attention reaches tisra til (the eight-petalled lotus in Anda), and complete knowledge about it is acquired in Par Brahm (Daswan Dwar), where the soul has cast off all its coverings of mind and matter.

A person, therefore, whose attention is running outside the eye focus in the physical world, or is fixed in centres below the eyes, uses his intellect only to understand phenomena of the astral, causal, and spiritual planes of which he reads in scriptures or hears from seers. Intellect or reason comes into play when there is no direct perception.

Again, intellect is a variable factor. In childhood it is something, in youth it is different, and in old age it shows another aspect. It changes under the influence of kam, krodh, etc. So when the measure is variable, its measurements cannot be relied upon. By argument, therefore, inner phenomena can neither be proved nor disproved. One argument appeals to one set of people, and another satisfies a different lot. Both stand in need of direct perception. All the arguments given in —— to prove or disprove reincarnation, when judged in the way stated above, fall short of their purpose. Reincarnation is neither proved nor disproved.

Saints' foremost argument is: "Come with us and see." Few are ready for it. So the saints come down to the intellectual plane of men and talk to them in their terms. By their superior intellect they give people's belief a little shake-up and make them think afresh. Slowly and slowly they bring them up to the point of experimentation. They give initiation and the experiment begins.

Many prophets and avatars remained confined to the spheres of mind and maya, and did not go to higher regions. Some of the prophets did not reach even tisra til. For them, paradise is the last stage. The principle of reincarnation is a fact. It is part of the Creator's scheme. Continuation of life in the regions below Par Brahm is based on it. Souls here are functioning, covered in appropriate forms of mind and matter. They are never naked (free). These coverings continue changing to suit the actions to be performed in a life as determined by karmic law. Only through association with saints do the souls leave these regions and go to Par Brahm and higher regions; otherwise they continue struggling here, covered by mind and matter.

Brief observations on ——, subject to what has been said before:

1.   The merciful God is Sat Nam. He entrusted his creation for administration to Kal, who is just—reap as you shall

sow. Faults are told at the end of every life when the account is settled. When new life starts, faults and other facts of previous life slowly slip from memory.

2.   Nature is not extravagant. It gives that form to an individual in which he can best satisfy the unfulfilled hopes and desires of the past life. If, in human form, hopes and desires are created which befit an animal, the next birth must be degradation, and animal ought to be the most suitable form to satisfy those desires.

3.   After the physical body and the astral form are cast off, there is no chance for individuality because there is none left but the only Being. This would be possible if, at the time of breaking up of the human body and the astral form, there are no hopes and desires left unfulfilled and the mind is a clean slate, pralabdh karma has been undergone, and no kriyaman karma has been incurred. This is almost an impossibility. And what about sinchit karma, stored on the top of Trikuti?

The unfulfilled desires demand a new body for working out those desires. And where is a living person now who is anxious to merge in Him? Nobody is willingly ready even for the inevitable death—casting off the physical frame, be it worn out or worm eaten. The being in the frame is forcibly drawn out by some extraneous power—agents of Kal. When, after death, the being is in the hands of these agents, the treatment that he receives from them is no better than the treatment meted out to a prisoner.

Is it imaginable then, that after death, in such environments, a soul will run away to merge in Him? It is neither free now nor free after death. Enchained it comes in this world, and enchained it goes out at death, to come back again after replacing the worn out chain by a new and stronger one.

4. This cannot be said about all persons who speak of their past life. Cases are on record where small children, even in Muslim families, have given hints of their past life.

5. This is hair-splitting. This is justified when the main points of a problem are correctly grasped, not otherwise.

6. It is a new definition of reincarnation.

7. The analogy of bubble does not apply. The soul bubble never gets a chance to merge into its ocean so long as it is functioning in Brahmand up to the top of Trikuti, for it is covered by mind and maya in Brahmand.

~

117. The bell and conch sounds are already within you. They are not to come from outside. All that is needed is that you should get nearer, and within the eye focus, to differentiate them from the chirpings of all sorts and catch them. The trouble is that although the mind wishes to rise to the focus, yet it does not like to leave the attachments of things on this side of the focus, and thereby does not make headway in that direction. Simran is incomplete yet. So long as mind does not sit in the focus and does not make it its headquarters, but continues running away from the focus, it has not benefited by the simran practice. As a matter of fact, it is not doing the simran practice. It is doing something else, away from the focus, secreting all sorts of thoughts connected with worldly affairs, country affairs, professional affairs, household affairs, and other affairs. If the mind were busy in (1) repeating the names; and (2) repeating them at the focus, it would be said to be doing simran. But if tongue repeats names and mind is busy elsewhere, thinking of something else, then it is not simran. Repeating of names in the focus is simran, and remembering of something else elsewhere is simran of that something.

Simran of worldly things to which man is accustomed is
to be changed into simran of the names in the focus. This
must narrow down the mind and this is what is called concentration. And there is no reason, if the mind sticks to the
focus and is engaged therein in simran or hearing the current, that the extremities of the body—the hands, feet, arms,
legs—and finally the trunk of the body should not go numb.

There is nothing to feel disheartened about. We are up
against mind, the mind that keeps all souls out of the focus.
Kings, dictators, presidents, the commoners, and all are running outside the focus. Yogis, sanyasis, ascetics, and philosophers fail to catch it. War is the outcome of the mind running
wild. It prevents the soul from rising up. It is the veil that
hangs between our soul and our Creator. Now we have found
it out, its true nature. It is our enemy. We are at war with it
and we are to capture it. Guru, the experienced warrior and
veteran, is guiding and supporting us. He has armed us with
Nam—the sound current, the current that is finer than the
mind current. So long as our attention holds the sound current, the mind is still; and as our hold on it gets firmer, the
soul gets stronger and gains supremacy over the mind. In time
the position is reversed—the mind becomes a faithful servant of the soul.

In our ignorance and weakness we strengthen the lower
mind. The Master awakens the slumbering soul—develops
in us our latent strength, through the practice of simran and
Nam current, and makes us fight our weaknesses and overcome them here, thereby making us fit to enter the eye focus
and go beyond. Step by step he brings us to the pitch that
with the exception of the Guru and the Nam, everything else
becomes a superficiality and ceases to have a hold on us.

When we are away from the Master and the satsang, the
world imperceptibly impresses itself on us so much that, in

spite of our regularly giving time to simran and Nam, we often begin to feel discouraged, dry, and desolate. In such a state faith and love are our support; and if faith is firm, the Master responds. He is always with us—within us—watches as a mother watches her child. So long as we are on this side of the focus, we do not see him working. But he is doing his duty.

Your worries and cares are Master's worries and cares. Leave them to him to deal with. Having become carefree, your business is to cultivate his love. He is not going to let you drift. You will go up.

Examine your mind—the thoughts it secretes and the things it runs after. When in bhajan, the mind must do bhajan and nothing else. The door of the tenth gate opens automatically when mind and soul go in that direction and knock at it. If they run in another direction, the door remains shut.

Nam is the rendezvous for all beings. It cures all sorts of ills. Guru Nanak says, "The whole world is miserable. Only he is happy who has taken to Nam."

≈

118. The sound current never stops, as it is only by means of sound current that the soul stays in the body. When the sound current stops, the soul will go out. The reason for your not hearing the Sound is that your mind is so much engrossed in worldly matters that it does not allow the soul to go in. When the mind goes down it ceases to catch the Sound. The remedy is to bring about the concentration of the mind by means of careful repetition, which will make the mind and the soul still and collected and, therefore, able to catch the sound current. Sometimes people come to me complaining that the sound current is so loud and powerful that they cannot bear it, and that its pitch and intensity should be weakened.

It is only sound current which takes the soul up to higher regions. Indeed it is the grand trunk road between ourselves and the Kingdom of God. As the concentration increases, the Sound will become more tasteful and sweet. Therefore the first necessity is repetition, without which concentration cannot take place. And unless concentration has become so intense as to enable the soul and mind to cross the stars, the sun, and the moon, the sound current cannot lift the soul.

Do not think that you are stupid or unfit. The reason is that, owing to war conditions and consequent stoppage of correspondence with me, the pressure of work, lack of satsang, and the presence of anxieties and worries, the mind has lost concentration. Worries and anxieties prevent the soul from going into the magnetic field of the sound current. If this war had not intervened to prevent our correspondence, I would have urged you on to greater effort.

In the beginning, the mind fears and dislikes to go in, and the body also aches; but by degrees, these pains disappear and the mind acquires the habit of concentration. The preliminary stages in Sant Mat are difficult, but when they are traversed and the mind goes up, then meditation begins to yield pleasure, so much so that one is unable to give it up.

The numbness of the lower extremities of the body is a good sign. Before rising from your meditation, you should pause and massage your limbs. The whole body, up to the eyes, should feel benumbed as a result of the concentration.

In the beginning any sound that you catch, whether of bell or chirping of sparrows and the like, should be caught. As the concentration increases, the sound will clear up into the bell. Repetition is the foremost necessity. Try to repeat in bed, before going to sleep, and do repetition when you get up from sleep.

All the sages have laid stress on the point that unless one dies during life, he cannot go in. This means that one should, by means of concentration, try to make his body numb up to the eyes. When one feels tired in body and mind, after the day's work, it is best to ease the mind and body by doing repetition in a solitary room.

The one hour devoted by you to repetition is not enough. You should pinch out one hour more from your daily work so as to devote one and a half to repetition and half an hour to hearing the Sound.... If you cannot see light within, then you should fix your attention on the darkness and keep peeping into it. The darkness will change into light.

You are right. Unless a man has succeeded in meditation or, as a matter of fact, in any work, he cannot induce others to take it up.

If your faith and trust in the Master are full and complete, you need not be anxious for the future of your soul or that it will be subject to births and deaths. The soul goes where it feels attached. Your anxiety should be to perform meditation and repetition regularly.

There have been numerous sages in India, both among Hindus and Muslims, but all of them agree that there is no better method than that of the sound current, which is an ancient and natural science. It is designed by the Creator himself, is within every one of us, yet whole nations and entire countries of the world are ignorant of it.

I appreciate your spirit when you put the blame upon yourself for lack of spiritual progress. This will lead to success. Most people shift blame to the method, the teaching, or the Master. Do not be anxious. When you give greater time to meditation, you will succeed ... spiritual progress does not depend on length of time after initiation. It depends upon concentration.

Regarding lust, anger, pride, and so forth, your view is correct. Purity of character is the fundamental basis on which the edifice of spiritual progress is to be built. These five passions will become weaker and weaker as the bliss of the sound current increases. In the end, all these as well as the mind will come under the control of the soul. Now the soul is under the control of mind and passions. When, by means of repetition and meditation, the mind and soul acquire the habit of sitting quietly inside, then this world will lose its attraction, and the other world will become more attractive.

If we think, we find that at death no one goes with us— even the body has to be left behind. Only the Master and sound current go with us and therefore they are our only relatives. The Master is within you and is looking after you. Go in and you will be convinced of it.

... Do not allow the love of any other woman to enter your mind. Look upon all the women of the world either as your mother, sister, or daughter, so that you may make progress in your spiritual journey. Keep yourself under control. It will do you good. The sound current and the Master are within you. You need no other company.... The greater the solitude, the better. There is no better luck than solitude.... All the sages going into higher degrees have avoided woman so that they might get solitude and perform their meditation without interruption.... Do not be anxious.

Try to lift the veil within and try to taste the spiritual joy, compared to which all the worldly designs and inventions are insignificant and valueless. He who has torn the veil within and brought the mind under control has conquered all the world, and the whole world is under his order. Before searching the world for new medicines, it is better that one should cure one's own mind.

Sar Bachan's advice to a gurmukh will give greater pleasure when you go in. Do not doubt; the Lord looks after his own.

～

119.   No, we do not want to increase the number of followers for the sake of numbers as our mission is not political or social. Our mission is to assist true and earnest seekers after God, and we want no others in our fold. One earnest soul is worth a hundred wavering ones.

～

120.   Do not try to overwork yourself, please, and try to reserve your energies and save time for your meditation. You need not sacrifice your sleep, as you have heavy work to do. You can cut down your professional time to give longer time to your bhajan.

Yes, Kal is not only the lord of this physical world but of all the worlds below and above and surrounding it, up to Trikuti. His technical Hindu name is Brahm. He rules over Trikuti and Sahansdal Kanwal and all the regions below them. He is with every creature in the shape of mind!

The Hindu Shastras say that we are passing through the Kalyug or the Iron Age. For an account of Satyug, Treta, and Dwapar, you should read a good translation of Markand Puran or Padam Puran,[1] in which a detailed account of the cycle of the four yugas or ages is given, along with the method of calculating the duration of each age.

A *gurmukh* is a soul who has reached Par Brahm and has cast off the three coverings from itself. A *satsangi* is a soul that has been initiated by a Master. A *sanskari* is a true seeker after God.

---

1. Hindu scriptures of religio-historical stories describing the lives and deeds of gods, heroes, and great kings; there are eighteen Purans in all.

Yes, as pointed out to you during your initiation, there are five regions and each region has its own distinct sound or music which is called Word. There is no additional initiation. Full initiation has been given to you, but the music cannot be heard except by going to that region.

For those who have been initiated, the Guru never dies. If he leaves his physical frame, he is with his initiates in his astral and causal bodies, and takes care of them; though obviously he cannot deliver discourses and directions in the physical frame after his departure. His external guidance is carried on by his successor, but no second initiation is necessary. It is true that only a living Master can grant initiation and consequent salvation to non-initiates, and therefore it may be said that a Guru gives salvation only when alive. But this remark applies only to those who were not initiated by him in his lifetime.

Those disciples who follow the directions of the Master, and carry on their meditation accordingly, are taken care of at their death by the Master, and they feel happy to leave this world for higher regions in his company. Those who have not heard the sound current are taken care of after their souls leave their bodies, and are sent back to this world or taken up, according to their tendencies and desires.

~

121.   The sounds of different regions, indicated at the time of initiation, are meant to give a faint idea of the music pervading that region. As a matter of fact, the music of those regions has no counterpart in the physical world. Their joy and pleasure can be felt only by going into those regions. This is true of all the regions and not that of Sat Lok only.

The sound current or Nam or Shabd emanates from Sat Lok, from where the creation starts. There is sound in the regions above Sat Lok, but that sound is so very fine and exquisite that it cannot be understood without reaching Sat Lok.

The list is not exhaustive. It contains the names of the Masters *(Param Sants)* and their disciples who became Masters. It is not necessary that there should be only one Master in the whole world or even in a single country. There have been different Masters in different countries at the same time, and even in the same country. Thus Guru Nanak and Kabir were contemporaries, and so also Dadu and Guru Arjan. But their teaching is the same at all times and in every country.

... There is a time fixed for those who are to be initiated by a Master.

... In the Hindi literature of Sant Mat, detailed description is given about the passage of the soul from the physical body to the astral world after death.

When you throw away your old worn-out coat or garment, you do not care how it is disposed of. If anyone burns it or buries it, you do not mind. The same is the case with the body after death. Cremation requires less space than burial. In India, when we are sure that the soul has gone out of the body, we do not wait longer than the time required for preparation of cremation. Sometimes, when death takes place after sunset, the dead body is left overnight and cremated after sunrise.

~

122.   There is no doubt that unless one attains peace within himself, it is no use trying to proselytize others. Therefore it is better that you should work hard and go in....

Your complaint regarding the want of progress in meditation is due to your mind's fault, i.e., the want of satsang, and the mind having its own free way, worldly cravings more than necessary, and looking upon meditation as of second-ary importance. When by means of repetition the concentra-tion is deep enough, the body will begin to get senseless, as the soul leaves the nine portals of the body and goes up.

But all this will take place when you work hard with love and faith. The mind looks upon the world and its objects as more important than spiritual matters. Your mind is scat-tered. Worldly learning scatters the mind. Simple-minded folks go in easily. The hill people of this country are such, and in several cases their souls went in at once, as soon as the secret of concentration was imparted to them. Therefore, what is required in this path is simplicity of mind, faith, and love.

The bell sound is constantly going on within you day and night. There are five regions in your forehead, each one emit-ting a distinct and different music all the time. Man sleeps but the music does not. It will stop at death. You do not go within and get benefit of the music. Weakness of faith makes it difficult to go in, and faith also comes when one sees some-thing within. Your mind has not yet become motionless nor do you devote full time and labour to this work.

Your idea that you are not yet ready for spiritual progress is not right. There is eagerness in your mind, but you do not work hard. I appreciate your love, but you do not travel upon the path. As yet your mind has not become indifferent to worldly pleasures, and you have not practised the ABC of Sant Mat. The five passions are ruling and you cannot go in, not-withstanding all your learning, although rustic women and children can go in. Whatever you have said about X is quite true. If a patient gets medicine from a doctor but does not use it, he has only himself to blame if he does not recover. You should read your own letter with care and attention. It contains the reasons for slackness in spiritual progress....

I am glad to know that you are eager to go in. This is the only object of life, as no other object of the world goes with us at death. It is only the Master and progress in Nam that go with us.… No doubt you have increased your physical capacity of work by means of physical exercise, but that is different from spiritual exercise which causes the soul to go in and increases spiritual vigour. Had you devoted to spiritual work one-fourth of the time that you spent in worldly work, you would have succeeded in going in with the grace of the Master.

I have read with great satisfaction your account of your progress in your profession. Yet, were you the king of all of the —— of the world, that would avail you but little at death. The attention which is scattered in so many directions outside is no wonder difficult to collect.… Please do take care that your mind becomes motionless during meditation. If the mind keeps wandering during repetition, it is so much time wasted. You say that you spend one and a half hours every day in meditation. Even that should produce some result. If it has not, the conclusion is obvious that the mind does not stay in during meditation, but begins to wander outside.

… I could only wish that you would go in after getting concentration; and when the Master will begin to talk to you and reply to all your questions, inside, all miseries will be over.… So long as the Master is not visible inside, the soul remains off and on drooping and desponding.

Were the Master to talk with his followers in this world in the language of their own countries, it would be considered a miracle by the worldly people who would surround him and pester him with petitions for worldly things. Yet when a follower goes in, the Master talks with him there in his own mother tongue. Just go within and see what the Master is.

The followers who love the Master and have no desire in their mind for anything of this world shall not be reborn even if they have not made much spiritual progress while here. They will be made to stay at some intermediate station from where they will go up to their destination by degrees. On the other hand, those who have worldly desires left in their mind at death will have to be reborn, notwithstanding their devoting long hours to spiritual exercise. After rebirth they will be initiated by the Master then living and will get an opportunity to complete their course.

The Granth Sahib contains the songs of Guru Nanak and some of his successors. Included in it are also some of the songs of other sages of different times and different places who reached Sat Lok. By this inclusion it is intended to prove that God is one, and the way to reach him is the same, at all times and places. The structure of all human beings is the same, and therefore the way to reach God, who is inside every human being, is also one and the same.

~

123. A devotee is sometimes not conscious of his mind wandering out till later. He should keep watch over the mind, and if it goes out, he should bring it in again and again. Thus by constant practice, the mind will tire out and become motionless. It requires time and perseverance. It is not an easy task to make the mind still and to keep it motionless. But one should not despond. As the mind becomes quiet, the Sound will become clearer and the body will become numb.

A soldier is not responsible for his actions. It is the commander who directs and orders the killing who is responsible. The soldier is a mere tool. He incurs no karma in connection with his duties. This falls on the shoulders of the commandants.

Yes, there is a downward tendency also; from man to animal, plant, and so forth according to the actions performed in the human body. There are two streams, or rather a circle, moving like a wheel—the top being man and the bottom mineral.

Secluded life is better for concentration and meditation than the so-called social life.

Yes, Satguru is the lord and master of the destinies of his pupils, but he does not interfere in their pralabdh karma which results in bad or good circumstances in their lives, and after death rewards each according to his karma and devotion.

Krodh (anger) scatters the mind and this makes it difficult to collect and subdue. You should avoid it and, so far as practicable, try to engage the mind in repetition instead.

124.   As for the war, a satsangi should not feel agitated on its account and get his peace of mind disturbed, seeing that nothing happens without the ordinance of the Master. A satsangi performs actions without desiring their fruits and leaves the results to the sweet will of the Master. It is for us to do our best in everything and leave the results to his pleasure.

The matter which concerns you more closely is bhajan. That is the only purpose of our coming to this world. Your feeling sleepy means that you are weak in repetition. A devotee who is successful in repetition of the five holy names is successful in concentration and in listening to the sound current also.

Your main effort should be directed to stilling your mind, which is the result of repetition. Try to perform repetition in one posture, changing your position as little as possible. The mind does not become still without two hours repetition at a time. If one performs repetition while walking, going on errands, and the like, the mind will feel quieter when one sits for repetition.

While performing your daily repetition, do not lose sight of concentration upon the Form of the Master.

... To be able to go within requires love and faith in the Master and some indifference to worldly pain and pleasure. Go on doing your duty and increasing your love and faith in the Master. That is all you can do. The Master will do his duty of protecting you here and hereafter. Never despond of his mercy and grace. Spiritual progress is not the monopoly of any single individual or nation.

Please do not fail to read every day a portion of some book on the path, such as *Mysticism: The Spiritual Path, With a Great Master in India, Sar Bachan,* etc. They keep the mind fit and eager for bhajan.

~

125.   I have, with pain, read your complaint about your son. His wickedness and ingratitude seem to be due to impressions of past births which have become pralabdh karma for him in this birth. It is almost impossible to wash away these impressions of past lives. They must work themselves out, and are working out. Such things are not confined to your country only. I have had experience of such ingratitude and unfilial and patricidal conduct here also in our satsang.

Therefore, all the saints and pious men of every religion have laid stress on the advice that during human life we should lead pure and pious lives, free from enmity and hatred of others. If we fail to do this, then our impressions of hatred and animosity are liable to bear fruit in the next birth. It is useless to reason with such people. They will not listen to reason nor to appeals to their sentiment of gratitude and love. Only terror can restrain them from their unnatural course.

Consequently I will advise you to take steps to put yourself on the defensive so that his attacks, though they cannot fail to hurt your feelings and reputation, may not do you any further injury. Make your will power strong so that your bhajan and simran may not suffer. I am not acquainted with the law of your land. You may consult some lawyers who may put you on the defensive without taking up cudgels against him. Leave him to the Master. He will reap the results of his own actions, but defend yourself from his attacks. I have every sympathy for you. You might also pray to the Master within you to save you from this pest.

≈

126.   I am glad to learn about the welcome change in the life of your son. You may help him and try to give him light on Sant Mat so that his life may become pure.

≈

127.   I had hoped from your last letter that your son was changing for the better but I am sorry to find that he has become his old self again…. You have done more for him than your means allowed. In this old age you need money, comfort and solace, and some loving one to look after you. You cannot lose more money to him; and if you were to continue to help him, he would want more and more out of you. It is better to leave such a person alone so that he may not have an opportunity to do all the terrible things he had done to you previously. No one can interfere in his karma. He must live his allotted time, and bad society which he does not leave is causing his ruin. If he had given up his wicked associates and taken to good, respectable society, he might have improved….

Do not grieve on account of your sons and daughters who are neurotics or have gone wrong. This relationship is merely temporary and is, in fact, no relationship at all. True relatives are those who share our views, are kind and considerate and have sympathy in our struggle. Please go on doing your bhajan and simran daily, with love and faith.

～

128.   The boy has to work out his own karma while you have to undergo your own. Every soul is to render account of its own actions. No one can take upon himself the reactions of others. He has an account of previous births to settle with you. All persons with whom we had connection in previous lives have to take an account from us whether as sons, daughters, sisters, mothers, or other relatives. But please do not feel grief on his account, as worldly relatives do not go with us when we leave this world. Only the sound current goes with us. Catch hold of the sound current and leave the rest to take care of itself.

～

129.   Through His grace the Dera has remained safe during this communal upheaval. The Punjab is passing through hard times. We have been undergoing an exchange of population on an unprecedented scale. The rich and the poor are in the same boat of misery all around. What next, nobody can say. We abide by His will. Rumours and propaganda confuse the man in the street. Please rest assured that things happen as he wills it. Bad karma is at the root of this visitation. The karmic law is inexorable. The Dera has not only remained untouched but has become the residence of some two and a half thousand refugees who are now vacating to settle in villages and towns.

～

130. Man is the highest form of creation, including the angels. Man is the image of God. The Creator and all his creation are within him, and he has been given the privilege of meeting his Creator while alive. And this is the aim of coming into human life.

The whole secret is in the part of the head above the eyes. The *way* to meet the Creator is also within man, and this *way* is the basis of all important religions; but their followers are ignorant of it. They are content with rituals, ceremonies, reading of scriptures and prayers, doing charities, living a chaste life, working for the social and mental uplift of humanity—thereby feeling virtuous—but expect salvation as a reward after death. This is unwarranted.

The *way* is the Word in the Bible, the Kalma of Prophet Mohammed, the Shabd, Nam, Dhun, Akash Bani and so forth in Hinduism, and the Nad of the Vedas. These words are synonymous and refer to the same fundamental essence—the voice of God—which is going on all the time within us; and we have the capacity to hear it when the attention is held within, instead of letting it run out in the external world.

There is no artificiality in it. It is not man-made. It sustains our life. It sustains the whole creation. The Gospel of Saint John has attempted to explain it in terms of human experience in chapter 1, verses 1–14. The Word is the design of the Creator, intended for man to catch hold of it from the eye centre and follow it right up to its origin, and thereby become godlike.

To get more light on the subject, you may please study the Sant Mat literature. If you feel interested, I shall be very glad indeed to answer any inquiries on this subject.

~

131.   I am glad to read of your activities for the uplift of people and wish you success in your work.

Regarding initiation, I would advise you to consider over the matter more deeply, and be in no hurry. The path of the Masters is diametrically opposed to the path which the learned and the public follow. Their minds are engaged in literary pursuits and in the material and mental welfare of other people. Thus the mind works in the world outside and gets scattered. In the path of the Masters, the mind is to be withdrawn from the world around and also from the body below the eyes, and concentrated in the eye centre.

The whole secret lies in the part of the body above the eyes, and the search for truth is to be made therein and within. The mind of the learned is complex, for they have stored and daily store so much in it. To travel on the path of the Masters, a simple mind has a distinct advantage. This does not mean, however, that the learned and the public cannot follow the path of the Masters. The tone of the letter may appear discouraging, but all that is implied is that their own mind stands as a big hurdle in their way. They have to un-learn or unload their mind to come to the eye centre.

Again, the path of the Masters is a long one and it takes time to mould the mind. The withdrawal of the scattered attention into the eye centre requires patience, perseverance, and faith. The learned get impatient when they find them-selves helpless in controlling their mind. They begin to doubt the efficacy of the method given. They want quick results, little knowing that mind is a power which is moving the world, and the world dances to its tune. It expresses itself through lust, anger, greed, attachment, and pride, and who is free from them? To try to concentrate the mind in the eye centre is to pick up a quarrel with it, and it is a lifelong quarrel. If successful in this struggle, the prize is everlasting bliss. Then there is no more revolving on the wheel of births and deaths.

There is no artificiality in the method of the Masters. It is not man-made or man-designed. It is natural and is present in all. The Master is simply to point out the method, and the disciple is to work according to it. The student has his duty and the teacher has his. All the Masters in all the ages, no matter in what clime, have followed this one method—the sound current or the Word.

I believe you know that a follower of the path has to give up meat, eggs, and the foods which contain them, and also alcoholic drinks. They harden the mind and their use in the spiritual journey is not allowed.

132. You did quite right in sending the applicants the copies of letters as you did. It was kind of you to take the trouble, and I appreciate it. As you say, no doubt there will always be some who are not so very enthusiastic but, by and by, they will all come back. No need to worry. Let them take their time. It is better to do a little extra for them, doing our utmost to help and stimulate interest, rather than neglect any opportunity to do them a real service. Sometimes the weak ones need a little extra boosting and gentle reminders. You can always write and ask them if they would care for further literature. If they do not reply, then let them go.

As to X, she no doubt has had some difficulties and has felt discouraged. I think she needs all the encouragement she can get from you and the rest. She is all right, but has a hard struggle. Of course you did right in giving her the instructions. When you follow the inner light, you will make no mistake, and if that light is not definite or certain, then go ahead and give the instructions, always giving the candidate the benefit of doubt, unless you are positive they are not what they should be. Remember, there are many weak ones, and they need our help. We are not to turn them away because they are weak. But weak men and women are not always bad. They simply need the strong support of a real brother or sister, as well as the help of the Master. Let us always do what we can for them.

… You say, "The Master approaches each of the five deities in his own realm and unites with them, one after the other, and eventually partakes of their original essence," and so on. This is correct only when the Master was a student himself, making the upward journey for the first time. After he becomes a Master, he need not unite with them as he goes up. And a Master does not become a Master by partaking of the powers of the five deities in the several regions.

You say this is what mastership consists of. Not quite accurate. Mastership is reached when one reaches Sach Khand, and becomes merged with Sat Purush. Then only is a man a saint and Master. All that goes before that, is just a part of the process of getting trained for mastership—schooled and prepared as it were. And on the way up, the Master always retains his own Form—after he becomes a Master—and his Radiant Form becomes more radiant at each stage of his upward progress. But it is always his own Form, not that of any deity in the several regions.

As to how to worship properly, that will settle itself, as you infer. When you see the Master inside, you will instinctively know what to do. You will always love and worship your own Master. But of course, you will worship all saints, too. We all hold that there is no greater privilege than that of bowing at the feet of a true saint, and I am myself devoutly thankful that I may enjoy that holy sacrament.

133.   Flying in semi-conscious condition of mind is a good indication, but attempt should be made that the soul may leave the body in a fully conscious state and fly up. This will come about when you get concentration of mind. When you sit for meditation, please take care that the mind does not wander out. If it goes out, please bring it back so that it may begin to work inside. When the mind begins to stay in, then the soul and mind will begin to work inside and you feel happy. When you sit in meditation and close your external eyes, please try to peep into the darkness with the internal eye. By and by you will begin to perceive light. Please devote three-fourths of your total time of meditation to repetition of the five holy names, as it brings about concentration, and one-fourth to hearing the Sound from the right ear.

~

134.   Answering your question about spirits contacted in spiritualist seances, I may say that at such meetings, spirits of all sorts may be met with and they may give communications. They may be spirits of dead relatives, or they may be of strangers, or dwellers in some of the lower astral planes, who have been there for ages. They may be called *devas* or angels.

But one word of precaution must be noted. Such as appear in seances are not to be depended upon. There are too many chances of believing they are some beloved relatives. Even the medium may be deceived as to their identity. Tricks are sometimes played at such seances—and for that reason it is much better to stay away from all such seances.

It is only when you yourself enter the astral plane consciously and independently, that you can see for yourself and need no longer be deceived. But then you have no need for mediums or guides. You see and know by your own rights, independent of all others. And this is the only proper, constructive way to enter the upper regions.

It is not at all likely that such "personalities" as you contacted had ever been your own selves in any past life or lives. When you leave the astral or other plane for reincarnation, you leave behind no personality which could by any possibility communicate with you now. The astral "shells" thrown off could not hold intelligent communication with you now. Besides, when you return to earth life, you bring with you your real astral body. You have now the same astral body you had in the past life. It goes with you always until you rise to the second region—Trikuti—and there and then you discard the astral body, retaining only the causal body. When you go up to the third region you discard the causal body, and the soul stands naked (free) in all glory and light, and for the first time it realises that it is pure spirit. Its light then and there is equal to the light of twelve of our suns combined.

Regarding the use of the mind over matter, unconsciously, that can be done, no doubt. But it is not a safe thing to try to do it. Wait until you go up to the first region and there you will fully understand the laws of mind-control and will be able to use the mind constructively at all times, with no penalty. In any case, no miracle is ever to be attempted, even if you were able to do it. The penalty is sometimes severe; but, especially, it stops your upward progress, which must be safeguarded.

But in all your financial struggles, hold steady to the centre in your meditations, and you must get help, because you will grow stronger of will and more one-pointed in mind. The more perfect is one's concentration, the more power he has over all the forces of nature. The mind is a very great power, but before you can use it properly, you must conquer the mind itself. Master your own mind and then you are master of all else. Better never try to utilize any law until you have mastered your own mind, and then all laws of the world are under your feet.

~

135.   I trust you have grasped the essence of the teachings of the saints. Briefly, it is a practical method of separating the soul from its combination with the mind and the body, and then uniting it with its source, or the supreme Creator. It aims at the union of the soul with its origin. It does not aim at keeping the body free from disease, or prolonging its age, or influencing the minds of others, or doing miracles, as some other systems profess. These powers result from concentration of the mind.

Devotees of Sant Mat acquire these powers when they have succeeded in the concentration of their minds. But, in their own interest, they are not allowed to use or dissipate their energy in such pursuits. The energy is to be conserved for making further progress inward. In short, a devotee does not find the way to realms within as long as he has not subdued his dissipating tendencies, just as a father would not entrust his treasures to a prodigal son.

Sant Mat follows the natural course of the sound current, which is the connecting link between the Creator and the individual. The individual is ignorant of this current in him because his attention is outwardly directed and the current is within him.

When one is awake, the attention is attached to external objects. When asleep, one is unconscious, and in the dream state one has imperfect connection with the impressions of external objects. If, however, the attention is held within—at the centre of consciousness (a point above and behind the eyes, and called the third eye)—it will grasp the sound current and will be held by it in turn, provided there is no tendency of the attention to return to external objects again.

In the beginning, there is a hard struggle to bring the attention to the eye focus, and it may be a work of years with some, while cases are known to have gone within at once. But when the habit to reach the focus has been acquired, the glimpses of the inner world make this study interesting. A boy goes to school, usually reluctantly, but is reluctant to leave a university.

No period can be fixed as to when the attention of any person will begin to stay within the focus. It depends upon the longing, faith, perseverance, and his past record. In this system, there are no rituals or customs to be observed. It is an inward path, and everyone has to go within himself, independent of others.

This sound current is at the foundation of all great religions. Their founders practised this, and their books speak of the current. Their writings contain their experiences of the worlds within, when going on this current. The sound current liberates the soul from the bonds of the material world as well as from the snares of the mind, and leads the soul to Him. The first duty of man is to know himself, that is, to free his soul from the bonds of mind and body and then unite it with Him. This is the highest service.

In case you find yourself ready to receive the instructions and initiation, you may please communicate with X. I am writing to him accordingly. I hope you will be able to do without eggs, meats, and alcoholic drinks.

∽

136. I have read of your internal experiences. They are as yet of an initial kind. As you advance in concentration, you will see the wonderful phenomena within, unfolding themselves by degrees before your internal eye. You should not be afraid of going inside, as the Master is watching over you. Still, if you come across any cause of fear, you should repeat the five holy names given you, or think of the Master's Form. The fear will disappear.

You should not tell of your visions to anyone, not even your husband, though you may write your experiences to the Master. If you reveal your experiences to others, your progress will stop. This is like a steam engine which works better and more powerfully if all the outlets emitting steam are closed.

The affairs of this world cause sorrow or pleasure. In sorrow, do not become an image of grief and lose heart, as you have not done already during the long illness of your husband. At the same time, steps may be taken to remove the cause of the trouble, and maintain peaceful equilibrium of the mind.

I am very glad to learn of your keenness in pursuing practical spiritual lessons, and note your acknowledgment as your willingness to obey instructions. Obedience to the Master's instruction makes the student's path easier and facilitates progress. And the world has nothing higher to offer than the truth of Sant Mat. I am particularly pleased to learn that you are doing your bhajan and simran regularly, and are able to hear the sound current and the internal melodies. In fact, it is the sound current that holds the world together, and the higher harmonies will, by and by, take the soul up to the highest region. With faith and constant practice, you will contact the finer harmonies some day. Obstacles are bound to come, but as you have rightly remarked, they are only stepping stones if properly tackled. Our own mind is, in fact, our greatest enemy, and this has to be conquered. This is done by Shabd or sound current practice, which is an absolutely fool-proof method.

There is no reason to be afraid; think of the Master and repeat the five names, and if you again feel any difficulty or fear, help will come. It was a very good experience you had. As the student progresses, he sees, hears, and experiences so many things. With faith and confidence, move on and on.

Sant Mat Vows:

1. Chastity. You should look upon all men as your brothers or elderly relatives; likewise, men should look upon women as sisters or mothers.
2. Absolute abstinence from meat, fish, eggs, and alcoholic drinks.
3. Never render obeisance to any form that appears inside, while in meditation, except to the Form of the Master.

Moods depend upon mental as well as physiological conditions. The stars have their effect too, but we should remember that we are born under particular stars because of our past karmas. We ourselves are the architect of our fate. Again, when the positive power is exercising strong influence, there is always a desire to go higher, but when the negative power is in the ascendant, moods are bad and there is tendency to go down.

137.   No, you are not alone; the Master is always with you and watching over you. You should leave all anxiety and entrust your dear and near ones to the care of the Master. Give as much time as you can regularly to repetition with care and attention, and no thought should be allowed to rise in your mind at the time. As your concentration increases by repetition, you will get more peace and greater joy.

Regarding cremation, you may do as you like; just as when your shoes have become old and worn out, you no longer wear them, but dispose of them as convenient. The dead body is like a cast-off garment which may be disposed of as convenient. Sant Mat is concerned with the soul and not the body. Burial or cremation are merely customs.

~

138. Suffering and poverty are also preordained for everyone before his birth, according to the karma of his past birth. They have to be undergone, yet a Master's disciple who raises his soul becomes indifferent to external surroundings.

~

139. I am very glad to learn that your son has come out safe and sound from the ordeal of war.

No, after death the karma of one does not affect the other. The relationship is broken. The relationship was between two bodies. One body having perished, its soul cannot be seen by the surviving body. Sometimes the dead are attracted by the living on account of the love subsisting between the two. Yet the survivor cannot perceive the bodiless.

The Master is always with you. He is always present with his disciples in his Astral Form. In order to get more firmly rooted in your spiritual practice, you should work hard.

The bluish constellations and stars are at the threshold of the inner world. Try to penetrate within.

The progress does continue, though the Master may have left the earth plane forever. This is based on experience. My Master initiated a lady and soon after departed from this life. Several years after that, the lady's soul went inside very far.

~

140.   I was very glad to read its contents. Many of your questions have been answered by my reply to X, which it is expected you will read.

I am greatly pleased to find that you have already freed your mind from unnecessary attachments and activities. If you continue this process so as to throw out all desires and thoughts excepting necessary ones, then it is expected that you will begin to experience pleasure in concentrating, because when the mind becomes still, then in its interior is reflected the Form of the Master as well as the holy Sound; just as in a tank's surface are reflected the trees and houses standing on its bank, with such distinctness that the image looks real. But, on the other hand, if the surface is disturbed by wind, then the reflection disappears. In the same way our mental equanimity is disturbed every moment by desires and thoughts, and our mind and soul are always flowing outward so that therein the radiance of the Master's Form and the Sound cannot be reflected. This is the reason why our progress is so slow. When your mind, purified from all thoughts, becomes concentrated at one point, then the above-mentioned visions will be reflected in it.

All the objects of this world, except the soul and the holy Sound, are transitory. They are undergoing change every moment. This world is in the keeping of Kal, whom people call God or Brahm. All of us are in his custody. Our true home is the purely spiritual region (Sach Khand), and our true Father is Sat Nam. He is our ocean, of which we are mere drops, and every drop longs to join its ocean. As Sat Purush is imperishable, so is our soul. Kal cannot kill us, but we are subject to his command, and he is causing us great pain. He has tied us in the chains of desires and karma.

If we think deeply, then the creation appears to be a wonderful merry-go-round. All the souls inhabiting this material world are divided into five classes, according to the quantity of tattwas (essences or elements) in each:

The first comprises the vegetable kingdom, in which only water is the active principle (tattwa), while the four remaining tattwas are dormant.

Next comes the insect world, in which two tattwas are active, namely, fire and air—the remaining three being dormant.

The third class consists of egg-born creatures, in which water, fire, and air are active—the remaining two being inactive.

The fourth is the animal kingdom, in which only the akash tattwa is inactive while the remaining four are active. That is why the animals lack reason.

The fifth class consists of human beings, in which all the five tattwas are in their full activity.

These tattwas are not to be confounded with elements of chemical scientists. They refer to the condition of matter and not to its ingredients.

Now it will be seen that Kal has very cleverly entangled all these five classes in the net of karma, because in every class he has so provided that creatures should eat creatures. Take the case of the creatures of the sea—the biggest fish eat other big fish; the latter in their turn dine on small fish, and these eat up smaller fry which subsist on insects in the water. In short, in water one creature has to eat another, as no other food is provided. Now take the creatures on dry land—therein tigers, lions, and wolves kill goats, sheep, deer, and so forth, while the latter live on vegetation. The hawks eat sparrows, while the latter make the insects their food. Men live upon all kinds of birds, animals, and vegetables. Thus, in all the world, creatures eat creatures. Now, the rule is that those creatures that are eating others shall be eaten by those whom they eat. Thus, can there be any possibility of the debt of karma being cleared up?

Now take the souls inhabiting the higher regions of subtle matter. They are as much subject to pain, pleasure, and passion as the souls in the world of gross matter. Those whose karma is worst are made to suffer in the region of hell; others whose karma is a little better are made to wander as ghosts and evil spirits; those whose karma is still better reside in Deva Lok or Pitri Lok, while still higher souls enjoy themselves in Paradise. Those still purer reside in Baikunth (higher paradise), while the souls of incarnations, prophets of higher degrees, and yogis rest themselves in the region of Brahm (Trikuti). There they enjoy the pleasures of that region for a very long period of time, but in the end they, too, after running their course, have to be born in this material world.

Now, from Trikuti down to the vegetable kingdom is the sphere of Kal, in which are rotating all the souls according to their karma. The ruler of the circle is Kal (Brahm), who wishes to confine all these souls to his own domain, taking care not to let them go out of his own sphere, so that the latter may not become depopulated.

When Sat Purush, from whom all these souls had emanated, found them in trouble, he sent his saints from Sach Khand to initiate these souls in his path. Saints are always present in this world. Their mission is to take the soul from the sphere of Kal to Sach Khand. They do not meddle with the religions of the world. Their teaching is the same for all; namely, to make the soul attend to the holy Sound, as the current of Sound comes direct from the Supreme Being. Therefore, Sound is the direct route to Sach Khand.

As, by degrees, the mind and soul become enamoured of the Sound, the latter will burn out all our impurities and make them pure. When pure, they will be attracted by the Sound and will begin to ascend inwards. At last, when both reach Trikuti, the mind will become one with Brahm. It was

generated from this region, and will merge into it. Then the
soul, having separated from the mind, will go to the region
of Daswan Dwar (Par Brahm) and find itself free from all dis-
eases as well as from the sphere of Kal. Then Satguru will, by
degrees, take it to Sach Khand. Therefore, the only way to go
out of this world and leave the sphere of Kal is by listening to
the holy Sound and having love for the Satguru.

You will, perhaps, object that when nature has made creatures the food of creatures, then why is animal food forbidden and are we told to subsist on a vegetable diet? The answer is that sin, giving pain to the soul and mind, depends
upon the quantity of active tattwas. The vegetables and fruits
are recommended because they do not possess mind, or possess it in a dormant state, incapable of feeling pain and complaining. Destroying of insects is a greater sin than destroying vegetables, bird killing is worse than insect killing, and
animal killing is worse than bird killing, while man killing is
the worst of all. There is karma even in vegetable eating, but
not so heavy as in animal food. The holy Sound alone is po-
tent enough to wash away karma of all kinds. The lighter the
karma, the greater is the attraction of the soul towards the
Sound.

This letter is lengthy and may prove tedious; therefore it
may not be made longer. The remainder will come later, at
some other time.

～

141.   As for X, her karma is very defective and as saints do
not wish to give another incarnation in this world to their
followers, therefore it appears proper that her karma should
be washed out in this birth. There can be no doubt that she is
in great trouble; still, the debt of karma must be paid off—
otherwise it will become the cause of another birth. As a

mother takes her baby to the surgeon to get its abscess opened, and it is not her intention to cause pain to her child, but to obtain perfect health for it, and without undergoing pain the baby cannot recover, so the same is the case with X. Please encourage her so that she may not lose heart, but may bear her illness with patience and fortitude, taking it to be for her good.

Up to this time there is no English magazine bearing on this path. Any other English book that comes out of the press concerning Sant Mat will be sent to you.

Your statement that your husband and yourself, while travelling along the same path, have different experiences, is correct. The karma of each is separate, and hence it is that while both are going the same way yet the success and interruptions along the spiritual journey experienced by the one are different from those experienced by the other. Although much of your karma is similar to that of your husband, yet it cannot be so in its entirety and hence the difference in the journey. Just as when the wife is ill, the husband is not necessarily so, the karma of each is different.

If it is found inconvenient to sit in the prescribed posture, then one may sit in an easy chair with the hands in the prescribed position; or one may sit squatting and use a wooden bracket to support the elbows in the position. X need not take the prescribed posture, but let her take any convenient posture in her chair or bed and turn her attention to the Sound. The only thing is that a posture once taken should not be changed during a single sitting.

I greatly appreciate that you do not dislike to keep aloof from society. As none befriends us except holy Sound and Guru, and as at the time of death no society can serve us, then why should we fall in love with societies and the things of this world? They were meant for our comfort, and so we should take service from them according to our need but not make them idols of worship. True renunciation depends upon the attitude of the mind. A man who, while living in this world and doing its work keeps his mind free from it, can be said to have renounced the world; and one who, living in solitude, has his mind full of worldly desires, should be called a man of the world.

Your desire to visit India is welcome, but what I wish is that you may have no need for your physical hands, feet, and body, but travel without feet, speak without tongue, hear without ears, and see without eyes, and while sitting indoors visit not only India but the whole of Brahmand. If you saw India with the physical frame, what use, if you did not go beyond this world?

If you reply that you want to come to India for seeing your Guru, then it should be noted that the physical frame is not the real form of the Guru. It is a mere dress he has put on in this world and which will be put off here. The true form of the Guru is holy Sound, and in that form the Guru permeates every hair on your body and is seated within you. When you go above the eyes, then the Guru will meet you in his Radiant Form, and when you reach Trikuti, the Guru will accompany you in his Sound Form, even up to Sach Khand. Fly upwards upon the wings of faith and love so that you may talk to him every day and be with him always. This will come gradually, so you need not despair. Perform your devotion regularly, and one day all these powers shall be yours and you shall reach your true home.

~

142. I quite see the force of your point that for the Americans it is very hard to isolate the spiritual truth from the admixture of Theosophy and Christian Science and "healing

the sick" and "curing the blind." The incomplete grasp of the evolution as developed by present day-science is another stumbling block. Man is a mixture of matter, mind, spirit, and the truth.

This eye sees matter only, though it is aided by the telescope and the microscope. The eye that sees the mind and the spirit is different from this eye. This eye depends on the extraneous source of light for illumination. The other eye is self-luminous. Guru Nanak says: "The eyes that see the Lord are different from these eyes." When the attention is reversed and is held at the eye focus, that eye becomes active and begins to function, and sees the cause instead of the effect, and the higher the reversed attention rises, the more luminous and penetrating this inner eye becomes. Finally it sees the primal cause.

As members of this world we assume certain duties pertaining to the sphere of our activity. We should perform them as best we can, without losing ourselves in their performance. All the philosophers and mystics agree on the par excellence of man in creation. His superiority lies in that, as man, he can solve the riddle of the universe and isolate the cause from the effect. And if he did not solve this riddle, he came in vain. Therefore, repeatedly, I draw your attention to this important duty of man. You are on the high road of the current, and with love and faith and forced marches, travel on this road and reach the place of eternal peace and bliss.

Mind is the disturbing element. It connects spirit with matter by coming in between as a connecting link. When the tendency of the mind is outward, it is attached with matter, and when it looks inward, it gets detached from matter and tries to know the spirit, which naturally has an inward tendency. In proportion to the loosening of the union of mind with matter, the union of mind with soul strengthens.

Carefully, therefore, examine the tendencies of the mind
and study its weaknesses, and try to overcome them. So long
as there is dirt in the mind, it cannot stay within. Its attachments draw it out. Whichever pan of the balance is loaded,
that pan goes down always. Mind is our enemy and, like an
enemy, its movements should be watched.

The whole world—man, animal, bird, insect—dances to
the tune of mind. Every creature is being tossed up and down
by it. The only place where mind dances is when it is brought
before the current. Only then it becomes helpless. It cannot
be controlled by the study of scriptures nor by the performance of austerities. Neither the soldier nor the warrior, nor
the conqueror, nor the moralist, has succeeded against it. He
who ever succeeded against it, did so by catching the sound
current.

~

143.   I received your two letters in due course of time. About
a month ago a few copies of the pamphlets were sent to you
without any covering letter with them. No money is to be
sent for these, as the price is nominal. I shall be glad to supply more copies if needed.

Regarding the yogi and his forty-dollar course, X wrote
to me about him. I gave her an outline of the yoga course and
compared it with Sant Mat and, as usual, gave her full permission to satisfy her curiosity. There is nothing very wrong
with the system, in as far as they go. The point is that the
systems, when practically looked into, do not carry very far.
Almost all of the systems end at the first stage of Sant Mat
(that is, they end where we begin). Even this stage is reached
only by a few.

Again, there is no fixed time limit in any system, in which
time a practitioner will reach the stage. If anybody fixes the

time limit, he is deceiving himself and deceiving others. People become enamoured when they hear one say that by following this or that system, they will attain the goal in so much time, and are caught. They do not critically examine themselves. Mind is not a thing that can be switched off and on at will.

It cannot be taken away from its routine course in spite of one's best effort in a day, a month, or a year. It is a lifelong struggle. Those who have undergone this struggle, or who are engaged in it, understand what it is to conquer the mind. It is son, daughter, wife, husband, friend, wealth and poverty, attachment, greed, lust, anger, pride, and whatnot. It is attached to the outside world with ropes, double ropes, triple ropes, and manifold ropes, and has been held by these chains so long that it does not feel the irksomeness of its bonds. It likes them instead.

Mind has completely forgotten its origin. To the caged bird, its captivity is the normal run of life. What would a course of yoga do for such a mind? The tangled skein cannot be unravelled so easily. Just as a mother watches over and looks after her child, a devotee looks after his mind. Even then there is no time limit. In the words of a famous poet, that struggle with the mind is like the invitation to a lover to come ready for the extreme sacrifice (loss of his head), but there is no promise of even an interview from the beloved.

If it were an easy affair, Guru Nanak would not have sat on pebbles for twelve years. Christ would not have spent nineteen years in the Tibetan hills and Soami Ji himself would not have contemplated in a solitary, dark, back room for seventeen years. I need not write more. You know the struggle. Doctor has already said, "It is death in life." All that I would add is that there is no disappointment to those who are attached to the current within. Sooner or later the door will open.

X's tragic end was reported at the time in India's leading newspapers as well. Looking at it from the angle of vision of the matter-of-fact man of the world, it was a rash act. Aviation over seas is not safe yet.[1] Yet Lindberg succeeded where X failed.

Matter-of-fact men would say that X's machine was not as good or that he came across very foul weather and, on the whole, that X was not wise enough when he undertook this adventure. The matter-of-fact man has to give some reason to account for an occurrence. When a doctor fails to find any other reason for a death, he calls it heart failure, and there the matter ends. When the cause is known, the element of surprise disappears. Common occurrences do not produce surprise, for the cause is so apparent.

Similarly, those who see the past and future with the inner eye, and see the cause of a happening in this life in some distant past, are not surprised at the extraordinary happening, like X's tragedy. To them it is the result of a cause, a natural effect.

Destiny is, therefore, nothing extraordinary to the inner eye. It is simply a matter of routine. X was to end his present life like this. It was the result of his own doing at some previous time. He could not avoid it. When you say he was clean and sound and there was no necessity for him to hazard this, then you take away all blame from him, and have to admit that he must have been forced to undertake it unconsciously, by force of circumstances which he could not see or avoid. He was helpless. He probably undertook it with all the forethought he was capable of.

Saints, as a rule, do not interfere with what is happening. They live in the will of the Supreme. Because they see the

---

1. In 1930.

past, present, and future, there is nothing extraordinary for them. Knowing full well the past, present, and future, they pass their time unostentatiously. They intentionally pass as ignorant. They look at things from a much broader point of view, while we look at them from a comparatively narrow angle. Deaths and births are great events to us, and yet they are not equal to even a drop in the great ocean of creation.

A story goes that in the time of Guru Nanak, a man came to him, and in the course of conversation, the subject came up about saints living in the will of the Supreme. Nanak advocated the supremacy of His will and the safety of the individual in bringing himself into line with His will. The man advocated the superiority of reason and action. The long and the short of it was that the man asked Nanak if he could point out some one who lived up to this. Nanak gave the name of one Bhai Lalo, a carpenter, and gave him the other particulars. This man, in time, reached Lalo's place and found him working in his shop. Lalo greeted him and said that he would attend to him in fifteen minutes. The man continued watching Lalo who was preparing a wooden plank (bier) to carry the dead. After finishing it, he placed it in the shop and went out to the bazaar and soon returned with the other articles required in disposing of a dead body and put them aside with the bier.

Lalo was about to address his guest when a messenger came running from Lalo's house and said, "Your son fell down from the roof and is dead." Lalo was unperturbed and said, reflectively, "His will." The guest was watching Lalo all the time. Lalo quietly took out the bier and the other articles, carried them to his home and arranged, as is customary, for the disposal of a dead body.

After disposing of the body, and taking leave of the people assembled, Lalo returned to his shop with the man. He then apologized for his delay in attending to him. The man had been watching Lalo all the time and knew now that the plank which Lalo had been making was intended for the body of his son, and that Lalo knew all the time that the boy was to fall and die. He therefore accused Lalo of negligence in not going home in time and saving the child from the fall. Lalo repeatedly pointed out that the boy was to die like that, and that it was in the interest of the child that he was not saved; that his child's connection with himself was to end like that, that it was in the fitness of things that this had happened, and he was happy in His will.

Now Lalo's is not a negative attitude. It is a decidedly positive attitude, which is not attained as long as one is confined to the sphere of reason alone. Reason is blind and the activity based on reason is also blind, in comparison to what is seen by the inner eye. But so long as the inner eye is not seeing, one is in the sphere of reason or intellect, and has only this reason to guide him. Looked at from the point of view of reason, X was not wise in his adventure. Looked at from the point of view of the inner eye, he could not help it and it was to happen like this.

You ask, "Would he have been saved, if he had taken to the Sant Mat?" If death is an event of our life, then the initiation into the sound current is the event of events. The initiation is preordained. Those who are destined to receive it in this life get it, and not otherwise, no matter how close they may be to a Master. Death and initiation are in no way to be connected together. One is independent of the other.

The outward run of soul, covered by mind and matter, may be likened to a journey by stage on a long road. The journey from one station to another is the span of a single life. Now, assume that the journey is made in such a way that the covering is changed at every stage. The old covering is left behind, but the impressions of the last journey are there.

These impressions or experiences mould the onward course; and if there are many travellers on the road, one traveller impresses and is impressed by the others.

A traveller left behind may catch up again. A setback or a runback is not unusual. A skirmish in one stage may develop into a fight in another stage. The vanquished in one stage may turn out victorious in another. The impressions and experiences on a journey are the karmas. They influence reason as a magnet influences iron. X's reason was influenced by his past history, and so is the reason of everyone else. No two persons think alike, because the past history is never the same. On this journey, no traveller is one hundred percent fatalist or a free-willer. A fatalist makes feeble efforts, but is not always successful. In this journey, struggle is the rule.

We have been on this road ever since creation started—an endless period. We have not gone back to our home, the proof of which is that we are here now. The way hence is within us. That is the sound current, but we are disconnected from the sound current. Saints connect us with this current and see us back to our home. This is the mission of the saints. From the time of initiation, they are with the initiated at the eye focus, help him to come back to the focus and, from there go with him in His house.

There may be people who hold that, in spite of their great desire to go within, they do not seem to get the help. Such people have only to search their hearts a little deeply. They will find that what they call their great desire is very superficial. They do not want to go within and stay within, but wish as a matter of curiosity to return and play the tipster. When a soul really wishes to go back, there is nothing to prevent it. It is the law. Has any father given away his hard earned money to his son to squander away? Or has any father kept away his earnings from his deserving son?

Enclosed is a translation of a poem by Soami Ji Maharaj. I am proud of you both and of your work. With blessings from the Father.

> Soul, I know thou art in distress.
> From the day thou brokest contact with the Word,
> Thou hast formed attachments with the mind.
> Thy stupid mind has bound thee to the body,
> And in the snare of sensual pleasures holds thee.
>
> Thy kith and kin are a source of pain,
> Yet art thou tied fast to these.
> A living spirit thou, and false and lifeless these.
> Between these two how could there reconciliation be?
>
> Proper therefore to wake up now,
> Rather than be caught in the cycle of transmigration.
> Through Satsang seek the everlasting
> And cultivate the Master's love.
>
> From the Master learn the secret of the Word
> And climb up to the heaven again.
> Do this much in the present life;
> The Master will look to the rest.
>
> Even now take heed, says Radha Soami;
> Sorrows will vanish, and the secret
> Of eternal bliss stand revealed.

The first lines of the poem describe the outward run of the soul:

> Soul—mind—body—senses—objects.

Mind is stupid because it left Trikuti and degraded itself by coming down into the body. It did not stay there even, but, through the senses, is attached to objects exterior to itself.

The second stanza indicates the incompatibility of soul and matter. The "heaven" in the fourth stanza, means the eye focus. The fourth and fifth stanzas give hope and assurance.

~

144. I am very sorry that your letters have remained unreplied so long. The secretary misplaced all the American letters in May and found them this Christmas. I had gone out for two months in October and November. You must be feeling this delay, but I hope you will be generous.

You have recommended Marion Schumaker and Dr Johnson and Mr Myers…. I have written to Dr Johnson and Mr Myers to correspond with you for initiation and fix time if they are ready. You may please give all three the necessary instructions and initiation, if you find them ready. I hope they will be able to do without eggs, meats, and alcohol.

Regarding initiation of those who have not applied directly, I would say that you may give them initiation in special cases, if you consider them fit. But it would be better if you let them apply and wait for a reply. It is in your interest, for you may feel disappointed in case they go wrong.

It is difficult to make a true estimate of a man intellectually. What to say of others, one does not know aright himself. The mind changes with the impressions received, and sometimes without any apparent cause. "Coming events cast their shadows before." But what is in store yet, intellect cannot comprehend. At least, it only tries to guess. To follow the working of the mind, we must leave the physical or material zone and enter the mind zone; and, more than that, we should detach ourselves from the mind also, for only then can we see it dispassionately.

"To understand the laws regulating entrance to this faith," you must go within. You will then see that "all that shines is not gold," nor all that looks dull is base. As long as we are covered with mind and matter, we cannot see reality. When you have thrown off these coverings, you will be able to read others correctly at a glance. You will then find that everyone, good or bad, is working under a law, and whatever has happened or is happening is right.

Those who are to get initiation in this life are stamped already. Says Guru Nanak: "God has written on the forehead that this man will have faith in the Guru, will get initiation, meet the Creator, and be happy." The simple-minded accept quickly that Sant Mat is correct, and stick to it and succeed, while the so-called educated or the learned continue wandering. Their scattered minds are not at ease, and take long to settle. Their minds are to be tired out, so to say, before they get steady. For them it is a hard task.

You are familiar with the soil and rock strata. In some places the strata vary in quick succession, while in other places the same stratum continues quite deep. The same is the case with karma. Unless you are familiar with the strata, you cannot guess what lies underneath. The change may be sudden, or otherwise, from one stratum to another. Similarly, the change in man's temper may be sudden or slow, depending on the pile of karma. To understand the law, "know thyself."

You feel dejected when you find that people do not stick to the teaching. I would ask you not to make it a personal case. We are not creating a new religion or a new sect; there are plenty of them already. We are not making money out of it that we should feel sorry that, with the fall in numbers, there will be loss in income. We are not hankering after name or fame; they are poison in this path. You do it simply as a charity—giving or wasting your time for the good of others.

If you come across a real seeker, give him a hint. There is no necessity to go out of your way to influence others. Things happen when the time is ripe for them. Your talk with others leaves the impression on them. Sooner or later they will go deeper, and your talk will bear fruit. Let not the coming or going of others interfere in your own progress. I do not wish you to help others at the sacrifice of your own progress. Says Nanak: "He who preaches to others, but does not act upon it himself, will continue coming and going in births and deaths."

Everyone is actuated by his karma. If the Creator does not wish to bring a person on the path immediately, you may try your hardest, but he will not grasp the idea. And those whom He wishes to give to, accept it without hesitation. Go within and see this law. It is true that faith, like other things, varies in intensity. The only way to strengthen it is to have firsthand knowledge. Knowledge is within you. You have to go within yourself to get it. There is no other way.

The Christian religion and the Shabd Yoga or Sant Mat are two distinct things. Sant Mat is not a religion of customs and rituals, nor a theory and blind faith. It is a science which connects the soul with its source. Christ studied a branch of this science, but it is a pity that Christ did not leave behind any writings from which his philosophy or science could be traced. All the works on the Christian religion were written by his disciples.

The science of the Indian saints is given in their books, which are authentic. In their writings, they have described the inward journey of their soul. They say that they have seen Him and lead others to Him. Their system is quite clear. The disciples of Christ have mixed custom and ritual in his science. It has resulted in confusion. Saints do not care for outward customs and rituals. They neither abolish them nor create new ones. Their business is to go within. They emphasize pure spirituality. From the Bible we learn that Christ did follow the current. Even now, if you go within, you meet him on the way. To understand Christ and his science, let us go within and meet him.

If X has dropped out, it does not matter in the least. This seed (Word), once placed in a bosom, cannot die. It must germinate when watered and bear fruit when nourished—in this life or the next. There is no getting away. She complains that she is not cared for. Poor soul, she does not understand that pain and pleasure are necessary adjuncts of this life. Our life is a combination of good and bad karma.

Disease is due to karma—our own bad karma—and one should be happy that through disease the bad karma is being fulfilled. Disease is the unloading of the burden, and paying off the debt. When a child gets dirty, the mother cleans it and washes it, no matter how much the child may cry and weep. When He gives us disease, He wishes to clean us. If she were to go within, she could see what help is given, and how.

If X or anybody else wants proof, she must enter the laboratory where the experiment is going on. The laboratory is within the body, not outside it.

I am not familiar with the book *Eating for Health and Efficiency*. If it is good, you may recommend it to those who are starting on the path. Under separate cover I am sending you a small book, *Self-Restraint versus Self-Indulgence*, by Mahatma Gandhi. I hope it will be of some use to you.

≈

145. I have received your letters and also your pamphlet, *The Religion of Nature*. I am glad you took the earliest opportunity to go to the Brocks and got the initiation. Now you may consider that your outward inquiry as to what is truth and where it resides and how to get at it is over. The net result of your inquiry is: The truth is within you, and you have to go within yourself to get it. You have heard the Sound enough in its very feeble form. That should give you a start. The outward inquiry is over and the inward search should commence.

The first essential thing is concentration—bringing the scattered and scattering attention in the eye focus. It is the attention or sense of feeling, mind, and so forth, no matter what name you give it (for at this stage it is a combination of all), that is to see and hear within, just as it is seeing and hearing outwardly now. The same force which is working in the world outside, through eyes, ears, and so forth is to work within, through the inner eye and the inner ear, in the inner worlds.

Like the switching off and on of an electric current from one aperture to another, we should be able to switch off and on our attention from the physical, material world, or the physical body, to the inner, finer world and the inner, finer or astral body. The attention, like the current, is the same; but it is to work in different spheres. Collection and holding of the attention at the eye focus is to switch it off from the physical world and the physical body. When this is achieved, concentration is complete. We should then be entirely cut off from the material world and our own material body but conscious within.

Because our attention has been running wild, outwardly from the eye focus, not only during our present life since our birth but in our previous lives also, so to hold it at the eye focus is an arduous, uphill task. The habit of staying out from the focus has become second nature. But there is no reason why we should not be able to overcome a habit. It only needs effort and determination.

You may have observed that this attention is not permanently attached to any material object in this world. From childhood onward it has had its likes and dislikes. At one time it is attached to friends, at another to family, and so on. It has not stuck to one thing. Herein lies the remedy: the attention is detachable.

So what we do in our method of concentration is to place before our attention the vision of the inner worlds. By repeatedly putting those scenes before it, we bring it again and again into the focus. We are substituting the visions of the inner worlds in place of the outer and material world. Jot Niranjan, for example, when remembered, suggests the idea of candle light and bell sound, inside the eye focus; similarly, other names. The five names thus give us the main features of the path within, and when we remember these, we are, in a way, bringing our attention onto the inner path. It is only a matter of effort, longing, determination, and persistence in the face of failure, when this switching of the attention from the external, material world onto the inner worlds will become easy and a matter of routine. Sticking to the eye focus is essential.

The mind will often run away, and when you find it has run away, bring it back into the focus. Sometimes sleep intervenes. Sleep only means that the mind was withdrawn from the external world, but we did not stick to the focus, and instead the attention sank down to the lower focus—the throat or navel. So bring it up again to the eye focus.

If one sticks to the focus, then the mind, which runs wild in the beginning, slowly and slowly quiets down and it begins to feel as if sticking to the eye focus is not an unnatural thing. The current from the body then slowly begins to move towards the focus. (The body should not be disturbed from the posture). The first withdrawal is from the extremities—

the arms and legs. If the practice is prolonged, the body—the whole trunk—will lose the current, which will collect at the eye focus. Then one will be conscious within but unconscious of one's own body, what to say of the external world.

When you have stuck to this posture for as long as you could, and wish to change as a necessity, assume the posture in which the Sound is to be heard. Still sticking to the focus, try to catch the Sound, but do not leave the focus. The attention from the body below the eyes will also be withdrawn towards the focus. As this process is followed, you will feel the withdrawal of the current. When the current is withdrawn to the focus, one is unconscious of the body but is fully conscious within.

Some gaze on a statue or idol or picture, or a dot on a wall, or the tip of the nose. Now all these things are external to oneself. The attention will be concentrated where one holds it long enough. Having succeeded in concentration on external objects, the next step is to bring it within. So why not start from within?

The sound current starts from the eye focus. As long as the eye focus is not reached, the sound current is not audible. The moment one reaches the eye focus, he must hear the Sound. The Sound never stops; it is the attention that does not reach there. If a thing is lying on the roof of one's house, he cannot get it unless he goes up to the roof.

The soul is covered by mind and matter. We are a combination of soul, mind and matter. At present we are mostly matter, feebly mind, and imperceptibly soul. Our state is like that of iron covered by rust and then by mud. In this state iron does not behave as iron, and is not attracted by a magnet. Our attention does not catch the sound current because the attention is saturated with matter or the world of matter. When we will reach the eye focus, we will have washed away all matter and will be fit to catch the current. Reaching the eye focus is a prerequisite to catching the current.

Our attention is sticking to the body and the world like a fine silk cloth entangled in a prickly, thorny shrub. If one were to pull the cloth forcibly the cloth would be torn to pieces. But if one sits by patiently and disentangles it from pricks or thorns, bit by bit, one can succeed in removing the cloth intact. If you will pull out a single hair from the body, you feel the pain or the pull because the attention is there. No violent act will withdraw the attention. Withdrawal should be done gently.

Any act, therefore, that will make the attention stick to matter tenaciously, should be avoided. Discarding the sensual desires from the mind and being good, pure-minded, and honest in dealings with others, loosens the connection of the attention from the world. Concentration is the goal. Any act that assists in the achievement of this goal is right, and all those that keep the attention away from the focus are wrong. The nearer we are to concentration or the focus, the nearer we are to the light. Light, like Sound, is already within us. It never goes out. Only we do not reach the place where light is. The light is inside the focus and we are outside the focus. Says Guru Nanak, "The cure of all ills is the Word." Let us, therefore, go within the focus to catch the Word. Proceed patiently. The current of the soul should leave the body slowly. What to say of light, you will see innumerable worlds within, which you will cross on your way.

The five stages about which you have been told are the main stations on the road. In loose terminology, everything within the eye focus is called Brahmand. The part near to this side of the focus is often called Anda. Any number of subdivisions in Anda and Brahmand may be mentioned. Strictly speaking, the body, including the part below the eye focus, may be divided into five parts:

1. Pind, the part below the eyes;
2. Anda, from the eye focus up to the beginning of Trikuti, which has been explained to you as the second stage;
3. Brahmand, from the bottom of Trikuti up to the border of Daswan Dwar;
4. Par Brahm from the bottom of Daswan Dwar to the top of Bhanwar Gupha and lastly;
5. Sach Khand and the stages above it.

Sach Khand and the stages above it constitute the pure spiritual region. This is the only unchangeable part. Brahmand, Anda, and Pind are changeable, and therefore perishable. Leaving the pure spiritual region aside, the remaining parts—Brahmand, Anda, and Pind—are related to one another as the image is related to the object. Anda is the reflection of Brahmand, and Pind is the reflection of Anda, just as the sun and its reflection in water, and the reflection on a wall from the surface of water, are related to one another. The sun is above in the sky with all its magnificence and power. The image in the water has the appearance of the sun but has lost much of its magnificence. The reflection on the wall is only a hazy patch of light, distorted and devoid of glory. Pind is a copy of Anda, and Anda is a copy of Brahmand. The so-called man is thus a copy of the copy, leaving aside the pure spirit.

You may have seen in books the points and pictures describing the six lotuses in Pind, the part below the eye focus. It is unnecessary to go into this in detail, for it will serve no useful purpose. Suffice it to say that these six lotuses are the reflection of the corresponding six lotuses or centres of Anda, which are in turn the reflection of the six centres of Brahmand.

Just to give you an idea how the corresponding centres in Pind, Anda, and Brahmand resemble one another, like the sun and its images: the lowest centre in Pind is at the rectum, with red colour and four petals. The corresponding centre in Anda is the lowest centre, just above the eyes, with its red colour and four petals. The corresponding centre in Brahmand is Trikuti, with its red colour and four petals. The red sun of Trikuti is reflected in the four-petalled lotus of *antakaran*, just above the eyes, and this in turn is reflected down at the rectum as the dull, red-coloured, four-petalled lotus.

The majority of systems of concentration start from the rectum and then slowly work up the attention to the eye focus. Some start from the heart centre and then slowly work up to the eye centre; for in the case of ordinary men the headquarters of attention is not the eye centre but the heart. Man rises to the eye centre only when thinking deeply, and again sinks down below the eye centre. Dream and sleep states are caused by the attention sinking below the eye focus.

Sant Mat, or the system of the saints, starts with concentration from the eye focus. They do not concentrate at any centre below the eyes. The argument is simple. Man is normally working from the heart centre. With some effort he rises above this centre momentarily to do some deep thinking, and in relaxation goes back to the heart centre. So man is sitting at the middle of the mountain whose base is the rectum and the top is the eye centre, and the heart is the midway point. Going down to the rectum and then coming up is a waste of time and energy. So saints straightaway put the eye focus as the first goal to reach the top.

There is a natural capacity in man to rise up to the eyes, although he does not stick to it. This last thing is the only drawback. Saints, therefore, remove the drawback by repeatedly going up to the eye focus; and the eye focus, by practice, becomes the headquarters of attention. Changing the headquarters of attention upwards is going towards the light, step by step.

Power lies in concentration, no matter at what centre it is concentrated. But the higher the centre, the greater the power and the greater the peace. Entering and sticking to any centre in Pind or parts below the eyes is a study of the reflection of reflections. Saints have discarded entering into Pind. They sit at the eye focus, withdraw the current up to this centre, and start off to Anda and Brahmand.

Practice and actual experience gained in doing the process of concentration will automatically remove some of your doubts and difficulties. Please bear in mind that no strain is to be put on the eyes. It is not the material eye that sees within, for that is an organ like other organs which connect us with the external material world.

Your Master or Guru is within you at the eye focus, ready to receive you, and is awaiting your arrival. He is always within you. You can see him there by going into the eye focus. He will answer all of your questions and you will not stand in need of any outside agency.

Your *Religion of Nature* is very good, and you may give it out to the world. The world will benefit by it. But you will be well advised if you do not attempt another for some time, till you have actually seen something within and acquired first-hand knowledge. Write after storing energy.

146.   I quite agree with you when you say, "I feel that I can lift no higher than I can reach." Self-study is essential, therefore. To study the self, it will have to be isolated first from the material and ethereal coverings and from its connections with

the outside world. We are attached to the world through our attention. If we succeed in holding our attention within us, our connection with the world is cut off and we are independent of it for the time being. Similarly, if we hold our attention in the brain or in the third eye, our connection with the lower part of the body will be cut off and we will be independent of the body for the time being. So far we do it daily, although the duration is small.

When, after doing our duty, we return home, we have cut off our connection with the external world and narrowed down our sphere to the house only. When from the drawing room we retire to our own room, we have temporarily cut off our connection with the household. When we are about to sleep and our eyes are drowsy, our attention has contracted towards the eyes and left the extremities of the body. So far we are conscious. However, the attention does not stay in the eyes but, by habit, goes down from the eye focus, leaving us unconscious or semi-conscious. The lower it goes from the brain, the duller it becomes. Finally, we lie sleeping and unconscious.

Now, if we had held this attention in the eyes we would have remained conscious. And if we could raise it above the eye focus, within ourselves, we would be superconscious within, in the new world which is separate from the physical world and the physical body, with which we are not attached but are cut off from, for the time being. We have thrown off one covering, the coarse material sheath, from the self. When the attention returns to the body, and from there to the home and the world, we step by step are reconnected with the world. If the holding of the attention at the eye focus could be prolonged, we could remain connected with the inner world for longer periods, and correspondingly disconnected from the material world.

To remain connected with the outside world has become second nature by habit. To loosen this connection or to change this habit requires time and effort. It is a slow process. Violent methods do not succeed here. The attention is to be diverted, and second nature is to be altered.

When one succeeds in holding the attention undisturbed at the eye focus, the Word or the sound current (though audible feebly even before the eye focus is reached) begins to attract the attention, as a magnet draws iron. This current is the "royal road" that leads the attention onwards. This current is life. It is the essence. It is within us, for us.

Christ spoke of this current as Word. Mohammed called it Kalma, and saints have given it various names. It is the basis of all religions. The difference lies in the extent to which the founders of various religions followed it. Socrates said, "Know thyself." Christ separated his self from its coverings and could do it at will. It was a practical course with him. The present-day philosophy is theoretical only. It is more inclined to tackle world problems and ignore the practical study of the self. And that is why it does not succeed in solving its problems. Self-study is an individual study. Man came alone into this world and will leave alone. When he has solved the problems of coming and going for himself, he may help others in this line.

～

147. I have received both of your letters in due course of time, the latter having been written after initiation. In my last letter I had given you some hints on concentration, of which you were expected to get a clearer idea after initiation and application. You now have a better idea of your difficulties.

The posture is not easy for you, and the usual course with you is to sit upright in a chair. You occasionally lose consciousness and muscular control momentarily, and the head falls backward or sideways until it ends with a jerk which awakens you.

In the ordinary way, when one is about to sleep, what happens is that as attention withdraws from the eye focus, one loses muscular control, becomes unconscious of the body, and finally the eye centre gets vacant, and consciousness gives place to semi-consciousness and then to unconsciousness.

The loss of consciousness means that the attention did not stick to the eye focus but fell below this focus, onto the lower centres—the throat or the navel. At the throat centre it is almost in a semi-conscious state, causing dream; and at the navel centre, there is a complete loss of consciousness. If it were held to the eye focus and, instead of falling down, it had gone up to that centre, there ought to have been full consciousness and superconsciousness, not of the body or the external world but of what you were doing within—repetition or grasping the current, or seeing something within if anything was visible.

Therefore, loss of consciousness means ordinary sleep. There cannot be unconsciousness if the attention is at the eye focus, or at the centres above the eyes. When you say the jerk awakens you, it means that you were asleep. There is nothing unusual in this. Attention by habit goes down, and we wish to come up. It is here that the struggle commences. So when you get the jerk, start again. Consciously stick to the focus. When you are conscious of the focus, and repeatedly bring your attention to it when it goes off, you will, by and by, become unconscious of the surroundings and the body, and remain conscious of the focus or what lies in the focus.

It is a slow process and takes time. But rest assured, sooner or later you will succeed. This struggle for achieving concentration has been compared to the rise of an ant on a smooth wall. The ant rises and falls sometimes after a climb of a few inches only, and, not infrequently, when the roof is in sight. The withdrawal of the current from the body to the eye focus is like the climb of the ant—a struggle, but a struggle with determination.

The headquarters of the attention is at the eye focus, but its rays animate the whole body. They go beyond the physical body as well, into the sons, daughters, wife, and other relations, into movable and immovable property, and into the country. They have a long range. It takes time to withdraw these rays to the focus. It is only when the rays have been focused in the eye centre that man becomes a man. Otherwise he is akin to a beast.

When these rays of attention begin to collect at the eye centre, or the process of withdrawal starts, one feels the pricking sensation. It is a sign of concentration. It appears as if ants were moving on the skin. The inner waves are coming up, and as the waves come up they should bring in a state better than the state of wakefulness instead of unconsciousness.

You have not the habit to sit in the posture. We Indians have the habit. Only the fat people here find it difficult. But, like other things, posture is only a means to an end. The end in view is concentration or holding the attention in the focus.

The light and the sound are always present at the focus. They are never absent from the focus. We could not remain alive if the current were absent from the focus. To get them (light and sound) you must reach the focus.

Do not worry if you have not seen anything so far. You may worry about their absence when you reach the focus and do not find them there. Everything lies inside the focus. Your wildest dreams or imaginings cannot picture the grandeur of what lies within. But the treasure is yours and is there for you. You can have it whenever you go there. Take it from me, and once for all, that everything, including the Creator, is within you, and whosoever has attained it, has attained it by going inside the focus. There is no easier method to go within than the one of which you have been informed.

Please be not in a hurry. With patience and perseverance, complete the course of concentration. Going within takes time. The rise within is comparatively easier. This part of the course is tasteless. Taste comes with concentration. Slow but steady wins the race. That which is acquired after struggle is valued, and that which comes easily is often not valued.

The natural tendency of the soul is to rise up, for it is a bird of a different sphere. The mind and the body keep it down. The cream in milk automatically rises when the milk is left alone. The moment the body and the mind are stationary, the soul begins to rise up towards the focus. It is the disturbances of the mind and the body that keep it down, just the cream does not rise if the milk is disturbed.

There are three bodies with corresponding minds: The physical body, the astral body, and the causal body. We are all familiar with the physical body. We can have some idea of the astral from the forms we see in dreams, but with this difference, that the dream is a state of attention below the eyes, and the astral sphere is above the eyes. The idea of the causal body cannot be grasped as long as the attention does not go within the focus, but it may be compared to the tiny plant in the seed itself. Inside the physical is the astral, and inside the astral is the causal.

When the attention reaches the eye focus, it has cast off the physical frame, and for the time being it is free and separate from it—just as we take off our coats. At the top of Sahansdal Kanwal, the attention casts off the astral form; and at the top of Trikuti, it casts off the causal form. These three bodies are controlled or moved by their corresponding minds.

So long as the soul is within the sphere of these bodies and minds, it is subject to births and deaths. At every death it changes the body, although itself is imperishable. The body dies, or changes, but not the soul. The change in the form of the body is determined by the fruit of our past actions, which is our karma. There is no "body" without action, and there is no action without "body." Every action that has been done has left an impression behind on the mind. It may not be in the memory for the time being, but may flash itself at any time. The point is that the impression remains, which will manifest itself in its own time.

Now, so long as all the impressions (received ever since the soul entered into the spheres of minds and bodies) have not been removed, the soul is not free, and till then shall remain subject to karma. It performs actions only when it activates the mind, and this happens only when it leaves the sound current and associates itself with the mind. It is free from the mind as long as it is catching the current.

So practically the whole of humanity—leaving aside other creation—is disconnected from the current and performs actions, leaving their impressions behind and becoming the cause of rebirths.

At birth, a definite number of actions or impressions are allotted to the soul. They form, in a way, the mould in which the new life has been cast. They determine the temperament, span of life, and the trend of activities during life.

During the lifetime, therefore, these impressions have been worked out, and new impressions have been received. These new impressions, together with the unallotted old impressions, are sorted again, and a definite number assigned to run another span of life. The process is therefore unending, and evidently there does not seem to be any way out of this cycle.

But saints show us a way out. They say that the impressions that you brought with you in this life, form your fate, and you have to undergo this.

There is no escape from this, and if it were to terminate somehow immediately, death would ensue. Therefore, there should be no interference with them. They cannot be altered or modified.

But the new actions that you do, you may do, not as an independent, but as an agent of the Master. As agent, you are not held responsible. A faithful agent does not misuse the powers and the property entrusted to him. Suppose that we take the body, the mind, and the worldly properties we possess as a trust from the Master, and work with them as his agents—then there is little possibility of our using them in ill ways. The new actions, therefore, will not be binding. The agent is responsible to the primary, and if he has done his work honestly and to the best of his ability, then for all his actions as agent, the primary is responsible.

In addition, the saints put us onto the current. By these means they free us from the new impressions, and the assigned impressions are worked out during the lifetime. The unassigned impressions, saints take upon themselves, and themselves render account. Saints have the capacity to render account for the unassigned actions, for they come from a zone beyond the limits of mind. Without the help of saints and the travel on the sound current, there is no escape from the impressions.

The range of mind extends up to the top of Trikuti; and so long as the soul is in or below Trikuti, it is subject to transmigration. Souls that have taken shelter with the saints, sooner or later—sooner if they follow their advice—go beyond Trikuti to Sach Khand.

You will thus see that the law of karma is universally applicable, while forgiveness is the speciality of saints. Christ forgave those whom he initiated, and not those who did not come in contact with him. Christianity is wrong wherein it supposes that, in the name of Christ, they are forgiven. It is blind faith and self-deception. Christ played his part when he was present on this earth in the flesh.

There are in our satsang Freemasons up to the twelfth degree. They say that in Freemasonry there is no such thing as actual concentration of the attention, nor the rise of the soul into the higher planes. They call Freemasonry a society more inclined towards charity. They do not find any spirituality there. As to the journey within, there is no stage which is crossed by the show of passwords, mantras, signs, or grips. Words finish at the third eye. The journey is travelled by the force of love and longing.

Religion means union of the individual soul with its source. In actual practice, it is the concentration of the attention at the eye focus and by rising up by following the sound current. It is therefore an individual affair. Everybody for himself. You are to go within yourself. I am to go within myself. To do this, no outward ceremony is needed. The moment one begins to concentrate his attention, he cuts off his connections from others. All outward ceremonies are meaningless. True religion admits of no external ways of devotion. Burning of incense, human and blood sacrifice, eating bread, and drinking wine are non-essentials. Human and blood sacrifice indicate not only ignorance, but show perverted mentality.

Idol worship, blood sacrifice, grave worship, pilgrimage to so-called holy places, and many other customs are common in India, and some of them in other countries as well. How they originated is not difficult to trace. Take the case of idol worship in India. A being, by actual concentration, went inside the focus, saw the thousand-petalled lotus (let us say) with its big central light and the other subsidiary lights, together with the various sounds that are going on there. As an artist, he expresses that in wood or stone, or paint and brush. No wonder that he, having seen the deity within, may bow his head to what he himself has made. He gives the idea to others. The sluggards, instead of rising up within, remain contented with bowing their heads outwardly. Some of the outward forms of worship are thus explained. But they are all meaningless.

Saints, if they like, may pass their magnetism to others. Christ, as we read in the Bible, passed it on to others. He cured the blind and the invalid. saints may use their power, if they wish, through word, touch, or look. They may not use the external organs but, instead, may use the mind or even the soul, and affect the mind or the soul of the other, without the other person even being made aware of it. These latter ways are the rule rather than the exception.

Christ passed his magnetism to bread and water, and whosoever partook of it received the magnetism. The value lay in Christ, and not in the process. Christians now perform the ceremony but the magnetism of Christ is absent. To get the magnetism, rise to the spheres within and be Christlike.

～

148.   I am ready to help you, if you find yourself ready to travel into the inner worlds. You are to do your duty and the "guide" will do his. Naturally, the journey will take a long time if there is no longing to reach the other end, as the scenery on the roadside causes frequent halts, or some other considerations stop the progress, or too much unnecessary load is carried.

The journey lies through the astral, mental, and spiritual regions. The sound current not only connects these, but makes these regions. They are its offshoots. If a soul were to stick to the current, and not look aside or go off the current, and were to leave behind the memory of this world, there is no power that can keep it here for a second, or that can stop it on the way. The memory of this world pulls it down and keeps it down, and the scenery of the inner regions throws it off the current.

So long as the mind is filled with me and mine (my wife, my sons, my daughters, my property, my honour, my wealth, my country, my nation, my wisdom, and so forth), it cannot pass through the narrow way. To make the mind go through this narrow way, is to bring it up before the narrow gateway and make it struggle and force its way. By actual struggle and experience, it will very soon learn what keeps it from going in. Only then will it feel the superfluity of what it is carrying with itself and, as a necessity, will have to shed it. Then it becomes light and humble, and will pass through the narrow way very easily.

At present the mind is active in this world, making its connections with it through the organs of senses, and if we try to hold it at the centre of concentration above the eyes, we fail, because the memory of me and mine pulls it out again. How long it will take to wipe off this memory at will depends on its past history or karma. But just as we have learned other things by practice, we can, by practice, train the mind to this new habit. When it has made its way through the gate, it will be able to catch the current; and the guide will be there inside the gate to lead on. The only load that we need carry is the implicit faith in the guide and the intense longing to reach the other end. All else is superficial and non-essential.

This world is the plane of struggle. There has never been peace here, nor will there be. Problems of today give place to problems of tomorrow. In a place where mind and matter are active, there can never be peace. Sorrows and wars of nations or communities, or individuals, shall continue. The soul must seek other planes to find peace. To find peace is the business of the individual. Everybody has to seek it within himself. The neighbours cannot help in this. We came into this world as individuals, and as individuals we leave it, and each one leaves it by the same common method—the process of death—the withdrawal of attention from the extremities, and then from the body, and finally up through the eye focus. When the attention descends from the eye focus and activates the body, we are born; and when the attention goes back through this focus, the body is senseless and we are dead. The spiritual devotees are born daily and die daily. To them death is a routine affair.

Meats, eggs, and alcoholic drinks have to be given up by the practitioner. These articles of diet dull the soul.

~

149.   I have received your letter dated October 3rd, asking for initiation. Dr Johnson and Dr Brock, both have recommended you. There are others too in California who are interested in this system. I am asking the Brocks if they can go south and arrange to give the initiation. Mrs Brock has not been keeping fit for some time, but she is improving. On her recovery, I hope Dr Brock will be able to undertake the journey and give you the instructions.

Meanwhile, I would request you to continue the study of books and, whenever opportunity offers, to consult Dr Johnson. It is better to have a clearer idea of the system and to grasp thoroughly what it aims at. It aims at the union of the individual soul with its source, by freeing it from the combination of mind and matter, which combination has held it separate and apart from its source—no one can say for how long—ever since creation started. That separation has been the cause of its miseries and wanderings in the various forms of creation. It has been longing for peace but has not found it so far.

The way to peace lies within. Within us lies the royal Word, the sound current, which mystics have called by various names but which means the same thing. Everybody has to go within himself to attain that peace. The worldly objects do not satisfy desire very long. Today we want this thing, but tomorrow that thing has lost its charm and we want something else. Whatever we see with our eyes here is transitory and is subject to change. Thus it is clear that a changing state of affairs cannot bring it permanent peace. In a state of change, struggle is the rule.

Man has the capacity to detach himself from the world and its objects. We are detached from it daily, when we go to sleep. In shorter periods, we get detached frequently. When we give up one thought and take up another, we have passed through the gate of detachment; only the duration was small. This duration can be prolonged at will. Of course this requires practice. When attention can be detached from one side, it should also be possible to attach it to something else. The practice of Surat Shabd Yoga lies in detaching the mind from external objects and attaching it to what lies within, and then catching the sound current and travelling on it. This current connects the individual with its source. This practice does not interfere with any normal routine of life. There are no rituals or customs. One has to deal with himself:

Meats, eggs, and alcoholic drinks are prohibited.

⁓

150. I have received your letter of October 28, wherein you have asked for initiation. Dr Brock is likely to come south to give the instructions, but coming entirely depends on the recovery of Mrs Brock, who I learn, is making good progress. You may please communicate with him and find out when he is likely to come.

There is no hesitation on my part to put you on the path, but spiritual development requires great sacrifice. It is a fight against the mind. The mind connects us with the world, and we function in this world through the mind. So long as we are functioning here, in this material world, we are materialistic. In the state of wakefulness the connection with matter is direct, and in the state of dream the connection is also there, for the dream is simply the carrying over of impressions gathered in the wakeful state. In deep sleep the connection is cut off, and this state is the state of dullness or ignorance.

Compared with the wakeful state, the dream state is bad, and the state of deep sleep is worse. In these three states man passes his life. He is either awake, dreaming, or in deep sleep. Leaving out of consideration the last two states of semi- and complete unconsciousness, and examining the state of mind in the wakeful state, we find that, like a bee, our mind is running from one object to another and is never at rest. It finds momentary pleasures but is soon disappointed. The transitory nature of the worldly objects, no matter how dear and near, gives it no lasting peace. When the objects are gone, the mind feels uneasy. In the so-called wakeful state, therefore, there is no possibility of attaining lasting peace, no matter whether man is barbaric or civilized, brave or cowardly, ruler or the ruled, rich or poor.

There are other worlds inside of man, not made up of this coarse material but of stuff which can be called nonmaterial. These worlds cannot be seen as long as the mind is shaking. We are connected with this outer material world through our organs of sense. Through eyes we see, through ears we hear, and so on. Suppose our mind does not run outward through these organs of senses. Then our body is a mere object like other objects, and we, for the time being, are entirely cut off from this world—in other words, as good as dead. When we let the mind go down through the organs of sense, we again become alive as far as the world is concerned. If we go a step further—that is, direct the mind inwardly, after disconnecting it from the organs of sense—the inner worlds will become visible. When this practice of disconnecting from the external organs of sense and connecting with the inner worlds becomes a habit, then man can function at will either in this material world or in the inner, nonmaterial world.

At present we are dead as far as the inner worlds are concerned, and we are alive here. Thus, we will be alive in the inner worlds when functioning there, and alive here when functioning here. Our sphere of activity has widened. We have discovered a new world, just as Columbus discovered America. So long as the mind has not developed the capacity to throw away, at will, the impressions of this world, it cannot sit inside, disconnected from this world, nor can it have access to the inner world. But it has the capacity to do so and it has to be trained. It is a slow affair, requires patience, perseverance, and faith.

Ever since creation started, the mind has been running in the above-mentioned three states and has not gone within, nor has it found peace and rest. The task, therefore, is difficult, but it can be successfully completed, and this is the object of our life. If man is the highest achievement of creation, his responsibility is great also. Man is born so that he may merge his soul in its source and not be born a second time (in this world). The greatest service one can render is to merge his soul, by freeing it from the attachment of mind and matter, in that ocean of peace and bliss of which it is a particle or drop.

I have written this in a little detail so that you may understand the magnitude of the problem you are undertaking to solve. The ups and downs of life cause hindrances, but where there is a will there is a way. There is no obstruction which love and faith cannot overcome.

Meat, eggs, and alcoholic drinks have to be given up, for they make the spirit coarse and dull.

~

151.   The truth lies within you, within everybody. Without that truth, we could not live for a second. Just as the sun is in the sky but its rays illuminate the earth, similarly truth is within us—in the brain, behind the eye focus—but its rays activate the entire body. If we could hold our attention in the eye focus, our attention would then be able to grasp the truth. So long as the attention is scattered in the body or out of the body in the world outside, our face is turned away from truth. No matter how much progress—individual or national—we might make in the outside world, we are not a jot nearer the truth. The mind will remain dissatisfied. It will still be feeling the want of something. When the scattered attention will be withdrawn from the outside world to within the body, and then from the body to the eye focus, our connection with the outer world and the body will have been cut off for the time being. Then the attention will be able to grasp the truth which is vibrating within us and is self-luminous and audible as sound current.

The truth has been within us always. It is present in the teacher as well as in the student. The only difference between the teacher and the student is that the teacher has, by concentrating his attention, established his connection with truth and studied it, while the student is yet disconnected. The teacher is to point out the way and guide, while the student is to work diligently with longing. A boy goes to school. The knowledge was lying dormant in him. Under the guidance of the teacher, he works, develops, and digs up his knowledge from within himself.

People spend years in schools and universities to study a limited number of subjects, and even then "are picking pebbles on the seashore." You are going to study the self and its relation to the grand truth. You are to isolate the self from the mind and matter, and then trace it to the source of all. It is comparatively a difficult subject. Implicit faith in the guide or teacher, and longing, as of a lover when he is out to meet his beloved, are prerequisites on this path. And where there is a will there is a way. You are welcome to study this subject. Meats, eggs, and alcoholic drinks are prohibited.

~

152. I assure you that I do not mean to neglect any of our American satsangis. I think I answered your last letter; it may have gone astray. But in any case, you should write to me every few months and give full account of your progress and ask any questions you may wish to ask. I shall be glad to hear of your inner progress on the path. No doubt you are making some headway and I am anxious to see you go inside, truly, and find the great light and joy which awaits you there.

There is nothing equal to this *way*, and it gives more real joy and satisfaction than all else in the world. But to get that you have to go inside. It cannot be realised outside. All the world is seeking it in books, holy places, and association with people, but it has to be found inside. That is gained by steadfast meditation and holding your attention in the eye focus, without wavering. When you learn to do this, the treasure, which is yours already, will come into conscious possession, and you will realise more than you can dream of. Let nothing stop or hinder you. Let no earthly obstacles stand in your way of going inside. Set your mind steadfastly upon that and make all else subordinate to that, and other things will melt away and leave you free.

I am well aware that you have struggles. You have some things within yourself to overcome and some things outside of yourself which must be surmounted. But you can do it. If you have full confidence in the inner Master, he will always help you. And often when you find the difficulties greatest and the hour darkest, the light will appear and you will see that you are free. Let nothing discourage you. This is no light proposition, but your getting Nam means more than if you had inherited a million dollars, or many millions. You are one of the lucky sons of Sat Purush, and he has chosen you to get Nam and go with the Master to Sach Khand. You must reach there. Nothing can prevent you. But you can hasten the progress or retard it, as you like.

Do your utmost now to remove all difficulties within and without yourself, and then sit as many hours as you possibly can. Hold your attention fixed at the focus, not allowing the mind to run away or to waver in the least. If the mind runs away, bring it back instantly and hold it at the focus. By and by, if your attention is steadfast, you will see a blue sky and the stars and suns and moon, and then you will see the great *jyoti*, the thousand-petalled lotus, and the Master's Radiant Form. You must see these things. Look steadily for them and permit no doubt or question to enter your mind. It is certain.

When you have entered the first region, you will get the full benefit of the sound current. It will come to you clear and sweet, and its music will fill you with joy, and that of itself will enable you to overcome all your remaining difficulties and weaknesses. That is the one thing that makes you strong against all foes and makes your victory absolutely certain. With the melodious sounds ringing in your ears, your success is absolutely certain.

You must reach the supreme goal in due time. Some reach it sooner, others later, according to their own individual efforts and the karma they have to overcome. But you should not have a long battle. You have already overcome much, and the inner Master is always with you, eagerly waiting for your arrival at the gates within, to receive and welcome you. When you meet him inside and talk to him face to face, as man to man, then he will always be ready to answer all your questions and to guide you all along the path. He is there now, but you cannot see him until you remove the intervening curtains. But you can easily do that. Go ahead and do it. Great will be your reward.

～

153.　Regarding the hearing of the sound current, it is a matter of steadfast, fixed attention and perfect concentration. When you have attained that, you may be sure you will hear the perfect sound current. The real Shabd is heard only after reaching Sahansdal Kanwal. Before that, you get only a feeble reflection of it. Go on until you hear the perfect bell sound, clear and sweet, and most delightful. Only when concentration is perfect will you hear it. Do not be discouraged.

The treasure of initiation cannot be wholly taken from the disciple. He can never lose it for all time. It is there, and he will come back to the path in the next life, or as the Master wishes. The Master who gives the initiation must take care of him or her, and must deliver the disciple at last in Sach Khand.

A saint usually does not compel his disciples to return to this world for another incarnation. But in some cases such as the one you refer to, the disciples may be brought back here for another birth, in order to give them a better position on the path. Then they will readily rise above all of this downward pull. Be sure that the Master never wants to leave his disciples, and he never does leave them, even though they may leave him. A wandering child is still the child of his father, and is always loved and taken care of, even though he brings suffering upon himself by his own conduct.

We are expecting much from America. The average person in America is much nearer to this teaching than in any portion of Europe. The day will come when your people will turn to Sant Mat.... Some day the great work there will assume much larger proportions. You may look confidently for it, in your own time. Be ready for it.

~

154. Answering your question as to the best way to reach and hold the focus, I can only repeat the substance of what you already have been given.

You also ask for the method I worked out for myself during my own early experiences. In regard to that, I may say that I never worked out any method for myself. I took instructions from my own Guru and he gave me the exact method. That method is the same as all saints use, which is simply the concentrated attention held firmly at the given centre. What else can we say? It is all a matter of unwavering attention. Every ray of attention must be centred there and held there. If one strays away for a time, one has lost the advantage. It may be said safely that if any earnest student should hold his attention fully upon the given centre for three hours, without wavering, he must go inside. But that is not so easy without long practice. However, by and by, the mind becomes accustomed to staying in the centre. It rebels less and less, and finally yields to the demand to hold to the centre. Then your victory is won.

Before that, the mind will not remain still for a long time. It jumps around like a monkey. But after a time it will give in and settle down. It is a matter of *will* to hold to the centre, also not to forget nor allow the attention to go off after some other thought or experiences. One easily forgets and then the mind drops down. A keenly awakened intelligence must hold to the centre, steadily, every moment. If any thought enters the consciousness, jerk the mind back to the centre and hold it there. Make the spirit, instead of the mind, the commander of the situation. The mind is tricky and will run out if permitted. Conquer it. But to conquer it is not easy, of course, and it takes time. The problem is not complicated at all. The whole thing is just *attention*, and then unbroken attention, *at the eye centre*, allowing no other thought to intrude itself into the consciousness and lead you away from the centre.

This was the method by which I won my way inside and it is the method by which you must win your way. It is the old method of all saints. The reason you nearly reach it, as you say, and then lose it, is because you cannot hold the mind still. It is somewhat like a wild animal which has been accustomed to run about in the forest. When captured, it is in great distress if held still in the hands of the captor. But like that animal, by and by it will yield and obey if we persist in our efforts.

The repetition of the names is to help in holding the mind at the eye centre. That is the value of the names. Whatever goes with the names is a thing to hold the thought in the centre. If we think intently of a place (during the day but not at the time of bhajan and simran), we form a sort of mental picture of that place, of what is there, of its ruling spirit or power; then, as we continue, we begin to desire to go toward that centre. We must enter it if we persist. All the powers of the spirit, the real *atma* in man, gather at the focus by means of this concentrated thought; and then, by means of accumulated force (through bhajan and simran), we break through the curtain and enter the light.

You should not try to listen to the sound current at the same time as you repeat the names. Do the repetition first for about two-thirds of the time set for your meditation period and then direct your attention to listening for or to the Sound. One thing at a time—that is best.

∾

155. If in dreams or while in devotion you come across a fearful sight which causes terror, begin to repeat the five holy names, and all fear will vanish at once. Nothing evil can stand before the holy names.

About taking meat diet as directed by medical men: my advice is not to take it on any account. It is a great hindrance in our spiritual progress. We are governed by a very severe law of karma. To kill an animal is a heinous offense under natural law, and its punishment is very severe. The saints have strictly forbidden taking any sort of life in any way.

As you see lights and have begun to hear the bell sounds, I write down a few instructions for your future guidance:

1. Sometimes, during practice, Satan appears in the form of the Master, and in order to mislead the soul he offers miraculous powers and many worldly blessings. So when you see the Master within you, repeat the five holy names in order to see whether it is the Master or Satan. If it is Satan, he will disappear instantly on hearing the holy names. You should never ask anything from the Master except his eternal home. He bestows upon us, without our asking, all that we want and is proper for us.

2.   Never pay any attention to any sound on the left. It is always misleading. Always hear the bell sound to the right. The more your attention becomes rapt in the Sound and you take pleasure in it, the more will hidden secrets become known to you.

3.   Take care not to disclose to anyone whatever you may see within yourself. The reason is that, in the first place, telling it to other people produces vanity in us; secondly, it is absurd to disclose such secrets to those who cannot value them.

The most important thing you can do is to draw your attention away from all the worldly things and to concentrate it wholly in the Sound, forgetting the world and your own self till you reach the Master's "holy feet" and attain his eternal home. The Father's home is full of love and light. Try to reach that abode.

～

156.   So far as circumstances allow, a devotee must give time to satsang. Please devote some time daily without fail to Sound practice and repetition, as this is the only fruit of our life which we will take with us on leaving this world; whereas, even the kingships of this earth shall have to be abandoned when death overtakes us. Therefore, it is necessary that we should add to our spiritual wealth, which is the only thing to help us at the time of departing. And the only way to increase our spiritual power is by means of Sound practice and repetition. The greater our love for holy Sound, the greater will be our peace of mind and spiritual progress. As far as possible, we should try to make the focus above the eyes, in the brain, our resting place. Just as a man, weary with the day's work, resorts to his home to take rest, so we habituate our soul, on being tired with worldly work, to take rest in the holy Sound.

The attention has to be brought inside, and when it likes to rest there, like the wanderer coming home, it will find peace within. This bringing in of the attention is done by repetition, with the attention at the eye focus. Repetition without fixing the attention is no good. Repetition with attention impresses on your mind the idea of what lies within you and tries to take you to those for whom the names stand. By this process we are leaving outside objects and perceiving those that lie within.

The moment we are within, the sound current is there to take charge of us. The Astral Form of the Master is at the eye focus and is always ready to do the necessary work or guidance. In this process, the limbs and gradually the entire body below the eyes will become senseless. Breathing will continue normally as in sleep; only the attention, instead of being without, will be within. There will be full consciousness within of internal objects, but unconsciousness so far as the outer world is concerned.

Those who complain of sleep at the time of taking exercises usually sit halfheartedly and only as a matter of routine. Tell these people to keep the mind's attention directed toward the eye focus, even during working hours. Work needs attention only momentarily. Most of the time the mind is off the work anyway. This inner utilization of the attention within will not hinder work; in fact, the work will go on better.

Good gust

~

157. I received your two letters.... They are full of questions and analyses, as you say. I like them. I appreciate the great pains you have taken to study the literature available,

also your spirit of inquiry, aiming to clear up doubts and get at the root of things.

Limitation of books and book knowledge: Books that matter, as distinguished from trash, are an account of the experiences of persons, reduced to writing for the benefit of others. If anyone wishes to learn, say chemistry, he studies books on chemistry; thus he learns something about chemistry. But if he gets instructions directly from a chemist, he obtains a better grasp of the subject. Again, if he sets up a laboratory and begins to experiment, he will gain still better knowledge of the subject. And last of all, if he carries on his experiments under the personal direction of an expert chemist, he will avoid many a pitfall and will, in due time, become a chemist.

Again, one book on chemistry may appeal to one student and may not appeal to another, for the mental make-up of the two may not be the same. One may have his analytical faculty developed, while in the other, the synthetical faculty may predominate. A book, therefore, is not all-comprehensive. The author has written it from the angle characteristic of himself, and it will appeal only to persons having a touch of the same qualities. Also the same book may appeal to a person at one time and may not appeal to him at another time; for man is a variable creature, and his intellect is a variable factor.

Again, there is the difficulty of exact expression and of correct understanding. You cannot convey a correct idea of a railway train or a modern motor car to a person familiar with only bullock carts as a means of conveyance. A radio agent, without receiving apparatus, will carry but little conviction as to the marvels of radio among persons who never before heard of the radio. Even with a radio set at hand, he is likely to be taken as a juggler.

So when ideas about material things cannot be conveyed

correctly in words, either written or spoken, ideas about non-material things, such as mental and spiritual experiences, cannot possibly be expressed with any degree of clearness and exactitude to persons who never have had any such experiences. Yet mental and spiritual experiences on the mental and spiritual planes are as real as are the experiences of anyone on the physical plane.

A boy who leaves school after learning the three R's says, "Knowledge is unlimited." A student who completes the common school course, but who has not yet entered the university, also says, "Knowledge is unlimited." The graduate of the university also says, "Knowledge is unlimited." A university professor who has encompassed the limits of learning afforded by all universities also says, "Knowledge is unlimited." Now the boy, the student, the graduate, and the professor all use the same expression, but evidently they do not mean the same thing at all. The boy's idea of knowledge is very shallow, while the idea of knowledge as held by the professor is deep—a sea compared to a pond.

Books, therefore, convey but little at best, and are often misunderstood. The more critically a beginner examines books, the more discrepancies he finds, and the result is usually confusion of thought. Hence the need for association with a living teacher; also the need for actual experience of converting theory into fact, or individual realisation. So, books, by their very nature, are imperfect and serve but a limited purpose.

Man himself is the perfect book, for all books have come out of him. Inside of him is the Creator with all his creation. The study of books gives secondhand information, while the study of man gives firsthand information—that is, the study of what lies within ourselves. So why not enter within ourselves and see what is there?

From books we are to grasp the central or the basic idea upon which they are based. If you examine books in that spirit (I am not defending all books, and I am sorry to say that the English language is poor in real literature on spiritual subjects) you will find that the central idea of Sant Mat, and of other religions, also, is the practice of the sound current. Many different names are used to express the idea. Christ, Mohammed and Vedic rishis practised and preached the same. It may be said that they had studied, or risen on this current to different heights; but the fundamental idea of all of their teachings is this sound current.

The type of the language, or the setting in which this basic idea is given, depends upon the place and the people the Masters work among—their customs, the manner of their presentation, and their own intellectual development. And as these customs, manners, and so forth change with time, their books go out of date. Hence the necessity of giving the same principle of the sound current afresh. The message must be kept modern, and so adapted to the times and people to whom it is offered.

This current is present in man—all human beings. It is natural in man, not artificial. It can be neither altered nor modified, nor added to nor subtracted from. All else in this world is changeable, and changes continually, but not this current. It is an emanation from, or wave of, the great source of all—the supreme Creator, by whatever name you wish to speak of him. Each individual is a spark or a drop of that same infinite source.

The Creator is at the top of this current and the individual soul is at the other end, the current thus acting as the connecting link between them. By that current, the life—even the very existence—of the individual is sustained. The individual feels no touch with it on account of the thick veils of

mind and matter which cover it at this end. But it is there—
in man and in all forms of creation—in the eye focus, whence
it permeates the whole body below the eyes, and then goes
out from the body, through the various sense organs. To catch
it, the scattered and scattering attention must be controlled
and held in the focus where connection is established with
the astral, the mental, and the spiritual planes; and the same
finally merges into its source at the other end.

*The first essential thing, therefore, is to enter this labora-
tory within ourselves,* by bringing our scattered attention inside of the eye focus. This is a slow process. But we are not
justified in saying that we cannot do it, or that it is impossible, or that it is useless. Here is a worthy pursuit for the
application of our critical and other faculties. If we cannot
control and subdue our thoughts, arising within us, who else
will? It is our job and we must do it; and we must do it now,
in this very lifetime, while we are men, for man is the highest
form of creation.

There are many ways of doing this; but from experience,
saints find that repetition, called simran, done in the manner explained at the time of initiation, is the best and most
effective way, as well as the simplest way. If thoughts of
the material world take us out of the focus, thoughts of
the inner worlds will take us in that direction. When we are
inside of the focus, we have disconnected ourselves from the
material world and are on the threshold of the astral world.
We too have cast off our material frame, and we are of the
same stuff as the astral world, and are now in a position to
function there. The same attention that was working in the
material world is now capable of working in the astral
world. And just as we now call this lower world real, we will
find the astral world as real, or more real, than we now find
this one.

After reaching the astral plane, the same attention, now purified from the material dross, hangs onto the sound current, becomes further purified and rises on it to reach the spiritual planes. With every inch of ascent inwards and upwards, the soul is casting off the coverings of mind and matter and is awakening from the deep sleep of ages. Needless to say that in this process the soul is not helpless, but it goes in and stays in, and comes out at will.

We may look at this matter in another way: The Creator is existence, knowledge and bliss—or power, wisdom, and love. An atom or a spark of this essence of existence is the soul which, encased in its coverings of mind and matter, forms the individual man. If the coverings were removed from the individual, the soul would be naked and would be qualified to know its Creator. The individual will know itself—attain self-realisation—and will in turn, be able to know its Creator. Wrapped in its coverings, the soul merely hears of its source from others or reads about the Creator in books, makes guesses and draws imaginary pictures to satisfy its intellectual curiosity. It also manufactures creeds.

If a lantern were wrapped in a thin muslin cloth, its light would be dimmed. If there is another envelope of thick, coarse cloth over the muslin, the light will be cut off entirely and the lantern will cease to serve the purpose of a lantern. Man is much like a covered lantern. There is light in him. There is the spark of pure existence, knowledge, and bliss in him; but the envelopes of mind and matter dim his light and he gropes in darkness. Real existence has degenerated and appears in him as reason, intellect, and instinct. Bliss has degenerated into fleeting experiences of pleasure and pain.

Clothed in our dark coverings, we are incapable of understanding our source. And the extent to which we succeed in removing our coverings marks the degree of our capacity to understand our source. These remarks about the books, the Creator, the individual, and the sound current, will help us in answering your threefold question:

1. The original home so often referred to, whence we came;
2. Why we left that home;
3. Will we ever leave it again?

The individual, as he is constituted now, is incapable of understanding what happened or is happening at the source. The saints who come from that end, and have access to that end at will, know what is going on at that end; but, by the very nature of things they are handicapped in trying to convey information to the individual at this end. They attempt, in various ways, to satisfy their audiences. Some are convinced and some are not. No matter what answer is given to these questions, we can always find fault with it, and even if reason and intellect are satisfied for the time being, the necessity for converting theory into facts of experience and personal realisation still remains.

But the point is that saints do not wish to satisfy their audiences by empty words. They offer to take the inquirer to the other end and thus give him firsthand knowledge. One beauty of it is that, at that end, these questions do not arise. So if the curious questioner would exercise a little patience and faith, most of his questions would be answered automatically as his experiences increase.

Suppose a man finds himself at the bottom of a deep well, where he is very lonely and uncomfortable. Another man happens to pass that well. He carries a long rope. Finding this man in the well, he lets down his rope and offers to pull the man up, if only he will catch on to the end of the rope. But

our man in the well enters into argument with the man above
and demands to know just how he came to fall into that well,
and what is the guarantee that he may not fall into the well
again, if he is pulled up. The utmost that the man with the
rope can say is that he will take him out of the well and then
he can study the situation for himself. But if the man in the
well does not take advantage of this opportunity, it only
means that his time has not yet come to escape from his
imprisonment.

Predestination versus free will: A will is free only so long as
it has not acted. Once it acts, then that very act becomes binding on it. The second time it acts, it does not act as free will,
but as a "calculating will," for it carries the experience of the
first act with it. And a calculating will is not a free will but a
limited will. The very creations, or acts of a free will, work as
limiting factors upon it and guide it in its future activity. So
the more actions one performs, the more his will is guided
and thus limited. And this is real predestination.

There is thus no antagonism between predestination, fate,
karma, and free will. We were free at one time. We acted, and
then our acts became binding upon us. They curtailed our
initial freedom. They now act upon us as unavoidable fate.
Since our experiences have become complex and varied, these
experiences now appear in us as joys and fears, hopes and
desires, each of which, in its turn, moulds or fashions our
reason and intellect.

Intellect, reason, and feeling, being what they have been
fashioned to be, now determine our actions and make us
choose the predestined course. Thus the acts of one life determine the framework of the next life. Like farmers, we are
now living on the crop we gathered last, while we are preparing the soil and putting in the seed of the new crop. Although
we must undergo our fate, there being no escape from it, yet

all is not lost if we use the little freedom we have in such a manner as to lead to our ultimate rescue.

We wish this age-long wandering from life to life to come to an end. And so it will, if we choose the means of escape. The easiest, the safest and, in fact, the only way out is association with the free. Saints are free by virtue of their practice of the sound current. And they come among us with one single mission—that of connecting us with the sound current and so making us free. And this is the only path of spiritual freedom.

Facts versus theories: That which may be a fact to one man may not necessarily be a fact to another. And it will not become a fact to him until he has had a similar experience. Facts of Sant Mat are reproducible, like facts of any science, and can be demonstrated in the laboratory of Sant Mat. The laboratory of Sant Mat, as said before, is inside of man. Anybody who enters this laboratory (brings his scattered attention within himself at the eye focus) can see, feel, and realise what the saints say, and he can repeat the experiment as often as he likes.

Sant Mat deals with facts only, not with theories or beliefs. It lays down a practical course for its devotees. It is practical through and through, and it can be executed by young or old, male or female, wise or simple-minded—while, at the same time, they are enjoying the fullness of home life.

Life duties: Sant Mat is natural, hence it is rational. It expects its devotees to live a normal life and to do their duties better than others. Sluggards do not make any headway here or elsewhere. Sant Mat creates detachment in attachment, living in the world and yet not of the world. With mind under control, stimulated by a personal knowledge of other and better worlds, the disciple's viewpoint of life and of its duties and responsibilities changes.

The life here actually becomes unreal and its values are assessed accordingly. Things which others lay much stress upon become of little value to the disciple. And often that which others may consider valueless, and even foolish, may become of more value to the disciple than life itself. This is because he looks down upon life from a higher viewpoint. But this does not mean that anyone may neglect a real duty. Compared with life in the worlds above the eye focus, the life below the eye focus (our present condition) is no better than a dream.

If people would go inside the focus and enter the upper worlds, they would become eternally happy. Empty talk would cease. They would contemplate the grand reality. So first you are to control your mind and rise within yourself to the eye focus, and the other man is to do the same within himself. When inside the eye focus, you and he have both cast off the material coverings, and matter is now no longer a hindrance in your study and upward march. Neither is it a hindrance in your communications with each other, while you are both above the eye focus.

To do this, it is not necessary to leave home or country. Anybody who goes inside of his focus is independent of time and space, and he can, from his own experience, give guidance to another who has not reached so far. He who rises still higher and has access to other and higher worlds is capable of guiding others to those higher worlds.

As in all other branches of study, a student who occasionally meets his teacher and converses freely with him, has a distinct advantage over one who takes only a correspondence course. The same is the case here in Sant Mat and the development on this path. But the beauty of it is that, when you gain access to the inner light and the worlds of light within, the elements of time and distance so completely disappear that you stand face to face with your teacher and Master, and he will always remain right there to instruct and to lead you as well as to strengthen you.

You need not accept anything which does not appeal to you in books, or even in my letters. You may leave aside, for the time being, the ultimate object of life and its how and why. You may start your inquiry from this end, and then take as your objective the attack upon the eye focus. Reach that point as best you can, by this or any other method. Draw up your own plans, if you wish. Only make and execute some plan to reach that objective. Bring your plan into action. That is the main thing. And then if you find it does not work so well, come back to this plan. The main point is to reach the eye focus somehow. You will be dealing with your own attention. If you succeed in holding it inside of the focus, you have won the battle of life.

You say in eight weeks since your initiation you have made no progress. Sant Mat does not fix any time limit. Let us appreciate the situation. Ever since our birth, at which time we left the eye focus and came out of it and established our connections with this world, we have not gone inside of it. Sometimes, when we have a deep, intricate problem to solve, we close our eyes and try to think by holding all our attention in the eye centre. We do it for a short time, but soon run out again because we have acquired the bad habit of always remaining away from the focus.

Poets, painters, and musicians receive inspiration from this point. All great thinkers get their ideas clarified here. Whatever scientific progress the world has made, it has all been derived from this source. This focus, back of the eyes, is the fountain of all inspiration which has produced the world's masterpieces. And whatever further progress is to be made in the future, the source of information and inspiration will still be this point. Here is where Divinity comes down to meet the struggling man.

And what holds us outside this focus? Why does not everybody in the world rush, with his utmost ability, to enter this magic fountain of inspiration and wisdom? Because our attention has always been, and is yet, attached to our bodies, to our near relations, to our homes, to our countries, and to our pleasures—sometimes to our pains and sorrows. We have so much identified ourselves with these things that we have lost our identity. Unless now we start detaching ourselves from these outside connections, begin to develop the capacity to switch our attention on and off at will, we can make but little progress on the path.

We are to re-establish our identity, to assert our supremacy over our minds and bodies. The mind must be made to work when we wish it to, and to remain motionless when we wish it to do so. We must become able to enter this body when we wish, to function in this world when necessary, and then to go out of it at will, when we wish to function in another world. It is the attention which is to go inside and see, and so long as it is running outside, who is to see inside? If the owner of a house sits always outside of his house and complains that he cannot see what is going on inside, his complaint is not justified.

This detaching the attention from the external connections is a slow affair. Habits become second nature. It takes time to form new habits. But slow and steady wins the race, and practice makes perfect. Follow your mind for a minute and see what keeps it away from its headquarters. Avoid whatever interferes, and accept what helps in reaching your objective. I have already given you the saints' method, based on long, long experience.

If anyone is sure that he is on the right path, then if he takes but one step a day, he is still approaching his destination and is sure to get there some day, no matter how distant his destination may be. You will perhaps say, "How am I to know that I am on the right path?" I give you the means of proving it for yourself. Until you have proved it for yourself, you must, of necessity, accept something on faith. You would have to do the same if you were building a bridge.

We have taken as the objective the eye focus. In a way, we experience this daily. We come to this focus every time we pass from the wakeful to the sleep state, and return. When we are going to sleep, our attention is drawn toward the eyes, and then the whole body goes senseless. We do not (our attention does not) stay at the eyes, but rapidly the attention passes down to the heart or the navel centre and becomes dull there, and we become completely unconscious.

When engaged in talk and you become overpowered by sleep, you may have said to your friends, "My eyes are getting heavy. I have sleep in my eyes." You may watch your attention going first to the eyes, when you pass from the conscious to the sleep condition. You may study the behaviour of a child when he is about to go to sleep, or return from the sleep state. A student reading his book, when overpowered by sleep, struggles to keep his attention in the eyes.

Now, if you wish to go inside and prove this truth, fix your attention inside of the focus; hold it there by force of a determined will. Let the body become senseless, but hold your consciousness at the focus, becoming unconscious of the lower world but fully conscious of all that is going on at the focus. Then enter the astral world and pass on to still higher regions, enjoying a condition of superconsciousness and great delight.

Lucky, indeed, is he who spends his short life in the Master's company. "If a man is a true seeker, he should give himself up to the Satguru and drop all else." It has been said already, how the attention of man is attached to all sorts of worldly relationships and things. There is hardly any attention left for the study of self and for seeking God. Look about you. Who has time for all the needs of his own soul? He should take time, but he thinks he cannot. His attention is so monopolized by trifles that he has no time for most vital concerns.

A true seeker who gives undivided attention to the things of the spirit is a rare bird. But men follow after that which they love best. A lover cannot be kept separated from his beloved, for he has given himself over to his beloved. His beloved is his life. The quoted passages only point to the ideal. A saint is lucky if he gets one or two genuine seekers during his whole lifetime.

Facts about eating: Everyone may eat as often and as much as is necessary in carrying out the work in which he is engaged. As far as possible, the body is to be kept fit and in perfect health. A lumberman's food is different from that of a soldier, and a soldier's food is different from that of a singer or a philosopher. The same rule applies here. Sant Mat is not a profession and its devotees need not be set apart in a separate class. They come from and belong to all classes. Sant Mat exercises are to be practised while one is carrying on his duties, in whatever sphere he may be placed. My own Master was a soldier.

I have answered most of your questions by giving you the underlying principles. If, however, you have any further doubts, you are free to ask such questions as may occur to you. There is no need to quote passages from books. Put your questions straightaway. That will save you time and trouble.

∾

158. One point is not to be overlooked at this time. In America every man and woman who is initiated is selected by the Satguru under the direction of Sat Purush for a definite twofold purpose:

First, that the disciple himself may be freed from the bondage of the wheel, and taken to his own home in Sach Khand.

Second, that he may perform a definite service in laying the foundation and carrying forward the work intended by the Father for Sant Mat in America. There is a very great possibility there, and we hope and expect much from all of you.

If anyone selected falls by the wayside and fails to carry out the work intended for him, that is his great loss. He will one day see how much he has lost by his failure. But those of you who remain faithful and go on working to the best of your ability must one day realise how great is the work you have done and how great is the reward which awaits you. It is my wish and hope that each one who is fortunate enough to get Nam in your country may be very useful in the hands of the Supreme in doing this very great work.

Keep always love and harmony among yourselves, and allow nothing to sidetrack you. Hold fast to the sound current and let no fancy scheme of the negative power draw anyone aside. Above all, be faithful to your bhajan and sit with mind fixed upon the centre. It is thus you will all get strength enough to withstand every assault of the opposing powers. You will carry on until victory is attained, and thousands in your country see the great light.

$\sim$

159. "If there are Masters in India and they know the highest truths, why do they not do more to elevate the poor and ignorant masses of their own country?" Saints are the

treasurers of the wealth of Nam. Their mission is to take souls
from this place and see them in Sach Khand. To remove economic poverty and so-called intellectual ignorance is the
business of the worldly kings and rulers, or monarchies or
democracies. The spiritual uplift is not dependent upon economic nor upon intellectual development. Neither is spiritual development a national affair. It is the affair of the individual. He enters the world alone and goes out alone. The
current is present in everyone, irrespective of his financial
position or intellectual development, and everyone is free to
rise up within himself.

The department of the saints is entirely different. The
question of rich and poor does not arise, nor is there a question of whether one is ignorant or intellectually developed.
The commodity of the saints is Nam or current. It sells rather
dear. The price they demand is body, mind, and property.
Few are prepared to buy goods of the saints at this price. Perhaps this requires a little explanation. An individual is a combination of soul, mind, body, and property. So long as mind,
body, and property have not been sacrificed, the soul is not
free. So long as the soul is not free, it does not enter the pure
spiritual zone.

When an individual discards attachment to property, it is
not difficult for his attention to leave the objects of senses
and come back to the centre of senses in the body. When the
individual discards attachment of the body, his attention is at
the eye focus. When he has dissolved the individual mind in
Trikuti—the universal mind—he has discarded the attachment
of mind. He is soul now, free from mind and matter in all
their phases. The soul is now fit to enter the pure spiritual zone.

Saints do not want the property, the body, or the mind of
the disciple, but ask him to give up attachment to them, to
use his property like an agent and not as a primary; so that if

there is a loss, it is the primary that suffers, and not the agent; to use his mind with care, and not let it wander about. Saints do not take a pie from the disciple.[1] The above is a means to free the disciple from his attachments. I hope you will get at my meaning.

Saints know all about the past, present, and future. When you will go within, you will begin to know. The knowledge is within. The current is knowledge, for everything is derived from it. The more you rise on it, the better informed you will be. That will be your firsthand knowledge.

But this knowledge is not to be utilized in the shaping of worldly affairs, whether personal or of others. This knowledge is to be utilized for advancement within. If one begins to use the acquired power, the mind naturally turns outward and gets scattered. And not only does further progress stop, but there is an actual setback. This is natural.

Saints use no will of their own. They live in Him. They are His servants, not equals or co-sharers. They do not assert themselves against His will. It is bhakti yoga. As His dear children, He gives them everything. You will value the saints when you will go within and see for yourself what the Master does for the disciple, and how, through the maze of mind and matter, he lifts the soul.

You have my full permission to give copies of these letters to whomsoever you think is likely to benefit thereby.

There is considerable literature in Gurmukhi, but much more in Hindi. It will be very good indeed if you could learn Hindi or Gurmukhi—Hindi, preferably. Both are very much allied. The Gurmukhi script is easier, for there are fewer letters. You may please pick up whatever facilities are available. It is difficult to acquire proficiency in a foreign language, but

---

1. *Pie*—paisa: the smallest coin.

it will be of great help to you later on when you may choose
to render our literature into English.

~

160. I am much pleased at your inner progress. It shows
that you are doing some real bhajan, and that your process of
"mind purification" is going on nicely. Keep up the good
work you are doing. There is great light ahead. You shall have
all the help possible.

Please keep one point in mind constantly, and urge all
satsangis to do the same. (I think you should send out this
letter to all satsangis, so that these points may be impressed
again and again upon the minds of all.)

With love and humility, forget each other's apparent mistakes or faults, and make due allowance for differences of
opinion. Let no one ever try to establish his own opinion or
set his own way against the will of the majority. Love and
harmony are vastly more important than the opinion of anyone. As Jesus said, so long ago, so I now repeat to you: "By
this shall all men know that ye are my disciples, that ye love
one another!"

He who forgets this law and injects into the satsang the
least element of discord is no longer my disciple in spirit and
in love. He is simply a disobedient child. All of you have my
unstinted love and blessing, and I hope that the law of love
shall be your supreme law and your guiding principle. Remember that one man's opinion is of no importance whatsoever, when set over against the principle of love and harmony.
No matter whether any one of you likes anything that is done or
not, keep sweet harmony and love, and let the majority govern.

... You never will make a mistake, so long as you keep in
mind to act simply as the Master's agent. Then let him take
care of all results which may follow.

Satsang has more than one meaning. First, it means the meeting of the Master and a disciple; second, it means the meeting of all satsangis who may attend, whether the Guru is present in body or not. There is no formality about it, none at all. It is a simple meeting of all disciples who can attend. We avoid formality and anything that may have the appearance of a rigid organization. The less organization, the better. And there must be no idea of leadership. The only leader in Sant Mat is the Guru. Just the Master and his disciples meeting together is the only organization we have.

~

161. Do not set your affection on things of this world, for it is to be dissolved. This world is not durable. What is the value of loving that which must perish? Neither should you give your affections to people of this world. What is the use in loving those who are not going along with us? Indeed, give to all such treatment as times and circumstances require, but give not your affections to them, nor form with them permanent attachment. We should live in relation to this world just as a nurse is related to her charges. If the child she is caring for dies, she has only the concern of looking for another position. It is the mother alone who must weep for her child. But the nurse has no real sorrow.

Do not give to the world and the people of the world a value equal to that of your own ideal. Wherever your desire is, there must your residence be. Because our love is all for this world, that is the very reason why we must come back into this world again and again. But if we give our love to the Lord, we attain salvation. The Lord and the world are in the scales, and that side to which you give your love will go down (outweigh the other). The world is to be dissolved and her people also. When the Gurmukh detaches his love from this world and its people, and has taken the path from the Master, he should give his love to the Lord. If we give to him our true love, then no one can ever bring us back into this world.

The friend of this world is the *manmukh* (devotee of the mind). For this reason he is sometimes happy and sometimes filled with grief. Burning with the worldly passions he comes, and burning with them he goes. Having entangled himself in sensual pleasures by following the dictates of his own mind, at the time of death, the messenger of death takes him away. And after examination by the Dharam Rai (king-judge) he is placed in hell. This is the fruit of the friendship of this world. But the *gurmukh*, having taken the path from the Satguru, attains the *Shabd Rup* (Word Form), and for him there is no more coming and going.

In this path, there is no difference between the educated and the uneducated. All preference is given to love only. Without this, one is like a parrot (repeating words which mean nothing to him). Life is made better only through love of the Lord and of Nam, and work for them. Only in the spirit does God manifest himself and does the drop become merged in the ocean. Whoever has not gone inside and attached himself to Nam is a manmukh (devotee of the mind, of the world). Without Nam, no one can attain peace of mind, though he may read millions of books. Contentment comes only from Nam. By that alone is the curtain of darkness lifted.

Nam is universal in the whole world. Nam is of two kinds: varnatmak and dhunatmak. Varnatmak is that which may be spoken or written. Dhunatmak cannot be spoken or written. (The latter is the reality of which the former is the symbol.) When the spirit is attached to Nam, it draws one toward itself, and the door is opened. Until this happens, no one need think he can get it.

∼

162. Those who form friendship with bad people and regard saints with enmity, sink themselves, and their entire families drown with them. Speaking evil of others is the greatest sin, and they who do it are fools. This sin is without relish. The man who indulges in it is on his way to hell and he gets nothing in return.

Oh mind, whatever actions you perform, you will get that sort of fruit! If you sow wheat, you will get wheat. If barley, you will get barley. If you plant a thorn tree, you will not gather grapes. From wool, you will not get silk. The fruit of vice is hell, and a low sort of life only. Even your dreams arise from similar actions of the mind.

Talking of Maha Purush (the Supreme Lord) brings ecstasy to the soul. The Guru's sayings and works are of the quality of heavenly nectar. There are fountains of that nectar, and in them there is no selfishness. Fortunate, indeed, is he who gets it by working hard, and devotes himself to it. O men, if there is one of you who says, "I will not work," then bread he cannot eat. Finally, his pralabdh karma maps out his life, and so he is reborn. But whoever works shall of necessity get bread. In him is the true Lord of the whole creation. Seek him, and make him manifest in your life.

When a man reaches Sat Purush, then only is he a saint and Master. All that goes before this is only part of the process of getting trained, schooled, and prepared for mastership. And on the way up, the Master always retains his own form, after he becomes a Master. His Radiant Form becomes more radiant at each stage of his upward progress. But it is always his own form, not that of any deity in the several regions.

∾

163. I was so glad to receive your letter and Christmas card, both reflections of your heart. Goodness is its own reward.

The message of the Man of Nazareth is the Word, the Creator of all, and by which everything is sustained. It is the life of all. It is within us all in the form of the sound current. The individual soul is its part, and the part knows no rest until it is one with the whole.... The essence of the Bible is the Word, and it is for you to catch it and hold onto it. The Master is within, at the eye focus.

Below this stage Kal sometimes appears in the form of the Master, but is distinguishable from him by his narrow forehead, and eyes having yellow and red lines. The Master has a broad forehead, and his eyes are bright and shining. The form of Kal disappears when the holy names are repeated.

Karma is physical as well as mental. Gross karma is washed out by means of external methods, such as satsang, reading of the holy books, and so forth, as well as by the presence of the Master. Subtle karma is removed by internal Sound practice. Try to still the vibrations of the mind, and when it stands collected in the eye centre, as instructed, you will pass on to the regions of light.

There is no racial karma. Karma is individual. The satisfactory answer to your question is: Go inside and see; and if you labour, you will succeed. The path is long but can be travelled. If you do not travel in your time, that is, in this life, the Master will take charge of you at death and will bring you inward and upward; but then you shall have to remain at the stages within and do the exercises there.

As regards your dreams: In the state of sleep, the soul travels upward where it meets with delightful experiences, but when it drops downward, on account of the weight of karma, it experiences dreadful scenes. It is all the result of good or bad karma. As you progress spiritually, these dreams will become less frequent.

∼

164.   We are to leave this world one day, and if we are loving, obedient disciples, and have made proper preparations in this lifetime, we do not have the transition which we call death. While others weep, the spiritually developed soul departs happy—happier than a bridegroom on his wedding day.

The time of death is a critical one in our experience, when our friends and relatives are helpless to render any assistance; but for the followers of Sant Mat, it is the happiest time of all. The Master appears and takes the departing soul with him, and puts it in its upward journey at the place for which it is fit. There is no rendering of accounts with Kal, provided there have been love for and obedience to the Master. The departing soul is happier than it has ever been before. There is absolutely no fear of death. The Master's presence within breaks all worldly connections, and the mind is free to continue the upward journey.

Referring to seeing departed ones at the time of death: Some souls, when disembodied, remain for a time in the psychic realm, according to their earthly karma; and at the time of death (of a disciple), as the spirit is drawn upward, a glimpse of this plane is given. There is no spiritual progress on this plane, of which mediums sometimes catch glimpses. And anyone who has had connection with this plane can see it at the time of death or get a hurried, fleeting view of friends and relatives who are still on this plane; but not of those who have gone on, nor of those who have reincarnated. As long as there is the "I", "He" does not reveal Himself, but when self is gone, He alone remains.

It is incorrect that A saw B after the latter's death. It was simply the reflection of A's own mind. When the initiated soul passes out of the body, it immediately ascends upward with the Master, even if it has to take a second birth. In that case it is stopped at the first stage—not lower than that. It seldom happens that the soul of a follower of Sant Mat is sent back from that place for which it is fit. After it has undergone purification, it is gradually taken up higher.

Memory of previous births is generally withheld until the first or second stage is crossed. This is for the reason that old attachments may not revive and hinder progress. But when the second stage is crossed, then the soul is powerful, mind is subdued, and there is no danger from old memories. Then there is knowledge of all previous births—not only of himself alone, but of all others.

～

165.   Now that you have diverted your mind from the world, and given up all aspiration and hopes—except the hope to reach the region of pure spirituality—make a firm determination to gain the Radha Soami region. It is impossible for anyone to hinder you, or to call you to render an account of yourself. Such is the law.

The devotee should keep his love for the Master active, day and night, asleep or awake. When a soul has made its seat in the eye focus, it is always awake and moves ever upward instead of downward, even while the body below the eyes sleeps. To put it briefly, that centre or portion of the body is active where, for the moment, the soul is concentrated. When the upper centres are reached, the lower ones are asleep. The whole world is asleep as far as the centres above the eyes are concerned.

There are three minds: *pindi, brahmandi,* and *nij.* Pindi mind works in the body below the eye focus. It has low desires, is outward and downward in its tendencies, and has connection with the senses. The intimacy of the soul with it lowers and debases her. The brahmandi mind has good desires. It helps in the uplift, has an inward and upward tendency, and works in Brahmand. The nij mind is as a drop of the second stage, Trikuti, and in it lies the seed of all creation below Trikuti. All three of these minds have to be conquered.

Initiation is sowing the seed, which needs the water of satsang and concentration for sprouting. Love and faith are necessary for its growth. If an initiated soul fails to get this water and is attracted towards the world, the seed will not become a plant; but it is never destroyed. The weight of karma becomes heavier and obstructs its growth. But when this weight of karma becomes light, some day the seed will begin to sprout. Karma is removed by Sound practice. Therefore, every initiated soul should not fail in spiritual practice, and should give up worldly pursuits and desires, in order to hasten purification.

~

166. The saints love all creatures. They do not look upon anyone as an enemy.

It is our duty to obey the instructions of the Master, and spiritual exercises are his instructions. It is also the direction of the Supreme Father that we should be moral, honest, and laborious in the spiritual practices. And, if we do not obey his instructions, we cannot escape the consequences. We must turn from the world and obey with love and faith. His power is unlimited and He will save us.

~

167. Regarding the propaganda for increasing the number of members, there is no need for it. Saints have never lectured in the sense in which people lecture at the present time. They hold their satsangs, and everybody is welcome to attend. If you come across a real inquirer and seeker of truth you may try to explain the principles of Sant Mat as best you

can, but the five names and the method of practice are to be kept secret.

The Name, which is the Word or the sound current, belongs to the Master. It is his property and it cannot be grasped without his will. The five stages and their presiding deities, in fact, whatever was imparted to you at the time of initiation, is secret. The sound current is in the Master's hands, and he himself will arrange for those whom he thinks fit for his fold.

You may say, when discussing the principles of Sant Mat, that as long as the attention is not fixed on the sound current, a man is but a working animal and he cannot find rest. Rest is beyond the mind, in the sound current, but how to look for it is secret.

Our aim is not the propagation of a religious system, nor the accumulation of funds for private or charitable purposes. Our aim is to help earnest seekers of truth which is present within every one of us.

The saints really have only one message to give, and that message they give in the manner which suits the times. Their message is: "Soul, thou hast forgotten thy source. That source is in Sach Khand, and the sound current within you is the way to it, and we guide you to that."

Modern Vedanta speaks of three centres only—the eyes, the throat, and the heart—and all three are in Pind, below the eye centre. Old Vedanta rose higher than the eyes, but only up to Sahansdal Kanwal, and seldom reached Trikuti—the stage of Om. The Vedantists do not catch the sound current, but follow the inner light. As long as the bell sound is not caught, the sound current cannot be grasped. Sounds below this are mixed sounds of tattwas (elements). The bell sound is attractive and pulls upward, which is not the case with the lower sounds; and we have to bypass them.

168.   Man is the top of creation, and the Master is the top of humanity, for he has broken through the shackles of mind and matter, and is one with the universal Lord. By bringing our attention in him, we begin to love him, and he responds—not as ordinary human beings do, but like the looking-glass, reflecting our own image. The attention is thus withdrawn from worldly affairs and from our relatives; we are cured of the ills of attachment, and the mind comes within and rests in the focus of the eyes.

Incarnation of saints in India: India, at the present time, is the only country where people are largely vegetarian and shun animal food and, in many ways (following different methods), try to conquer the mind practically. Such people are the raw material for saints to work upon. This is not the case in other countries where the energies are directed outward, as opposed to the inward tendency of the Indians. But it cannot be said that India has always been like this and will continue in this way. In the world of Pind and matter, change is the order of the day and will continue to be so.

It is not advisable to speak of one's internal experiences to anyone except the Master, and it is positively harmful to speak of them to those who are less developed spiritually than oneself. In revealing secrets there is the risk of the element of pride coming in, which hinders progress. Strength lies in keeping the secret locked, not in giving it out. Others may benefit, but he who is giving out is the loser.

Breathing and meditation: Concentration, is to be done without giving any thought to breathing. If you are thinking of breathing who then is doing the concentration? Do not think of breathing at all. Breathing is going on of its own accord. It is automatic. You do so many other kinds of work during the day, but you never think of breathing; then why should you think about it when meditating?

The mind, which is running loose, is to be brought within. Yogis control breathing in order to conquer the six ganglia situated in the body below the eyes. They simply hold the attention within the eyes and withdraw the current from below. Concentration is quite independent of breathing. Let breathing take care of itself, as it is doing all the other times, and direct your attention to the light or darkness in the focus of the eyes. No force of any kind should be applied to keep the spine straight. The trunk of the body should be held straight (in a natural position), so that the breath comes and goes freely.

Names are to be repeated mentally and not audibly. The mind is to do the thing, not the tongue.... The main thing is to keep to the focus. Repetition is simply to bring the mind in.

Mediums: You are quite right in keeping aloof from so-called spiritual mediums, and the thoughts you have expressed about them are also correct. These phenomena are all mental, not spiritual, though they are called spiritual by the ignorant. They employ mind force, not soul force. That which responds to their call is universal mind *(brahmandi manas)*. Their action is limited to the lowest planes, where souls still have all their coverings, except the gross physical ones.

What power have they to call a soul from the supreme joy of even the spiritual-material regions, to attend to their worldly questions? And how can they contact a dead relative who, in most cases, has already incarnated in some sort of physical form? These are childish tricks. The messages delivered to X are merely nonsensical. Your opinion is quite right. A disciple of a perfect Master has no need to go after these "spiritualistic" mediums, when he expects to see these things for himself in due course of time (from pure spiritual vision) and go to planes too high even to be dreamed of by mediums.

Kundalini is a force in the ganglia in the body below the eyes. Saints do not deal with such powers. There is no force stronger than the soul force. The saints go by Sound; the others by light or sound of the second degree—that is, of the left ear.

The second stage lies within the scope of Kal and Maya. And the coverings of all three bodies—physical, astral, and mental—cannot be removed until the third stage is reached. Therefore, the souls are not so pure and powerful against temptation while in the lower stages of development, and must come back to earth again and again. In the path of Sant Mat, the soul is cured of all the impurities of Kal and Maya (Brahm), and gains greater strength at every step or stage of the journey, until it reaches the eighth stage and is one with the Supreme Father. Thus the soul need never come back. All other religions end at the second stage.

As your concentration at the third eye becomes stronger, many mysteries will be solved for you, and you will get more pleasure from meditation. You will also have fore-flashes of light and knowledge. Solitude brings peace and help in spiritual progress. Many complain of the mind wandering during exercises. The mind feels pleasure in roaming at large, and does not like to give up its liberty until it has attained higher joy in exchange for its present pleasures. But constant practice will compel it to give up its former habits.

Kal does not brook interference with his work, and your maxim of relieving suffering when it comes your way is the appropriate one. A practitioner related to me that he happened to see a large crowd of ants biting to death a big worm. He took pity on the creature and, freeing it from those tyrants, placed the worm beyond their reach. Afterwards, while taking his exercises, these ants (in subtle form) began to bite his feet, saying they were taking their revenge, and it was no business of his to interfere with them.

The student you mention seems to be somewhat over-anxious in expecting appreciable results from exercises during a short period. The first step is to accustom the mind to give up its wanderings—at least during devotions—so that it may become habituated to collect in the eye centre. Until this is accomplished, one cannot expect to have any flash of the subtle regions which begin from the eyes upward. The person who is sitting in the lower story of a house cannot expect to have a glimpse of the higher stories until he spends time and labour to ascend. However, one need not worry. Everything will come in time. The way seems long and full of difficulties, and were it not for the Father's merciful guidance and protection—which is all-powerful to nullify the snares of Kal and Maya—no one could hope to make any headway.

The soul of every true follower is progressing internally even when he is not aware of the progress. Yes, the soul can enter Brahmand when he is unconscious of it.

~

169.   As to transmigration, if you cannot grasp it, give it up for the time being and discard it as groundless. When you go inward and can see the law working within, with your own eyes, then you will understand it and grasp it. But just to say a word about it:

Where lies the difference in the major part of humanity and the animals, except in outward forms? Both eat, sleep, fear, and reproduce alike. The difference in intellect and reason is only in quantity and not in quality. Man's life work is to find his "where" and "whence." And if he has not done that, he will be reborn in the form best suited to his desires.

"As you sow, so shall you reap." If man does the actions of animals, why should he not go back to the animal form? After undergoing punishment in the lower forms of life for his actions, he was born as a man. And if he does the actions of animals, he will go back again to that level and suffer. Study humanity and its tendencies more closely and you will not hold to your view so tenaciously. Try to concentrate and rise inwardly, so that you may see for yourself.

I am glad to learn that you three are happy in the company of one another, and look at vital things from the same viewpoint. It is well that you have decided to shift to the country and nature, and earn your living from the farm produce instead of passing a busy, nerve-racking life in the city. These are preliminary steps for leading a life of meditation. Meditation is possible only when mind is at ease.

You have undertaken a great responsibility in leading an unmarried life and devoting it to your spiritual development. It is therefore imperative that you always be alert and keep constant watch over your mind. Consider that meditation is your first and foremost work, and keep the mind directed toward the focus of the eyes.

I do not wish that your business should suffer or your earning ability be reduced in any way. Work with the body, but use the mind in concentration. A workman on a machine may be attending to his work and singing at the same time. Meditation is the work of mind and soul; the body has nothing to do with it. Mind and soul are free for the entire twenty-four hours (day and night) and only when one is thinking deeply on a problem does the mind focus inwardly. Otherwise it is running its race unchecked. Concentration is not a hindrance in carrying on worldly affairs. Satsang is to meditation what a fence is to a crop.

Meditation on the Form of the Master: I told you to concentrate on the candlelight or darkness in the focus of the eyes, and purposely avoided the mention of concentration on the form of the Master, because you cannot concentrate on a thing you have not seen and of which you have no mental picture. Those who have seen the Master can certainly concentrate on that form. Those who have no opportunity of seeing the physical form of the Master should concentrate on the candlelight or the darkness in the focus of the eyes.

Photographic reproductions—though allowed by some to concentrate on—are objectionable, because photographs do not represent the original. They act as an extraneous object between you and the Master.

~

170.   I never gave permission to anyone to eat meat in my life. A mother does not administer poison to her own children. In Sant Mat animal food cannot be allowed under any conditions. It hardens the heart and makes the soul dull and heavy.

Those who have been accustomed to mediumistic work must give it up, and if they take pains with the exercises, they will surely give up those practices. The trouble is that they do not attend properly to their devotional exercises or they would willingly give up both, mediumistic practices and animal food.

The ideals of Sant Mat are very high, and are free from every sort of selfishness and hypocrisy. If these things exist in any mind, then it may be concluded that Sant Mat has not touched it as yet. Those who enjoy the real spiritual pleasures would never care for those other things. He who follows the dictates of his own mind and does not go to the Master for spiritual help causes much loss to himself.

… At the same time explain that trance and mediumistic practices must be avoided.

~

171. It is not difficult for the Master to take a soul upward, but premature uplifting causes harm. Just as fine silk cloth, when spread upon a thorny hedge, is torn to pieces if suddenly pulled away, so the soul, entangled in the thorns of karma, which penetrate every cell in the body, must be gradually purified by the Master's love. By his grace the soul is freed from these thorns and the karma is slowly sifted out from every cell in the body.

You will get everything you wish—things more wonderful and remarkable than you ever dreamed of. He who has to give you all, is sitting inside, in the third eye. He is simply waiting for the cleanliness of your mind and is watching your every action.

The repetition of the names should be performed with love and faith. Fix your attention in the eye centre (without putting any pressure on the eyes), and keep in one position, if possible, so that you become unconscious of the body below the eyes, and the attention does not wander from the eye focus.

Try to enjoy the exercise. By doing this, you will first behold the star, after it the white light, the sun, and the moon; then at the third eye, the Form of the Master will become visible to you. As your love increases, this Form will begin to talk to you and answer your inquiries. Afterwards, the real Sound that has the attracting power will come. The sound which you now hear is mixed with the sounds of the five elements (tattwas) and does not have much power of attraction.

There is no doubt we are weak and have neither faith nor love, but there is also one hope to sustain us—that he may take pity on us and forgive our sins. We have taken refuge at his holy feet and, deservedly or undeservedly, we are His children. Therefore, it behooves you to perform your devotions every day, without fail. Do not engage in discussions with others, but go on pursuing the path while attending to the daily business of life, with peace and precaution. The Master is ever ready to help his children.

~

172.   I am very glad that you and your wife are working together on this path, helping each other, and passing on to the supreme region with mutual love. It is my wish that you both may travel toward your goal with still greater zeal and perseverance.

Do not let illness dishearten you. Troubles are tokens of the holy Master's grace and the result of your own past actions. Continue devotion as far as possible, under the circumstances. This is the duty of the disciple who no longer cares for the changing scenes of mind and matter. Pain and pleasure, honour and dishonour, poverty and wealth—none of these can influence the attitude of his mind. He does not pray that troubles shall be removed, but rather that his heart be always filled with love and gratitude. As Guru Nanak said, "If you send me hunger, I shall be filled with Thy Name. If you send me miseries, I shall enjoy them as pleasures. If you grant me happiness, I shall bow to Thee in gratitude."

Although the above applies to the state of mind of a perfect disciple, you should try your best to attain it, and I am glad that you are labouring to reach this goal.

Instead of controlling the senses, the soul is now subject to them, and thus constantly wanders from one object to another without anything to rest upon. In the guise of doing good to others, it deceives itself, and in its ignorance it does not realise that valuable time is thus being lost. A votary, marching on the spiritual path, will eventually learn that this world—with all its attachments—is nothing but a deception practised by Kal. Innumerable worlds are worthless, compared to one atom of spirituality.

First "know thyself" and then preach. It is not proper to teach a thing of which one has no proof or knowledge.

When you come across an erring brother, with love and tact, explain his shortcomings to him. If he persists in erring, he will undergo the consequences. Such persons are not pardoned until they repent for their past actions. Attribute their conduct to the fact that they have not yet tasted the sweetness of Shabd.

It is not advisable to prevail upon members who have lost interest in Sant Mat. If you see anyone going astray, speak to him very lovingly and remind him of the high mission of human life; and if your words fall on deaf ears, do not feel annoyed or perturbed. It is no fault of his. When the cycle of bad actions has passed away, such souls will revert to goodness of their own accord.

≈

173. You say you are not much encouraged with your meditations. You should devote more time to the practices, until thoughts cease and soul and mind collect in the eye centre and then go inward. All knowledge is within. As long as the mind wavers, it is not seen, just as one cannot see his reflection in muddy and disturbed water. Our minds are dirty with low and outward desires, and are constantly wavering. They are ignorant of what lies within. Concentration is the first step of the soul's inward journey.

Repetition of the holy names during one's daily routine work is very useful. One is thinking about a thing within oneself; therefore, when one sits for devotional practices, the mind is naturally turned in this direction.

You are right when you say that the Western mind is trained from the beginning for the material things, and it is very difficult to withdraw it from worldly objects. The power

lies in controlling the mind, because mind is the curtain between us and the Supreme Being.

When you have controlled the mind and it raises no
thought, but is lost in the sound current, you will then see
spiritually within. As you have such an earnest desire for going within and seeing the Master, rest assured that you will
one day succeed. Increase time for devotional exercises.

Knowledge is within you. Sound current is the knowledge. Sound current is independent of its surroundings. It
stands by itself. It is the essence, and all else sprang from it.
Humanity is entangled with matter and does not even study
the mind, not to mention the sound current or the spirit behind the mind. On account of its association with changeable things, it is subject to change, dies, and is reborn. This
will continue as long as it does not catch the unchangeable. It
must rise on the sound current and reach Sach Khand, the
place of perpetual bliss.

Do strengthen your faith, make the mind motionless; and
when it becomes motionless, it will begin to see within. For
instance, if you shut a boy indoors, the first thing he does is
to break the doors and windows; and when he cannot find a
way out, he gets tired and sits quietly. He then begins to see
what lies in the room. Mind is like the restless boy. It has to
be closed in against its will and, when it acquires a taste for
the interior, it does not go outside.

~

174.   If one's faith is firm and unshakable, and one daily
gives time to the practices, and has no worldly desires, then
there is no power which can bring one back to this plane.
There is no rebirth for such souls. Birth is for those who die
weeping with desires unfulfilled. Desires are the cause of suffering, and he alone is poor who has unfulfilled desires. He

who is free from desires is richest. All desires arise in the mind, and when the mind is subdued and is merged in the sound current, the game is won.

Soul is enveloped by the mind, and mind by the body. Soul is powerless in the clutches of the mind, and mind is helpless before the senses. A beautiful object attracts it, and sweet music holds it. The soul within is pure, but suffers on account of its association with the mind. While this association lasts, the cycle of change and births will continue— whether the body is material, astral, or causal. The causal form has a longer duration, but is also subject to decay. In Sahansdal Kanwal the soul's connection is with astral forms, and in Trikuti it is with causal forms. When reversion from the causal form takes place, the soul comes to the human form or lower down, depending upon its spiritual status.

A child goes to school and attends class. He is entitled to promotion if he has been doing his work regularly and is fit for promotion. On the other hand, if he has been attending the class but does not learn, he will be kept back. Suppose, instead of learning his work, he develops bad habits and consequently loses in efficiency. Surely he will be put back to a lower grade.

In the same way, if a man, during his lifetime, does the actions becoming a man, he will be kept as man in the next birth. If he has attempted to seek the source of his being, and has received the instructions from a Master, he will be promoted to spiritual regions and there is no rebirth. But if instead he has done the actions of animals and not of man, he will go back to the class of animals.

It is not the karma of this life alone which determines the next birth. I explained in one of my letters that karma is divided into three divisions:

1. Kriyaman—fresh actions;
2. Pralabdh—past actions which have to be undergone now;
3. Sinchit—the store or reserve stock.

During lifetime, pralabdh is finished and death ensues. For rebirth, part of kriyaman of the previous life becomes pralabdh in the new life, and the rest of kriyaman goes to sinchit. Some old sinchit is also added to pralabdh—a very complicated affair, but I just wish to show that it is not the actions in this life alone which determine the next birth.

There are some people who are not fully acquainted with principles of satsang, and who are fond of keeping up external appearances. They complain that though a long time has passed since they were initiated, they have had no spiritual vision nor gained any spiritual power. Their grievance is unjust. How can these people, who do not labour on the exercises, expect to reach the exalted state, which is the result of long and continuous work? They do not control the mind and senses nor obey the Satguru's commands.

The mind is the most powerful, clever, and cunning of enemies. And to release the spirit from its bondage, it is necessary to break the mind's attachment to alluring material objects, which are not ours, but have been evolved by matter and maya. Be on your guard against its deceits. Do not listen to the mind, but always try to bring it under the rule of the Master. The more you look after it, the more you will go in, in internal practice.

This physical body of ours is not enduring; yet the mind has become so accustomed to this form through numerous incarnations that even now, after the Master has graciously revealed to us the secret of the holy Name and Sound practice, we are reluctant to give up worldly enjoyments and turn inward.

～

175. You want knowledge. Knowledge lies within you. Sound current is knowledge. The more you study it, the higher you rise and the wiser you become. And this knowledge is complete in Sach Khand. So first withdraw your attention; bring it inward by repetition. Sit in the eye focus and catch the bell sound, then follow it to the fifth stage. The path may appear long and unattractive to begin with, but there is no other way. God is one, his instructions are one, and they are the sound current.

The path lies within you. The sound current is the direct road. The Lord himself is within you. Only he who has gone within can appreciate and comprehend this. Others have no idea of it. With repetition of the holy names, bring in the scattered mind; and with the help of the Master, ride on the current and reach the home of eternal bliss, beyond the mind and maya.

It is given to Man (human beings) only to rise upward. In no other form, not even that of angels, is this possible. Man is the top of creation. Hence every moment is valuable, and it is the duty of man to utilize it. Only the time spent in this path will count. This is my New Year's message. This New Year's Day, my message is that you give as much time as you can to catch the Word, and see the Man of Nazareth face to face, on your way to the shore of eternal peace and bliss.

∼

176. Wealth or poverty depends upon the absence or presence of desires, respectively. He who has no desires is rich. He who does not desire anything is a sovereign.

∼

177. Character is the foundation upon which rises the spiritual edifice. As long as one is a slave of the senses, talk of

spirituality is a mockery. A magnet would attract shining iron, but not rust. Similarly, the Sound will attract a pure mind, which is free from passion's dross. But when the mind is steeped in the mud of passion and desire, it is like iron that is covered with rust and mud. The first essential step to a spiritual life is character. One may deceive one's friends, relatives, and even oneself, but the power within is not deceived. It is the duty of a devotee to keep constant watch over his mind and never let it loose. As a mother looks after her child, so does a true devotee watch his mind.

... Brave is he who has control over his mind and senses, for the inward progress is in proportion to this control. It is the repetition that brings the mind in, and the sound current that draws it up. There are inexhaustible treasures within us all.

~

178. I am sure you will realise that the first aim and purpose of this work is to perfect your own mind and soul so that you may rise from this material plane to higher regions and eventually arrive at your own real home, in the supreme region. That is vastly more important than having a home or husband, even more important than helping others. If your own soul becomes a brilliant and strong magnet, it will help and draw others. They will love you. But the best way to get the love of others is first to give great love to others. Then they cannot resist coming to you.

This work is to develop the divine life that is within you, and will exalt you. Then all else will follow. This work is not to help people in this world so much as to prepare them for their eternal home above. All of this it will do. If this meets with your full approval, you may have the initiation. Write me if you have any further questions.

~

179. *The karmic law of the vegetarian diet:* A human being cannot comprehend the existence of God and his creation until he has succeeded in freeing his soul from the bondage of the five tattwas, the twenty-five prakritis, the three gunas, maya, and mind—all of which are enveloping it here. Not until he has emancipated his soul from every one of these covers and taken it beyond the sphere of mind and intellect, and opened his internal vision, is the soul able to know itself and understand what it is made of. After that it becomes fit to seek its Creator and to find the ocean from which it originally descended as well as the means to regain it. Consequently, before a disciple has succeeded in getting rid of these chains, it will be sufficient for him to know that this world can be divided into two parts: land and water.

Every grain, every plant, has life in it. Hindu philosophy has acknowledged this fact since very ancient times. Dr Bose has demonstrated this fact to the world by his experiments, showing that plants feel and breathe, and have souls. If a ray of light is allowed to penetrate a dark room, it reveals numberless germs floating in the air of that room. The whole room seems to be full of this germ life. When we breathe, these tiny creatures go inside of us and die. When we walk, numberless creatures are killed by contact with us, and countless others are crushed beneath our feet. The same is true when we drink water. The microscope reveals myriads of tiny creatures in a tumbler of water, and these we drink to their death every day. Souls would appear to be literally packed together in all space in our world. If we put down a needle point on the earth, countless germs may be found beneath its point.

And so, in our world, life is everywhere destroying life. In such a world where one creature is destroying another, it is impossible to expect either justice or peace of mind. There is no rest or security anywhere. Therefore, when the ancient sages found that in this world creatures were destroying each other, they decided that it was better to give up the world. They found that in such a world there could be no peace of mind, and that it was impossible to find peace of mind in any worldly object, and that happiness lies within oneself and in that ocean of which one is a drop. Therefore, the sages thought, so long as they were confined in the prison of this world, they would adopt the course which was the least harmful; that is, they would subsist on creatures the killing of which was the least sinful.

They discovered that all living beings in this world could be divided into five classes as regards the composition of their bodies—the number of elements they contain. By "elements" they did not mean the ninety or so elements discovered by modern scientists, but the main conditions or divisions of matter. There are five such classes of substances. According to their classification:

Under class one came all of those creatures in whom all five of these substances are active, that is, man.

In the next class came those in which only four substances are active, and one is dormant; that is the quadrupeds. In them there is no sense of discrimination, as the akash tattwa is dormant.

In the third class fell creatures in which only three substances are active; namely, air, water, and fire. It includes birds. They lack earth and akash.

The fourth class is made up of reptiles, in which only two substances are active—earth and fire.

Then comes the last class, the fifth, in which only one element or substance is active; that is the vegetable kingdom. In them, water is the only active element. Experts have proved that in many vegetables there is as much as ninety-five percent water.

When creatures of the other four classes are killed or injured, they cry out in pain. But not so the vegetables, though they have life. So the sages concluded that the eating of vegetables was the least sinful (the least burdened with karma). Although the eating of vegetables produces some karma, yet it is of a light nature, which can be worked off easily by spiritual exercises. They thus chose the course of least resistance, and so abstained from the killing of higher forms of life.

The method of practice of the sound current is the only method by which to escape this jail into which we are born. This method is natural, and it was not designed by man. It is as old as the beginning of creation. The Creator is one, and therefore the way to reach Him is one, and it is in the interior of every human being. It is incapable of alteration, addition, modification, or improvement.

Man is to reach the ocean of his origin by means of ascending the sound current, irrespective of caste, creed, nationality, or sex. It is a practice for the awakening of powers within us. By slow degrees our soul will emerge from the grave of the body or vacate it. In the body there are nine outlets through which the soul communicates with this world, and these the soul learns to close and fix its attention in the eye centre. Then it begins to traverse higher planes. When it attains Turiya Pad, it will acquire control over the mind, senses, anger, lust, avarice, attachment, and egotism.

At present the soul is under the control of mind, which itself is under the control of the senses. When we reach the astral region, after leaving the material plane, the soul gains control over the mind. When we get to and beyond the astral region, as well as the heavens and hells which are within the astral regions, all of these are left behind. The soul will then hold these in contempt, and will go on to Brahm Lok—the causal plane.

Brahm is also below Par Brahm. Leaving Brahm, the soul will go to Par Brahm, where it will be freed from all its shackles. On reaching Par Brahm, all the material, astral, and causal coverings of mind and matter that envelop the soul are removed. Then the soul is pure spirit. This is self-realisation. Here there is no form, no cover, no shape, no youth nor old age—only the soul, shining in its pure radiance, a drop of existence, knowledge, and bliss, capable of comprehending the great ocean, its creator. Now the drop tries to reach and mingle with its ocean.

The Master is not a body only. He is the power which guides and helps us at every stage and in every region, during our inward spiritual journey. When we are in the physical body, he instructs us through his physical form, and as we proceed further; he assumes the form of each region—all the way up to Sach Khand.

~

180. Meeting a Master in this life is something unique, for after meeting a Master, there is no coming back in the cycle of life and death. To meet a Master in this life is to enter on the *way* to life eternal. Really fortunate are they who have come across a Master, have been connected by him with the sound current, and are practising the sound current.

To be devout, religious, and good-minded is one thing. Meeting a Master is something else. There is no comparison between these two. The two belong to different species. Religious, devoted, and good-minded folk will get their reward, but will come back to this world to get it. If in any future life they get a chance to meet a Master, they too will reach their eternal home. In India also there are pure-minded persons who have not had the opportunity to meet a Master.

~

181. When the mind is free from little worries and can be put to bhajan smoothly, such opportunities should be utilized for bhajan to the maximum advantage. But no matter in what circumstances one finds himself and what new problems one is facing, a devotee should not miss his bhajan. He may give only fifteen minutes or even five minutes to it daily, but he should be on it without a break. The moment he hears the current at this end, his presence is recorded at the other end—Sach Khand. By pressing the button of an electric bell, no matter how long the line, the bell at the other end of the line rings and indicates the press of the button.

As a mother is eager to see her child grow up and come into its own, so the Master is eager to see his initiates make their progress towards the eye focus and rise up on the sound current, and gain access to higher regions while in this life— so that what they had taken on faith becomes a fact to them.

Men are born, bred, and have their being in this world, and through their senses keep in touch with this world, and thereby their experience remains confined to this world. In the mother's womb and after birth, man grows on the coarse matter of this world; and he becomes coarse to function in this coarse world. Like to like is the rule.

If he were to shake off this coarse matter, or in other words, if he could withdraw his attention and separate it from the coarse matter, he would become fine and would be able to function in fine worlds—mind worlds—and by shaking off mind, he would be able to function in spiritual worlds. Because he does not attempt to become fine, he does not get experience of fine worlds; and naturally, of what he has no experience, he is doubtful. But for those who have made themselves fine, the fine worlds are as real as the coarse world is to the coarse.

Spirituality is real when one has experience of it, and unreal so long as he has not experienced it. Man has the capacity to experience it because man is a combination of spirit, mind, and matter: first, spirit; second, mind; third, matter.

~

182.   Attaching attention to anything is prayer to that thing. And prayer is good, for in prayer, mind contracts, and if done regularly with interest and for long periods, mind comes in concentration, and by concentration, mind becomes pure. The purity of mind expresses itself first in clear thinking, then in inspiration and in intuition.

Saints attach the attention to the sound current because, by experience, they have found that the sound current is the source of all else. It is the power at the back of all other powers, and from which all else has been derived.

~

183.   Just as there are angels, there are ghosts. They are residents of the astral plane, exactly as different nations with different characteristics reside on this earth. Like man, animals, and so forth, they are also a form of creation, which are, however, devoid of coarse matter and therefore function in the astral plane.

People who are very much given over to sexual and other low desires, and have not been able to satisfy their cravings, usually incarnate as ghosts. As disembodied forms, they attach themselves to weak folk having low desires. They do not go near strong-minded persons and dare not look at persons doing bhajan. Ghosts find no place even in a house occupied by a person who does bhajan.

~

184.   Helping others is not bad, but to help others when one is not sure of his own ground is risky. Keeping guard over other people's houses when our own house is left unguarded is not wisdom. Anybody who uses his spiritual powers for the betterment of this world does so at the expense of his powers. The spiritual power decreases and he loses his chance to attain higher spiritual powers. Conservation of spiritual powers is essential for further progress.

X's performances may be genuine, but where do they lead to? The healing power and such other demonstrations, however spectacular and impressive they might be, are really mental phenomena—a display of the powers of the lower or higher mind.

The use and display of such powers is discouraged by the saints, as they are a great hindrance in the way of higher spiritual attainment. Would you accept shells, however beautiful, or copper, however glittering, when you can get diamonds and precious stones?

Useful as his healing power may be to other people, it makes him work at a lower centre and keeps his attention centred on the outside, in the physical or phenomenal worlds. This prevents him from going within and piercing the veil, and mastering higher truths and greater mysteries. (But professional doctors, surgeons, and so on do not come into this discussion—their profession is their karma.)

His conceptions of a group soul are wrong. Plants and animals have individual souls, like men, and these souls may be born as humans in course of time or even in the next incarnation, owing to the special grace of a perfect Master. And a human soul may be incarnated in the body of an animal or a plant.

In the time of Rai Saligram, for instance, when an epidemic of plague broke out, the dearly loved son of a satsangi lay dying. The father was stricken with grief and would not be consoled, but the dying son was quite happy. "Grieve not, dear father, for I can see my past now, and know that death only means to me another opportunity to improve myself and complete what is begun. For in my previous life I was an acacia tree. A satsangi cut one of my twigs and offered it to a perfect saint—Soami Ji Maharaj—and I was, in consequence, given the human body, though I remained rather dull. In my next life I will develop still more. There is therefore no reason for you to weep or feel grieved." Similarly, men have been known to incarnate in lower bodies.

There are no bits of souls.

Yes, the mind and soul may go out in dream state and contact other planes.

This material plane on which we function is of the lowest order, and in comparison to this the astral and causal planes are much superior. One requires the assistance of some conveyance such as car, train, or plane to carry this material frame from one place to another, but no such contrivance is required for functioning on the astral or causal planes. There you have only to think of a place and you are there.

The delights of the spiritual planes above the causal are infinitely greater than what one is familiar with on the lower planes. Anybody having experience of the higher planes could not possibly desire to reincarnate on this material plane. Saints are here in obedience to the command of Sat Purush, to carry out his will to liberate the souls and bring them back to Sach Khand. A Param Sant soul, like Guru Nanak and

Soami Ji, comes direct from Anami and Sach Khand; but before he leaves his physical frame, he imparts spiritual powers to his successor who also becomes a saint.

~

185.   Any act that brings the attention towards the focus of attention—the third eye—and helps in making contact with the current and ascending on it, is a good act. Any act that breaks the contact with the current or brings it down from the eye focus to the lower centres, or throws it out and keeps it away, is a bad act.

The fall of the attention, therefore, no matter by what deed, is a crime. A violent act will naturally keep the attention tied down to lower centres and the man would be behaving like a beast, for manhood lies in the functioning of attention from the eye centre. A violent act, therefore, automatically registers itself in keeping the attention at centres below the eyes.

An ordinary person cannot perceive this change, but anybody who has access, even to the third eye, will experience the effect—what to say of violent acts—even of ordinary acts—and will be able to distinguish what is good and what is bad for him.

~

186.   I wish that you would go in and make conscious progress inside. If the way is long and slippery, faith in the Master and the practice of the sound current makes the footing firm, and perseverance and courage bring us nearer the road terminus.

You are right in praying for help inside, as the Master within is always ready to help, and does help, provided we ask for help in sincerity and earnestness.

187.   Regarding your view that evil is a lesser good: According to saints, both good and evil are given up when the mind and soul go beyond Brahm. In the view of saints, good and evil create shackles for binding the soul to this world, and therefore both are to be eschewed as parts of the scheme of Kal to keep the soul confined to this world. Higher up all is God and there is no evil or good, both of which are aspects of the mind.

~

188.   Nobody working in the mind zone (karmic zone) can alter the course of life. There is no such thing as premature death. Only saints who work from the pure spiritual plane, and are thus unaffected by karmic law, have the power to alter the course of life. That is why we go to them for complete and permanent salvation.

It is good to be kind to lower creatures, but if things are carried to extremes this life would be unlivable and unbearable. Sant Mat enjoins the observance of the laws of sanitation, but above all lays all the emphasis it can on the practice of the sound current, which is the only means of getting out of the sphere of karma.

~

189.   When a man falls ill, he consults a doctor according to his means, and follows his advice. When the circumstances in which he finds himself are out of his or the doctor's control, he leaves himself to nature. More or less the same applies to animals in the hands of animal lovers.

The animal lover has done his best when he has placed the animal in the hands of a vet. When the vet says that the disease is incurable and the presence of the animal is dangerous to other animals, the animal lover is helpless and so is the vet.

The karmic law is operative throughout and gives the final blow. The karma slowly and surely pushes the animal lover and the vet from the sphere of reason to the sphere of sentiment and inaction.

The theory of non-destruction of life under all circumstances is untenable in practice. If a farmer is to live, he must grow food by carrying on agricultural operations. In this he cannot help destroying insects and animals that destroy his crops. All hygienic operations, personal or public, are based on the destruction of life. The struggle for existence on the physical plane demands positive action. Sant Mat enjoins kindness to animals and forbids killing so long as the non-killing does not make life impracticable. Over and above everything else, Sant Mat recommends the giving up of the physical plane for good, by following the sound current, which is *par excellence* the cure of all ills and leads to life everlasting.

You are right when you say that to concentrate on an attribute or abstract quality, such as love, is a little too intangible. Let your friend seek the substance of which love is the attribute. The attribute does not exist without the substance. The substance lies behind the attribute. The sound current is the substance and love is its attribute. This current is present in all of us. When the current is grasped, the attribute—love—comes with it.

Your sorrow over your inability to come here is also bhajan. Never mind the distance. When the desire to come here is there in you, you are here with me. Satguru is always present with you in Shabd Form. He sees, he knows and responds.

~

190. I congratulate you on your achievements. Your efforts are bearing fruit. You are right when you say, "My concentration needs to be collected together very much more than I

am doing now." The greater the concentration, the deeper
the penetration into finer planes. The scenes you have wit-
nessed are good enough, but see that you do not get entangled
in them. A traveller who has a long journey ahead sticks to
the road. The spiritual journey is a long way, so keep on the
move and go ahead.

As to the casting out of evil spirits, a large majority of
such cases are cases of hysteria. Here and there, there is a
genuine case. And it is rather a rule that when persons afflicted by evil spirits come to a place of worship or to holy
and pious persons, the evil spirits leave the afflicted and go
away. Many such cases happen here with both men and
women. When they come here, the evil spirits say that they
have been captured or imprisoned, and, "Where shall we go
now and how? Have mercy on us. We will not come again."

There is not much in casting out devils. Evil spirits have
low desires—the unsatiated evil tendencies of the mind of a
past life. They do not like to come near good minds, just as
evil doers shun the society of good people. The devils haunt
and work from low astral planes, and run away when they
are confronted by a good and pure mind. To use spiritual
power or the power of Nam in casting out devils is, as you
say, using a steamroller to crush a leaf.

The spirit of Christ does not wander about on the material plane. He had had enough of it. Even if it were granted
for the sake of argument that the spirit of Christ works on
the material plane, the problem of coming in contact with
him still remains. To come in contact with him a Master is
needed. The way that Christ went to the Kingdom of his
Father in Heaven has been given to X and it is for him now to
go that way and meet Christ. Even if he were to meet Christ
on the material plane, would he ask him to give him power
to cast out devils and heal the sick, or would he ask him to

take him to the Father? Surely, if he were wise, he would ask the latter. And what would Christ say? His answer would be: "Here is the sound current or the Holy Ghost within you; fix your attention on it and follow it. But first vacate the body and cast out the mind 'devil' from you. There are no short cuts here."

You are perfectly right when you say that he should not ask you for help. He should develop the power within himself in the same manner in which you have developed it—by going within himself and becoming independent of you or anybody else. He should not expect any help from you.

～

191. Compared with Kabir's bold and fearless condemnation of extant religions, Dr Johnson's criticism of the organized churches of Christianity would appear to be very pale, mild, and weak. When you happen to come to me, I shall read to you, in the original Hindi, Kabir's poems criticizing idolatry, pantheism, and other vices of the Hindu and Muslim religions, as well as other poems teaching higher spiritual life, which X seems to have left out as he could not appreciate them. Kabir had reached the highest degree of sainthood, therefore he could not have described Brahm as the highest goal. Though it would be true to describe Brahm as the Lord of Triloki (three worlds), he is not the Lord of the fourth world, which is the pure spiritual region. X has failed to grasp the spiritual side of Kabir. What people generally call spirituality is nothing more than the fundamental moral code, which is a prerequisite to spirituality according to the teachings of Sant Mat.

The people who live in the nine apertures of the body and have not gone above the eyes, have ideas and religious views which are of no importance in the eyes of those who have gone higher. All the religions are to be condemned so long as they do not grasp the fundamental truth of the sound current; and when they have grasped this truth, they cease to be mere religions. So long as people are caught in the meshes of religion, their eyes will not open. The mission of the saints is to free people from the narrow-mindedness, prejudice, and selfishness of religion, and take them to higher planes. All the saints have raised their voices in condemnation of the bigotry and other evils of religions, as reform is not possible without this condemnation. If saints did not condemn idolatry, telling of beads, reading of holy books, and such other practices prevalent in almost all religions, as an end in itself, they would be failing in their duty and most people would be left in darkness.

~

192.   So long as the soul is within the boundary of Brahm and has not crossed the boundary into Par Brahm (Daswan Dwar), it is subject to the cycle of births and deaths. Only the saints are emanations from Sat Lok (the pure spiritual region), and they can take their followers beyond Brahm.

There is no harm in wearing fur or leather garments; only the killing and eating of living creatures is prohibited.

~

193.   It was learned on inquiry that you are feeling depressed. The cause of this depression is sadness and lack of concentration. You know that one comes to the satsang so that, attaining the wealth of *parmarth,* he should consider the world and worldly things of no value but should make use of them according to his needs. He should bear with contentment and gratitude all worldly shocks, sorrows and joys, health, sickness and trouble, and whatever comes his way. Rather, a

satsangi should so behave that he should not be overjoyed if he is granted the kingdom of the whole world, nor should he be the least bit concerned if it is taken away from him.

The *abhyasi* (devotee who performs his spiritual practice) has to navigate the whirlpools of pain and pleasure, honour and contempt, grief and joy—in the ocean of existence. If he is lily-livered, he will not succeed. He should fortify his heart (by spiritual practice) and face the vicissitudes of life with grit and patience. Recognizing the Supreme Being as the prime mover in all affairs, he should acquiesce in his will. So do not be weak-hearted. Hold patience and contentment in your heart, and perform your worldly duties. Forget all worries and do your job according to routine.

Whatever comes to man from the Lord is the result of his own actions, and the Lord makes him go through them for his own betterment. On such occasions, although it is sometimes a bitter pill, he should acquiesce in the will of the Lord. If, on the impact of worldly events, he loses concentration and becomes conscious of joys and sorrows, then it is apparent that satsang has had no effect on him so far. Take courage and strengthen and elevate your mind, and perform your duties faithfully.

∽

194. In your letter you gave a description of a dream and realised the force of repetition of the five names which dispersed the evil spirits, while the first name alone was not sufficient. Why? The sound current is continuous—from top to bottom—from the fifth stage down to the eye focus. The sound differs because it passes through different media; hence the five different sounds.

In the first and second planes there is maya—of course less in the second stage in comparison to the first—and for that reason the first two names are insufficient to release the soul from maya. In the third, fourth, and fifth stages there is no maya. These names, therefore, are effective. I am very glad to know that you remembered the names in your dream and succeeded in conquering evil influences.

Again you say, "Why did I not hear the Sound when I repeated with such one-pointedness?" In the waking or conscious state the soul is at the eye focus. In the dream state it is lower down, and in deep sleep it is in the heart and navel centres. As it goes away from the brain and descends down into Pind it grows duller. At the throat centre it is in a semiconscious state, and imperfect memory only remains. Below the eyes there is no Sound. Sound will be heard only above the eyes and in a state of consciousness, when the attention is in the sound current.

Soul is like a balloon, which has an upward tendency always. Like an inflated balloon, it is held here by chains of mind and matter and the paraphernalia of senses and objects. Sometimes it so happens in sleep that the mind grows dormant or is in a state of peace. At such times the soul, being free, begins to rise up alone. It sees the light and scenes in the upper planes but does not catch the Sound. Sound can be caught fully only in the superconscious state inside and above the eye focus, but the moment the attention is off the sound current and is directed towards the scenery of the astral plane, it is in a derailed condition. Thoughts of the external world keep the attention out, and thoughts of the internal world keep it in.

You are right when you say, "How helpless I am," and "It is impossible to travel on the path without the guidance of a Master." When you will rise to the inner planes you will see how powerful the Master is, what powers are under his control, and how he helps the devotee.

You ask, "Sound is a reality, all else is maya?" That is right. Sound is the only reality. Sound is knowledge, Sound is truth. In the first two stages pure or real Sound is not there. There is maya mixed in it in a very subtle form. From the third stage, the real sound current commences. You will understand the value of this path as you go within and rise. It is acquired by effort, by love and faith. It cannot be had by asking nor by paying dollars. Its price is selfless, pure love. It is within you. It is for you. It will come to you when you are fit to receive it. Make yourself fit for the reception.

As long as you are outward the thing looks dry. To go inward is rather difficult; but once in, the subject becomes tasteful and it will be easy. Through concentration, go inward once and the battle is won. I am glad that you have increased your time to one hour, but I must say that one hour is not sufficient. In three hours the mind is subdued, provided this time is given with love and devotion, and not as a duty.

To begin with, mind brings all kinds of thoughts and is running wild. If the devotee is patient and does not give up the effort, but continues increasing his time slowly and ultimately begins to take interest in this work, soon—such is the state of the devotee—that if by chance he misses a day, he then remains in a repenting mood over the loss.

Before sitting, see that there is nothing that will need your attention during this hour (or whatever length of time you intend sitting), so this one hour is a holiday from other business, and this other business will be looked into only after this hour. Make your time carefree for this interval. There should be no anxiety, no anger, and no hatred. Then sit in the exercises and repeat the names with the attention fixed in the eye focus, and, when feeling tired, then begin to listen to the Sound—as if it is coming from a distance. Do not go after it. When you go after it and leave the focus, then the attention gets scattered and the Sound is lost. Try to catch the fine sounds and not the coarse one.

We are to go in farther and farther. Coarse sound is of the outside but fine sounds are within. The sound you have referred to is not the real bell sound. There is a mixture of ten sounds here, and of these, the bell and the conch are the two sounds that lead up. The conch sound is caught after the bell sound. When you will catch the real bell sound, you will feel that it is audible at twelve miles or more, although it is within you, and the man standing next to you does not hear it. You will be hearing that all twenty-four hours of the day. Stick to the focus and catch the fine sounds. The bell sound will come in its time.

Again, when you see forms within, repeat the five names to see if it is from the positive or the negative power. Forms of the negative power must disappear on recollection of the five names. Concentration, by itself, is a great force. It brings in the scattered mind and soul. Pleasure and the power of miracles will be before you and the negative power will request you to use them, but they are not to be utilized. The time spent with them is time lost. They emanate from the negative power, and these are the means by which the negative power keeps the soul entangled and stops its progress. So, if someone offers anything within, it is not to be accepted, whether in dream or in the exercise.

195.   I am glad to receive your letter and to read that your faith in the Master is firm and you are busy with the exercises despite the infirmities of old age, and that you long to see the Master's Radiant Form and hear his melodious Voice. Rest assured that the Master is within you and is watching you, and will not leave you alone. He knows his part well and is playing it. Have courage. There is no room for despair here.

The Word is the foundation on which the whole visible and invisible structure of the universe is resting. Everything has sprung from this Word. The Master is the embodiment of this Word and is one with it. Your karmic debt is being paid up, and the more you pay here, the better, for then the rise hereafter will be unhindered. I fully realise your situation. When life ceases to have any charm but instead feels burdensome, when memory is failing and thoughts are not fixed, much of this life is gone and little remains. Try to surrender your will to his will, so that the moment he calls you, you are ready to go with him.

~

196.   I am glad to read that you can smile at it all now as childish nonsense. It was a shock to your attachment. Beauty lies in working without attachment. I do not mean calculated or reasoned detachment, but detachment which becomes a part of life. This is possible only when the mind is under control and saturated with the sweet music within.

The Californians are still beginners. They have not yet realised what satsang really means. In this line of work they are like ignorant children. By and by they will learn. As satsangis you should look at their souls and not at their minds. The evil is in the mind and is curable. I wish that you remain in correspondence with the Californians and meet them when convenient. They will be benefited by corresponding with you. Your clear, unbiased minds will tell upon them. Your loving and affectionate letters will induce love and affection in them, and their hearts will melt. Sant Mat is not a platform for debate. It is the glory of love. They will come round, and I think they will respond to love with love.

Saints look at the devotee's soul, and not at his mind or body, and that is the reason why saints are never disappointed. Attachment to the body ends in pain because the body is changeable and perishable. Mental attachments fare no better either. Man is endowed with the power of detaching himself from body and mind; hence it is incumbent upon him to develop this power and be free from the ills of body and mind. The easiest way to do this is to associate himself with something which is beyond the body and mind, and that is the sound current. The greater the association with the current, the greater the detachment from the body and the mind.

The world has never been kind to saints and their real followers. The great Guru Nanak was made to grind corn in a jail, was refused shelter by villagers, and so forth. Guru Arjan was made to sit on a hot iron plate. Shams-i-Tabriz was flayed alive. Mansur was blinded and then beheaded. Christ was crucified, what to say of the harsh words. But what was the response of these great men? Christ said, "Father, forgive them, for they know not what they do."

You may ask any question you like. There is no restriction. Your question as to whom to look to for guidance if the present Master goes out of life is very appropriate. The Master leaves the physical form in his own time as other people do, but remains with his devotees in the Astral Form as long as the devotee has not crossed the astral plane. All internal guidance will be given by him, and it is he who will come to take charge of the soul at the time of death. A devotee who rises above the eye centre now and meets him daily, will meet him inwardly there as usual.

The Master will continue to discharge his inner duties of guidance as before, only he cannot give instructions outwardly for the simple reason that he has left the physical vehicle. The functions which would be performed through the physical frame only, will now be done by his successor. All outward guidance will be done by the successor, and the devotees of the Master who is gone will love the successor no less. They will get the benefit of the outward instructions from the successor. Correspondence also will be done with the successor, and you will know who the successor is.

As to your inquiry about myself, I have asked the secretary to reply to you directly. I will, however, repeat that I am no incarnation. "Incarnation" usually means a representative of the power, Brahm. I am no adept either. I am an humble servant of the saints, and in Sant Mat no one says anything regarding himself. Guru Nanak says: "Father, I am at Thy feet. Have mercy upon me."

~

197. The Master, in his Astral Form, is always with you inside, and if you go in you can see him personally and even talk to him. The answers to your problems are:

1. Yes, the Master never dies. While living he helps his pupils externally by means of sound advice and guidance. He also helps them internally, in his Astral Form, after they have gone inside. When he leaves the physical frame, then his external work is carried on by a successor appointed by him, but he always helps his pupils internally in the Astral Form.

2. When the pupil dies, the inner Master has to decide as to whether he is again to be sent to the physical world or to be stationed in some intermediate region from where he can rise upwards. This depends on the pupil's tendencies and desires. If there is desire in the mind of the pupil for any worldly pleasure or worldly attachment, he has to be sent back to this world. As on rebirth the memory of his previous birth is washed away, he has to get initiation again from a living

Master. But on rebirth he is bound to get initiation and begin his course again from the point where he left it during the previous incarnation.

3.   Yes, the obligation does not come to an end until the pupil has reached Sat Lok. Even if the obligation is transferred, it does not matter to the pupil because the Masters are all one and the same. The real Master is Shabd (Word), which never dies.

4.   He need not know. When he gets initiation in the second incarnation, he will be guided by the then Master.

5.   Has already been replied in (2) above. When the pupil has crossed the second stage he need not be reborn.

It may be pointed out that after the Master has left the physical body and his successor has come in his place, the pupil initiated by the deceased Master need not contemplate and concentrate on the form of the successor. He may continue to contemplate and concentrate on the form of the Master who initiated him.

Posture: Any posture in which you can sit comfortably will do. You can get a chair made with cushioned arms on which you can rest each elbow, and close your ears and eyes with your fingers. The object is to get concentration, and any posture which can bring it about is sufficient. But sitting on the feet is considered to be helpful in concentration, and in this posture the Sound is clearer. The reason seems to be that in this posture one remains free from sloth and feels alert.

No doubt it is difficult for you but I could give three hours at a stretch in this posture. You may give only so much time in this posture as you comfortably can. The distance between the feet should be so much as to keep the spine erect and straight. At first it seems very difficult, but as the concentration grows the position naturally becomes right.

No particular posture is prescribed by the Masters excepting the one on the feet, but any other posture can be taken according to one's taste and convenience. Frequent change of posture hinders concentration.

Yes, not a single case of toppling over has come to my notice. In India a large proportion concentrate in the prescribed posture.

Food: Yes, extracts of cod liver and so forth are to be avoided. But they can be prescribed to non-initiates.

There is no restriction regarding wearing apparel.

The Master is not allowed to accept anything for his personal use or for his family. He lives upon his pension or private earnings.

At repetition, the five holy names are to be repeated without any thought of light or sound. Whether slowly or rapidly, does not matter. What matters is that no idea should be allowed to arise in the mind during repetition.

When alone, repetition may be done so that others cannot hear. This habit aids in concentration.

Listening to a gong does not aid in concentration. After practice in repetition, the Sound will become audible.

There is no *a* after *Sat* in *Sat Nam*, *ph* in *Gupha* should be pronounced like *ph* in *philosophy*, *ch* is to be uttered as *ch* in *rich*.

Yes, Radha Soami is the name of the highest Master and is used in greetings here.

⁓

198.   I very much appreciate your spirit of inquiry, your devotion to spiritual work, and your anxiety to go within. My time is at the service of seekers after truth, therefore there is no question of annoying me by putting questions. A father is never annoyed with the sweet prattle of his children. He loves it. I welcome your questions. Some of them are answered below; others may be put again when you have made some progress, for then it will be easy for you to comprehend the answers, and perhaps it may not be necessary to put them. They will have been answered automatically.

1. As you are not accustomed to sit in this posture, you may, at present, take support of a wall or, better, place a cushion of suitable thickness under the hips to take the weight of the body off the feet. When you have adapted yourself to this posture, you will find it ideal for hearing the sound current.

2. As the vital current is withdrawn from the body, the arms and legs should go to sleep, and finally the whole body. In the beginning one feels pain, and this is natural when the vital current leaves any portion of the body. This pain and benumbness of the limbs and the body are signs of the withdrawal of the vital current. But one should not mind this pain and should bear it. Attempt should be to pay no attention to it. If the attention is held in the eye focus, the pain is not felt. With the increase in practice, the pain will disappear and you will enjoy this sensation of benumbness. One should not be afraid of the pain or the withdrawal of the vital current. No person has died so far when sitting in bhajan. In time, light will appear in the eye centre, and the soul will find its way in, and you will feel that this body is not yours—you are separate from it and the body is the dead body of someone else.

3. When your concentration is almost complete, then, in place of darkness in the eye centre, sparks and fleeting flashes of light will begin to appear, and then light will be steady and the soul automatically will leave the body and enter the tisra til. You should continue looking at the light and repeating the names so that the mind does not wander.

As said above, you should simply look at the light and continue repetition, and should not put any pressure or strain on the eyes of the body. Please make no attempt to take the soul up by force. The soul will find its own way.

4.   You may not think of the optic nerves and the pineal gland, and there is no need to rest in an imaginary position. When the soul is coming in concentration, it will find its own way. If the mind is engaged in imaginary tracing of nerves and locating the pineal gland, or in other ways, the repetition will be interfered with. The mind's movements are to be restricted and it should not be allowed to go loose. The mind wishes to run away, and if you give it the latitude to do this or that, then it has won. The point is to keep it engaged in repetition with a view to eliminate other thoughts.

5.   The real Form of the Master will be met when the attention has entered the eye centre and penetrated the starry sky, the sun, and the moon in succession. This Form will always remain with the disciple and answer all his inquiries. Before this point is reached, the form of the Master contemplated from a photograph or his physical form is the reflection of one's own mind—just as when one fixes his gaze at any electric bulb for half a minute or so, and then closes his eyes, he sees the bulb inside. But it disappears when the mind wavers. The same applies to the imagined form of the Master.

6.   Keeping your attention in between the two eyebrows—the centre of thinking—continue repeating the names; and when the vital current from the part of the body below the eyes has reached this point, the soul will find its way inwards of its own accord. You simply hold your attention there and continue repetition or hearing the Sound— one at a time—and the soul will be lifted up automatically. And the Sound will leave both the sides—the right and the left of the head—and will come from the middle of the head.

7.   The body is alive on account of the presence of the soul current in it. The soul is a drop and the Shabd is the

ocean. The soul is sustained in the body by Shabd, and the body in its turn by the soul. But, so long as the soul is not lifted up to the higher stages, it remains associated with the mind in the lower stages. In the process of concentration, both the mind and the soul—they are closely associated—are lifted. At the second stage of the spiritual journey, the individual mind will have become purified to such an extent that it will no longer be individual, but will have acquired the characteristics of the universal mind. It has no place in the third stage. From there the soul alone goes up. The soul is the positive power and the mind the negative.

The *a* at the end of *Shabda* is silent. It is pronounced as *Shabd.*

8.   In man, in his ordinary state, the soul is hopelessly and helplessly entangled in a most complicated snare. There are chains of lust, anger, greed, attachment, and pride; there are the three states of tranquility, activity, and sloth of the mind; there are the twenty-five conditions like weeping, smiling, and so forth to which he is subject; there are the three bodies: the physical, the astral, and the causal, which serve as cages; and there are the three minds, or the three aspects of one mind, working one in each body or cage.

The object of bhajan is to free the soul from this snare. The current of the holy Shabd alone, which is not part of this snare but which has an independent existence—though penetrating the snare—and is yet separate from it—and keeps the soul fertile and green—is the one and only one power which cuts the chains and frees the soul from this snare. When one is connected with this Shabd current by a Master, and one hears this Shabd in the manner explained to him, and brings his attention nearer and nearer to the Shabd current, he is cutting the bonds, the soul is becoming free, and finally merges in the Shabd ocean of which it is a drop.

There are two currents of the soul: *surat,* which knows and hears, and *nirat,* which sees.

The nirat goes ahead of the surat in the spiritual journey, just as a person on a journey first looks at the path ahead and then follows it. Pandit Ji has complicated this subject in his attempt to clarify it. You may ignore it. When you will go within, the whole thing will be clear to you.

This spiritual uplift consists of three steps:

a. By repetition, bringing into concentration in the third eye the scattered attention and the vital current from the part of the body below the eyes;

b. Holding the attention in the third eye by making contact with the Astral Form of the Master; and

c. Lifting the soul up by attaching it to the bell sound.

This work is just the opposite of what we have been doing before. The soul was disconnected from the Shabd. It had forgotten it altogether and had associated itself with the mind, and was running wild in the downward and outward direction. Now this course is to be reversed. We are to do the about turn. Old habits are given up slowly, and new habits are not formed quickly either. Consequently the spiritual uplift is a slow affair, and "slow and steady wins the race" applies here most appropriately. So with firm faith and steady work, approach it with a calm and cool mind and avoid hurry.

Please take good care of your health.

9.   It is good to repeat the five names together in preference to one at a time. Please understand the object of the repetition. Everybody is engaged in doing repetition—contemplation of his work. A lecturer thinks of his lecture course; a farmer of his fields and cattle; and a businessman of his business and so on; and on whatever one is contemplating,

its picture is before the mind's eye. At the time of death the same scenes appear before us which we have been fixing in our mind during our lifetime. These very scenes or thoughts, as they are connected with this world, bring us back to this world after death and are the cause of our rebirth.

Saints say people have been doing this sort of repetition, as stated above, from birth after birth and have remained confined to this world. If they take to repeating names of the lords of the stages on the spiritual journey which lies within them, then their attention will be withdrawn from this world, the power of the mind and the senses will decrease, the soul will become powerful, light will appear, and there will be a new kind of sweetness which the mind has never tasted before. Finally the soul will discard this world of sensation, catch the Shabd, and will be lifted up. Therefore, there is no simpler way for concentrating the scattered attention than the repetition of the names. Of course the yogis tried *pranayam* and other methods, but without success. They do not take us very far on the spiritual journey and cannot be practised by family people. Repetition of names is for concentration only.

At the time of repetition, the Shabd is not to be heard. One thing at a time. The course of repetition is a long one. The starry sky, the sun, and the moon regions are to be crossed by repetition only, and contact with the Astral Form of the Master is to be made by this very process. And this is the end of it. Repetition would not take us any further. During this course, give three-fourths of the time—but not less than two hours—to repetition, and only one-quarter to hearing the Shabd.

During this repetition course, Shabd is heard just to keep contact with it. The Shabd at this stage does not pull up or lift the soul because the Shabd current is feeble and the soul is firmly held by the senses and the objects thereof. The feeble current has not much pull in it. When the soul will have contacted the Astral Form of the Master it has loosened the bonds and has come nearer to the Shabd, where the current is now powerful and has the power to lift up the soul. The spiritual journey will start from there. Shabd is the road, Satguru is the guide, and soul is the traveller. There is no danger of any kind. The soul will travel stage by stage and, from the description of the lights and the sounds of the spiritual stages, will know the progress made.

Important hints have been given here. More when some progress has been made.

So in the preliminary stage, repetition should receive full attention. People are apt to ignore it and pay more attention to hearing the Shabd. In the preliminary stage, repetition comes first and Shabd next.

When repeating names, no imagination is to be used in associating sounds and lights with each Name. If the mind goes after making lights and sounds, it has gone loose. Keep the mind engaged in repeating the names in the eye centre. No option is to be given to the mind.

10.   When we come out into this world from the mother's womb, we bring our fate with us. This fate, whether we are to be rich or poor, tall or short, healthy or diseased, black, yellow, or white, high or low, and so on, is the result or fruit of our past-life actions. We reap as we had sown. We get what we have earned. Therefore, we should work and play our full part with diligence and effort in the struggle of life and, without worrying, be contented with our lot and bear it cheerfully. And if there is any power that cuts the bad karma, it is the Shabd. When, therefore, one gets a taste of Shabd and enjoys Shabd, innumerable bad karmas are destroyed. The object of devotion to and love for the Master and Shabd is to cut the very root of karma, so that the soul

disengages itself from the bonds of karma and becomes free to merge in Shabd.

11, 12, 13. These questions will be solved automatically when you have gone within and made contact with the Astral Form of the Master and have thereby cast off the physical frame and acquired the astral form. Or these questions may be asked again when contact with the Astral Form of the Master has been made.

There is no fixed time as to how long it takes the average departing soul to leave the body completely.

14. There are five elements—earth, water, fire, air, akash—of which the material world is made up, and according to elements there are five classes of creation. In man, all the five elements are active; in animals, four are active and one is dormant; in birds, three are active and two are dormant; in insects, two are active and three are dormant; and in vegetables, one is active and four are dormant. It is difficult to understand it intellectually, but it will be comprehended after going within. The rise from which animal to man, or fall from man to which animal, depends on karma. Good karma lifts up, and bad is the cause of fall.

15. So long as the soul is entangled in forms—physical, astral, or causal—it has sex. But in higher spheres, when it is free from bonds of mind and maya, there is no distinction of sex. The sex changes according to karma. Sex is not a fixed thing—that male shall always be male, and female always female.

The outlook on marriage, on male and female, on unions, love, likes and dislikes, and mine and thine, changes rapidly with the entry into the third eye, by contacting the Astral Form of the Master, and hearing the bell sound. What man had called his own, and had longed to be with, here and hereafter, now look like strangers. As many births, so many fathers and mothers did we have, and so many wives, and many more children. We had such relations when we were insects, birds, and other animals, and it is no achievement to be proud of if we have them when we are in human form.

If the human form is the top of creation, it is for the single reason that man has the capacity to catch the Shabd and rise on it to reach his origin. If this has not been done, man has missed the golden opportunity and has remained a two-legged animal, a slave of the senses and the objects of senses, like other forms of creation. He will be Man when he has risen above the senses; when he is no longer a slave of lust, anger, greed, attachment, and pride; when he has made his mind motionless; when he has entered the third eye and heard the bell.

With every step taken on the spiritual journey, he is coming into his own by casting off the heavy load of matter—physical, astral, or causal—which really is not a part of him but which the soul takes up as tools to function in the causal, astral, and physical worlds. When contact with the Astral Form of the Master has been made, the outlook, which is now based on the experience gained in the world and the worldly relations, is that the Master and the Shabd are the two real friends and companions who are here with us, and go with us after death. All others have their limitations. It does not mean that he has an aversion for others. He does his duty by them but knows their true worth. He is in the world but not worldly, outwardly attached but inwardly detached—like a duck in water and yet not wet.

In the experience of saints, one Shabd is the creator of all that has been created. All creation, to them, is Shabd. They see Shabd in action everywhere. All forms of creation in the highest and the lowest stages are different aspects of Shabd.

16. Just as on the physical plane there are continents and countries with their different types of population, the same is the case on the astral plane. One such place is the heaven inhabited by *houris*. Muslims call it Bahisht and Hindus call it Swarg—difference in name but place is the same. The place is subject to karmic law and transmigration. It is not a permanent abode and not worth living in, but a place to be shunned, a design of the negative power to prevent the soul from going up. The whole astral plane is subject to the five passions, the same as the physical plane.

17. Sant Mat does not advocate asceticism, nor is it helpful. A settled means of income with settled home life give comforts which are conducive to bhajan. They are denied to ascetics. As said elsewhere in this letter, old habits go slowly and new habits are not formed quickly either. The training of the mind, like the training of a horse or like the training of a child in making them useful, is a slow affair. It is a lifelong work. Slow and steady wins the race. When Shabd practice becomes tasteful, all other tastes become flat.

18. There is antagonism between Nam and kam. Nam is another name for Shabd, and kam means sex lust. Nam or Shabd lifts the soul inward and upward, and kam pulls it downward from the eye centre. The sexual relation of husband and wife has been very much misunderstood and abused. In this respect a biologist even treats man as an animal, and calls this relation a mere biological function and no better. He is yet ignorant of the higher potentialities of man. Those who are familiar with this great aspect of man have treated this sexual relation as something sacred, and laid down rules for preserving its sanctity. Man dissipates himself and his energies in sexual intercourse. He would be healthier if he were to conserve this energy and would be godlike if he were to use it in spiritual uplift.

With the longing to go within and the hearing of the sound current becoming tasteful, the indulgence or play in sex decreases and ultimately becomes hateful, and is automatically given up, like other bad habits, such as anger, greed, and so forth.

I want you to do bhajan and make progress in it. This will please me most. This is the present which the Master will always accept.

Jesus Christ initiated people by connecting them with the Holy Ghost—the Word—the Shabd. Therein lies his greatness. And naturally, only those who have some experience of this Shabd can appreciate what service he did for people. His Sermon on the Mount is good. It is a moral teaching which can be lived in practice on the strength of Shabd only. If Shabd is missing, no one can live up to this moral teaching. I wish you could make the eye centre your home, make contact with the Shabd, and become a true Christian.

The simran or the repetition of the names will cleanse your abode in the eye centre, eliminating other thoughts. The stars, the sun, the moon, and the Master will decorate it.

There are ten different sounds going on ceaselessly in the eye centre. You have experienced some of them. Out of the ten, only two—the bell and the conch—are to be sought out; the other eight are to be rejected. The bell and the conch will take us to the regions above; others are local. But so long as the bell has not been grasped, any other sound that is audible is good enough and one should stick to it. When the concentration will increase, this audible sound will give place to some other finer than this, and that in its turn to something finer and sweeter still. Ultimately, the real bell will be audible.

The success depends upon the concentration. The nearer your attention to the eye centre, the louder and clearer will the sounds become, and that which is hidden and indistinct from a distance will be clear when you are near it. Light will also increase with the increase in concentration. All the instruments used in an orchestra are audible when we are close to it, but only the drum when we are far off. The same is the case here. When our attention is held in the body, we are far off from the eye centre, the place of the inner music, and when the attention has vacated the body and is concentrated in the eye centre, we are close to it. Every time we are in the eye centre we can sort out and catch the bell sound, but when away from this centre, we miss it and others as well. The sounds are there all the time, only we are out.

Regarding perspiring profusely (during meditation), particularly around the head, when the room is not hot: you attempt to go within by forcing your attention inward. Any strain or pressure or force, physical or mental, should be avoided in attempting to concentrate. Sit in the eye centre with an easy mind and repeat the names. Concentration will follow as a matter of course. Cycling is easy, but look at the man who is learning to ride a cycle. He is perspiring because he applies his force wrongly.

I am very pleased with your work. You may write as often as you like. Your letter is always welcome.

~

199.   Before sitting down for meditation, please clean your mind of all mental fogs and worldly attachments. Concentration would then be easy and quick.

Saints are Love personified, and they love not only their disciples but all creation and all around them. They look upon the whole creation with love and kindness.

To the Master, his spiritual children are dearer than the offspring of the flesh. The latter are entitled to his worldly property but his spiritual children would succeed to his spiritual wealth. You, as disciples, are dearer to me than my own sons.

It is not an easy job to reach the eye centre. It requires years of patience and persevering labour.

You are welcome to ask as many questions as you like, to clean the mind of all doubts. Please do repeat any question, the answer to which is not clear to you.

The Radiant Form of the Master may seem to be far away like the Evening Star of Wagner's opera, but still it is within you. It is not far away. There is a veil between you and it, and it will be torn by your love and labour.

Your two poems were read out and explained to me. Both are very pathetic and true. If the world were to follow Christ or Sant Mat there would be no war and strife.

~

200. Some of the questions in that letter are answered herein; others, as was said in my previous letter, should be left over till you have gone within.

With his physical form the Master comes in contact with people, gives the Creator's message that they have gone astray, that the path (Nam) lies within them, and that if they choose to go back to him they will get all the assistance right here in this world as well as on the inner journey. He removes their doubts, answers their queries, himself does what he preaches, and by his word and action creates confidence in people and attracts them to himself. Those who accept him, he initiates personally (or through some other chosen person), that is, connects them with Nam, and with his Radiant Form takes his seat in the eye centre of the disciple; and gives necessary (as he thinks proper) spiritual guidance which, of course, the disciple is not aware of, till he has entered the eye centre and made contact with his Radiant Form.

The physical form, therefore, is meant to explain the teaching of Sant Mat, clear the doubts and difficulties of people, and encourage the disciple in meditation.

As all people are held away from the eye centre and play on the sense plane because they are attached to forms, which are themselves playing on the sense plane, therefore it is natural that if people were to contemplate on and attach themselves to a form which does not play on the sense plane but plays on the spiritual plane, beyond the matter and the mind planes, they will be pulled up from the sense plane into the eye centre. It pulls up while other forms pull down.

Contemplation on the physical form of the Master, therefore, is a very great help in concentration and will take the soul upward to the Radiant Form. But it is not easy to hold onto this Form in contemplation. The mind, being dirty, runs again and again to dirt-laden forms and does not stick to it. To hold on to it in contemplation depends on the purity of the mind or, in other words, on the love of the disciple for the Master.

There are cases of pure souls which have gone in concentration at the very time of initiation. But such cases are rare. Therefore, the usual method of repetition of names is recommended for purifying the mind and bringing concentration. If this is done with love, and has been intellectually grasped as correct, it brings in concentration, and one can feel daily how far the attention has been withdrawn from the body.

By repetition one can cross the stars, the sun, and the moon regions, and make contact with the Radiant Form of the Master. This is as far as repetition will take the attention. The course of repetition ends here.

Dhyan is to make the attention stay there. This Form, being so beautiful, attracts the attention; and this attraction, when fully developed, gives the attention the power to stay there. So long as dhyan is incomplete, the soul goes that far with the help of repetition, but comes back. When one has merged his petty self in it and lost his "I-ness," then the Radiant Form talks as we talk here outside, and replies to enquiries and guides him to the higher regions. The sweet bell sound exercises its magnetic influence and the soul commences the spiritual journey, the Master giving the necessary help and guidance and, step by step, taking him to the Creator in Sach Khand.

All this depends primarily on the disciple's love and effort. It can neither be purchased nor had for the asking. One has to detach himself from his possessions, his relations, his own body and mind; and, doing all his worldly duties, be detached in attachment, be in the world and yet not worldly.

If one succeeds in establishing himself in the Radiant Form during his lifetime, he should consider himself lucky. He sits at the top of the physical world. There is nothing in this world with which this state can be compared. It stands by itself. It gives a unique type of peace.

No limit can be placed as to how the Master awakens souls with his Astral Form. Sometimes a person is in one country and the Master is in another and the two have not met before. Even then the Astral Form of the Master has gone to him, come in contact with him, awakened him, and talked to him. But full explanation and secret of the path is given only when they meet. The person, on meeting, realises that he came in contact with this Form at such and such a place.

It is the business and duty of every disciple to make his mind motionless and reach the eye centre. The duty of the Master is to help and guide on the path. To control the mind and senses and open the tenth door depends on the disciple's efforts. If there is any difficult work in the world, it is the fight with the mind. Because the soul is positive and the mind is negative, therefore the teachings and satsangs of the Master are to encourage the soul and make it stand against the mind, fight it, and win the battle. When the mind has gone in, it tastes sweetness such as it has never before tasted in worldly objects. Then it becomes obedient and faithful. So long as it has not tasted that sweetness, there is no greater enemy.

The primary factor in this success is the effort of the disciple. Sometimes it so happens that the mind loses faith even in the Master and puts forth strange arguments in support of its case. This is the result of past bad karma. Even rishis and yogis have been deceived by this cunning mind.

The Master teaches and the disciple learns. The progress of the disciple depends upon how fast he learns his lessons. The efforts of the disciple and the grace of the Master go hand in hand. Effort is rewarded with grace, and grace brings more effort. When a labourer gets his wages after a day's work, is the Master so unjust that he will keep back his grace from a diligent disciple?

The Master's physical presence helps the disciple to attain concentration, if the disciple takes advantage of his presence. The inner Master gives all the grace and help that the disciple is capable of receiving, no matter where he may be. The Master is within him.

The photo is for recognizing the Master when any form appears, in time, inside. Contemplation of the photo will bring in concentration, but the photo only will come inside. It will not speak, nor will it give any guidance. It is lifeless, a reflection of one's own mind. A large part of the world contemplates on the pictures of Christ and Krishna and other religious leaders. The pictures appear inside but remain silent and do not lead. Contemplation of a photo is a very poor type of practice. Contemplation of a photo is not sufficient.

No good will result from contemplation of photos and pictures beyond concentration, and that too only if done for long periods.

The contemplation of pictures of past Masters long dead, where even the pictures are imaginary, is absolutely useless, and the picture of the living Master is useful only in recognizing him when any form appears inside. Therefore, for concentration, repetition is the normal method and photo is helpful only in recognizing him. The same principle applies to moving and talking pictures. There are no substitutes for the living Master. So long as one has not come face to face and talked to a Master, no contemplation is possible in the real sense of the term. When, by repetition, one goes inside and meets his Radiant Form beyond the sun and the moon regions, the photo will help in recognizing him.

Surat means soul. The bell sound is Shabd. When the soul hears the bell sound, it likes it and loves it. On hearing it, the mind and the soul begin to stay inside but the Sound will not lift them up because they are not in its magnetic sphere. It is heard from a distance and has no pulling power. Therefore, one has to go to it by crossing the stars, the sun, and the moon with the help of repetition, and stay there with the help of dhyan. The lifting of the soul to higher regions is the business of Shabd. The Master gives help and guidance, and Shabd lifts up. If there is no lift, there is not much good in hearing the Shabd from a distance. The hearer is in Pind and the Shabd comes from Anda. The hearer has no control over it.

If Sound is audible at the time of repetition, then pay no attention to it. Pay attention to repetition only. When listening to the Sound, then pay attention to Sound only and ignore repetition. One thing at a time. Only one work can be done at one time, attentively and successfully. One moment attention in Sound and the next moment in repetition is not proper.

The prayer wheel is a useless thing. We are to bring the mind and the soul in concentration within us. When attempt is to hold the attention inside, who is there to attend to the prayer wheel outside?

So long as the thousand-petalled lotus has not been reached, the bell sound is to be listened to and from this lotus onward, the conch. When one is in dream, the attention is in the throat centre, and when consciously awake, the attention is in the eye centre. So one can easily distinguish whether one was in dream or was awake.

There is no end to the scenes and sights within, in the region of the eye centre. The scenes are the creation of the five elements in their fine form, just as the scenes in the physical world are due to the coarse form of the five elements. One should not pay any attention to them. The progress on the journey stops when a traveller busies himself in sight seeing. If the scenes and sights come in the way, let them come, but pay no attention to them. Pay attention to repetition.

The soul rises on the current of Shabd and returns on the same current. It has four rates of speed, like that of:

1. the ant, in Pind,
2. the spider, in Anda,
3. the fish, in Brahmand, and
4. the bird, in Sach Khand, respectively.

The ant rises on the wall, falls and rises again—a slow and laborious process. This is our state in the process of withdrawing the current from Pind, that is, from the nine portals of the body to the Radiant Form of the Master. In Anda the soul is like the spider which comes down from the roof to the floor, goes up again on its own fibre, and is independent of the wall. In Brahmand the soul is like a fish which goes upstream. And in Sach Khand the soul is like a bird that comes from the top of a mountain, straight to the earth below, and rises up from the earth to the top without any hindrance. This last state is of saints who go like a bird from the physical plane to Sach Khand and come back from Sach Khand to the physical plane, unobstructed by mind and matter.

It is not necessary for every soul to go through the whole cycle of transmigration. For fuller understanding one should cross the second region.

Kabir did not descend lower than human life. He had to take up human form to teach humanity. This is the case with other Param Sants also.

… Every sage calls the lord of the region to which he has attained during his lifetime as his spiritual father, and the region as heaven. Allah is the same as Niranjan; Kali of Ramakrishna represents the divine energy; but these things one should see for himself rather than try to grasp them intellectually.

Your view that a soldier's career is inconsistent with Sant Mat is not sound. Guru Jaimal Singh had no hostile feeling towards the opposing combatants; in the evening he would go among them and they respected him as a sage. A soldier is like a sword in the hands of the commander. The sword is not responsible, and the soldiers have not to account for their actions before Kal. Again, whatever one does with the permission of his Master, the Master is responsible for the consequences.

The governance of this world is in the hand of Kal, and he has so arranged that no soul should go beyond his sphere. We should avoid injections so far as we can. Such minor points should not be stretched too far, for, if we do, we are soon lost in detail, life would become impracticable, and Sant Mat unworkable. Emphasis should be on the practice of Nam and on going within, anyhow. If we stick to the trunk, the leaves and branches will take care of themselves. And, after all, injections are not so mischievous as evil thoughts are.

... God is one; the structure of the human body is the same all the world over. The Way to reach God is through the human body. Nam is the Way within all, therefore it is one and the same for all creation.

~

201. I am glad to know that my last letter containing replies to some sixteen to seventeen questions at last reached you. No, I have no reason to be offended as it is my seva (service) to clear doubtful points to seekers. Your questions will always be welcome but you should not mind the delay in receiving the replies, as I have my hands full and so also are those of my secretaries. They have a great number of letters to reply to each day, besides other work which has been increased by the war controls. But it is a task of love and is carried out in the same spirit by us all.

~

202. This is in reply to your letter dated February 21st in which you repeat question 16 of your letter dated October 14th. "Imbued with the doctrine of non-resistance of Christianity".... "Resist not evil".... "Love your enemies and them that hate you and spitefully use you" ... "without thought of reward or punishment." Let us examine the fundamentals of this doctrine. Our only but deadly enemy is our mind. Lust, anger, greed, attachment, and pride are its agents. It is through these that the mind keeps us always out and on the move from our home in the eye centre, thereby binding us with this world; our actions becoming the cause of our rebirth and death and our eternal misfortune.

The positive qualities—continence (chastity), forgiveness, contentment, discrimination, and humility—remain suppressed and ineffective. Pious resolutions and so-called prayers afford us no protection against these agents. Looking a bit minutely we find that when man's attention is confined to the Pind part of the body, he is literally full of evil, as the attention is slave to the passions stated above. If this were not the case, there should be no difficulty in attaining concentration and going in and up. If man were not to resist these evils, then these evils would keep him tied to the wheel of life and death forever. The doctrine, therefore, serves no useful purpose and is positively harmful. The soul would forever remain slave to the mind and would never attain salvation.

If we carry this doctrine to its logical conclusion, then we should not be an active or passive participant in any war; we should not be a party to the manufacture of and the trade in armaments and other sinews of war, including the atom bomb; no taxation for conducting a war should be justified; even the police force would have to be disbanded, for what we do not want to do ourselves, we would not be right in getting it done through others. The right of self-defence, allowed in the law of all civilized countries, would have to go also. The farmer is at war with insects, birds, animals, and other enemies while raising crops; and if the farmer is to observe this doctrine in thought, word, and deed, then goodbye farmer and farming, and to all others who live on his produce. Again, we see that man is constantly at war with nature for self-preservation—in observing sanitation, and in the control and cure of disease; and if he is to ignore these, then man would soon come to his end. This way of interpreting the doctrine means that man and his civilization must disappear if the doctrine is to survive. So nothing has been gained from this hair-splitting, and the very object of human life has been missed. Surely this could not be the intention of the giver of this doctrine. The doctrine has been misunderstood. The evil has to be resisted and conquered. All saints, including Lord Jesus, give us the Word, the practice of which would lift man up from Pind to Anda and higher regions, thereby generating in him the strength to conquer the evil in him and attain salvation, which is the object of human life. When the key—the Word—is missing, the doctrine of "non-resistance to evil" remains a dead letter. It has been said in previous letters that our viewpoint on life changes rapidly with every little travel on the spiritual journey within ourselves.

The senses are detached from the objects; the mind no longer runs through senses; the attention is held by the Word within; the evils—lust, anger, and so forth—run out from within, finding the place too hot for them, and they go out one by one in the form of children, not secretly but declaring openly that in the presence of the Word they cannot remain within.

When the evils have been conquered and turned out, their place is taken by the positive qualities; then strife and struggle give place to peace and tranquility. And the higher the rise is within, the greater is the harmony with the Word and His creation. Then the doctrine of non-resistance to evil—or putting it positively and at a much higher level as the doctrine of charity, mercy, and love—is seen as the handmaid of the Word, and comes into action automatically. And when it becomes dynamic and dominating, the doctrine of non-resistance to evil acquires a new meaning.

The evil is seen as a mere weakness which is easily tolerated in the hope that, properly handled, it can be overcome. The parents' love, with their gentle but firm handling of their children, gives them good breeding. The teachers' love and handling makes them good citizens. The church does its bit.

But the saints' love and handling makes them saints. Parents, teachers, and church work in very narrow spheres and have their limitations. They teach toleration and do good work but do not eradicate evil; and without its eradication, the strength "to love your enemies and them that hate you and use you spitefully" does not develop.

The whole beauty, therefore, lies in the Word and its practice. Because the saints are rare and the Word cannot be had except from a living saint, and the practice of the Word is no joke, and without the grasp of the Word there is no awakening of the soul, no victory over the mind and senses, no development of the positive qualities and no banishment of evil; the man, no matter how intellectual, remains an animal. He imitates saints without the strength of saints, glibly talks of their doctrine but cannot live up to it, with the result that there is a clash in the doctrine and the facts of daily life and warfare.

Suffice it to say, therefore, that people abstain from adultery, meat, eggs, and intoxicants, particularly alcohol, and practise the sound current, go in, turn out the evils and take charge of their house, and thereby qualify themselves for observing the doctrine in practice—which means tolerating the weaknesses in others on the strength of the love and harmony generated by going within, and lifting them up more by example than by precept. A person with a good robust physique is an advertisement of strength which spontaneously induces and encourages the weak to be like him.

The uplift and the good that a saint does may be judged from the fact that if a true saint is walking, some insects must die if they happen to come under his feet, and these insects are lifted to the human stage in the next birth. If a saint sits under the shade of a tree or eats its fruit, or brings it or a part of it in his use, the tree is given the human status. The same applies to an animal in the service of a saint. Even a chance gaze by a saint on a bird is sufficient to lift the bird to the top rung of the evolutionary ladder; and when he initiates a person and connects him with the Word, he opens the way to salvation. Guru Nanak says a saint saves millions, by using only a tiny particle of Nam.

A word about "duty and action without thought of the fruit of action." The idea is good and appeals to reason. It is easily said. The difficulty is in bringing it into practice. So long as the attention is confined to Pind, we are under the influence of mind, and desire is its necessary concomitant. When the attention is attached to Nam and tastes its sweetness, the mind goes under and so does desire. Therefore, when the attention is firmly held by Nam, only then the action can be done without the thought of reward, and only then, while "doing" is one "not doing," but not earlier.

With this background it is evident that only the saints, who live in the spiritual regions beyond the mind spheres, live nonviolently. They emphasize the practice of the Word and advise people to live non-violently in the hope that a cool and charitable disposition would help in catching the sound current sooner. Persons engrossed in mind and matter, in lower regions, cannot live non-violently in thought, word, and deed.

A votary of Sant Mat, therefore, does his normal duty to his family, his town and country, and above all to himself and his Maker. If, for the preservation of peace, he is to enlist as a soldier, it is his duty to do so, for peace is a prelude to the practice of the Word. As a farmer he is justified in taking normal measures for the protection of crops, for the maintenance of human life.

Dairying is good, but the raising of stock for meat and fur, and work in slaughterhouses, are avoidable and should be avoided.

Transfusion of blood is becoming common in modern medicine and cannot be avoided, for doctors have no alternative.

Enough, therefore, if so long as the contact with the Master's Radiant Form has not been made, the restrictions laid down regarding food and drink are observed in practice, and the Word receives its full share of time with love and faith. When the contact has been made, the devotee will be sensitive enough to know for himself what is good for him and what is harmful and, if in doubt, can get a direct answer from the Master within.

Question 2.[*] Blood transfusion is permissible as it does not involve killing. To make a distinction in donors as meat eaters or otherwise may make it impracticable in emergency. The Word is the one cure for all contaminations, old and new.

Question 3. If the disciple sticks to the sound current, Kal does not interfere. The Master is there to guide him. When a person commits no offence he is not afraid of the law and jail.

Question 4. There is only one regent in each region. They are the guardians of the road of sound current on which the devotees of sound current go to their home in Sach Khand.

Question 5. Kal and the regent of Trikuti is one and the same. From Trikuti downward this negative power becomes more active, and in the two regions above Trikuti it is less active. The power of the soul increases enormously in higher regions.

The idea of typing any letter or a part of it by individuals for their own benefit is good.

---

* These question numbers correspond to specific questions posed by the disciple in an earlier letter, hence there is no reference to a "Question 1."

"Is there any way by which the feeling of the Holy Presence can be raised to the eye centre for concentration?" This feeling is itself the result of simran. So with the increase in time given in simran, and carefully watching that the mind remains engaged in simran and sticks to the eye centre, concentration will be achieved quickly.

"If one feels the current ... or their value?" This sensation is good and is a sign of the attention getting loose from matter. With further approach of the attention towards the eye centre, the separation from matter will be complete. Please see that there is no strain on breathing. Go in with love. When such feeling is there, the time in that posture should be increased.

... and was very glad to read your poem regarding the coming of the "noble guest".

The incident referred to in Dr Johnson's book took place many years ago on the occasion of my first visit to Rawalpindi, and the persons concerned were mostly Sikh priests who thought my sermon would adversely affect them. Before that, there had been no preaching on the internal philosophy of the Granth Sahib. It seemed to them new and a deviation from their orthodox beliefs. Subsequently, I have paid numerous visits to Rawalpindi, and now the gathering there is so large that our big satsang hall is insufficient to contain it, and the people hear the sermons with eagerness and calmness, and pray for initiation.

The will power becomes strong by repetition and concentration, and spiritual force is created, which awakens love and faith within, and that leads to personal magnetism which is present in a small or large degree in every human being and even in animals. This spiritual force is within every one of us but is awakened only by spiritual practice. Only those whose internal eye is open can feel it.

This personal magnetism of saints, sages, and prophets goes with them when they depart from this life. A man's teachings and discourses survive him, but his spiritual power goes with him. Therefore only the effect of Christ's teachings remained behind.

∾

203. "A Sinner's Prayer" is a beautiful composition and I very much appreciate it. Every thought that comes from you is full of love and is acceptable to the Guru. Father's love is bound with child's love. Kabir says, "I am His dog. He holds me by the chain (of love) round my neck and I follow wherever He leads."

∾

204. Man is the highest form of creation. He is the temple of the living God. His whole creation is also within the temple. Unfortunately man looks out from the temple and not in. When he begins to divert his attention inward he is, in a way, coming in tune and, like a radio in tune, receives messages. The better the tuning, the more efficient the machine. Your period of anxiety and tension reaching a climax on January 8th coincides with my condition. If you could go a little further up, you could know the cause of tension as well. A little more effort, a little way up, and a better tuning, then you would not feel and guess, but will know.

When there is suffering all around, everybody feels and helps according to his capacity. I am in the hands of my Master. Whatever duty He assigns me, I carry it out. To me there is no greater pleasure than that. Please have no anxiety. I do not mind any trouble to myself. I am very pleased with you.

∾

205.   I am very pleased with you both for the practical way in which you have moulded your lives and your attitude toward life. You provide a practical demonstration of what Sant Mat teaches in theory. You have met the ups and downs of life cheerfully, and your faith in the goodness of the Master has never wavered. In adversity and disease one gets an opportunity to test himself and his depth in his faith. Your letter written after—had recovered from the attack is creditable to you both. Sickness, if borne with patience, causes less trouble and worry to the patient as well as to those who have to look after the patient. Patience lies in the stillness of the mind, and the higher it has been raised the greater patience it brings.

You know we are not to live here forever, nor is it our wish to stay here on this plane of struggle and turmoil a minute longer than we can help. We are to go one day. We are to so mould ourselves that we do our allotted duties here to the best of our lights, and go straight with the Messenger when he gives the message and takes us home.... This is the time for preparation to meet that requirement. Again, why any hesitation in us? Our path to our home is lit with the brightest of suns and moons; our home is peace personified; and our Father is love and grace. I gladly repeat that you are living as a disciple should.

X says that in her last attack of disease she did not see the light and she experienced fear of passing in darkness. Doctor also thought that she may pass away any minute, but no Master had shown his face. Dear daughter, you will never die in darkness. The end is not yet due, and when dirty karma alone is being paid, the Master's Form does not show itself, so that the devotee in pain may not request for altering or modifying the course of the disease. The Master wishes that the karma be gone through and its bad effect neutralized. When the effect is neutralized, the Form may appear. But when the end is near, the Master does not forget the soul and remains with the soul, and gives so much sweetness in the Current that the attention is withdrawn from all directions and is held within.

When certain karma is being gone through, the Form is absent, and I will tell you the case of my mother: She had been initiated by my Master—Baba Jaimal Singh Ji—and once or twice a week she used to see her Master within. I was yet in service in the Himalayan Hills, some distance from her home. Like a good mother, she would write to me of good things but would never write to me of her illness so that I may not feel anxious about her. She fell sick and was sick for two months. I was sent for by telegram. On reaching home I found her better. On enquiry about the trouble, she said that the disease was not so painful as the absence of the Master (inside) for full two months. "But he is with me now for the last three days." On further enquiry about the cause of absence of the Master for two months, she replied that the Master said: "You are to go now. Your end has come. There was some karma which had to be gone through, as it is not intended to give you another birth. That karma has been gone through now and you will be taken away in three days' time." After three days, when the time came, she asked us (family members) to sit in meditation. When we were in meditation, she passed away. Dear daughter, don't you worry. You will not be taken away without notice.

Coming back here again or going up within after death depends on the tendency of the attention. Like the pan of the balance, that which carries the heavier load sinks. If this world is meaningless and has no value in your mind, and you really consider it perishable material that is not worth having and, instead, your mind is given to the love of the Guru and Sat Purush, and there is longing to go to Sach Khand, then there is no power which can bring you back.

If, due to some adverse conditions, much time has not been given to the current—but there has been a strong love for the Master and a wish to go within—even then rebirth is not given. The soul is taken to Trikuti or Daswan Dwar and made to make up the deficiency there and, in time, taken further up, to the end of the journey. If, on the other hand, love for Nam and the Master is nominal and the mind is given over to the world, then there is rebirth here. But this new birth is better suited for the spiritual work than the previous one. The mind is peaceful and the devotee gets initiation and opportunity to work up and replace the worldly desires by longing to live on the higher planes within.

Therefore, a devotee of the Current should never fear death. He is not going below the stage of man in transmigration. His efforts should be to finish his work here and now.

You are right when you say that it is our duty to lighten our karmic burden in this life by giving as much time to the Current as possible. The karma of innumerable lives has to be paid. It may look difficult but it is easier to pay it here. A creditor is contented to take something very much less than his due from a debtor who has made up his mind to go from the country and settle elsewhere, and who has the backing of a mighty emperor (Satguru).

I have said many a time before and repeat it again that once the seed of Nam (sound current) has been sown in a soil (heart) it will sprout one day, grow, become a tree, and bear fruit. It is impossible to destroy this seed. The devotee of the Current must reach Sach Khand. It is inevitable and no power can stop him.

… A boat held to its moorings will see the flood waters pass by; but detached from its moorings, may not survive the flood. The current is our base—our moorings. A soul that is attached to the current is safe.

No harm if she is to cook meat to keep a house. She must not eat it herself. But you know when meat is cooked it is not always easy to resist taking it. The world is a furnace in whose fires the soul is purified. She should look up and inside, and carry on in the circumstances as best she can. The current is within her and no outward circumstances stand in the way if she wishes to hear it.

... This life is for working out that fate. If in this life we give ourselves to devotion, we will not come again, but we will go back to our home. This life is for the purpose of ending our coming back into this world. I am glad you have grasped this truth yourselves, and have taught it to others also.

As I have said already, I am against the performance of miracles. Sant Mat gives no value to miracles. In Sant Mat, going by his will is much more creditable and honourable than doing miracles. But if any action has been interpreted by Dr Johnson as a miracle, that may be Dr Johnson's way of appreciation. I am ignorant of having done any such action ... Go within and see what wonderful powers the soul acquires in its rise. Sant Mat knows of only one miracle and that is to withdraw the soul of man from transmigration and unite it with its origin.

It is impossible to make an estimate of the powers of saints. They are unfathomable. They are dear "sons" of the dear Father who has entrusted them with all that He has.

∿

206. You write that you expect to come to India in January next. I shall be glad to see you and your dear wife, and we shall do all we can to make you both comfortable while you are here. We live here in an out-of-the-way place on the banks of the river Beas, twenty-seven miles from Amritsar, and about sixty miles from Lahore, which is the capital of the

Punjab province.[1] But few of the comforts to which you have probably been accustomed will be available here. In any case, we will welcome you and do all we can for you.

The highest and the easiest method that the greatest sages of different countries have followed and preached, for the liberation of the soul, is the path of *Surat Shabd Yoga*—which, for want of a better word in the English language, is usually translated as "sound current." The Muslim teachers have called it Sultan-ul-Azkar. *Sultan* means "king" and *azkar* means repetition of the holy Name, this word being the plural of *zikr.*

Once a soul has received initiation from the Master on this path, giving the full method of concentration and other spiritual exercises, the disciple cannot fail to attain ultimate realisation, provided he is faithful to the instructions given to him at the time of initiation and he sticks to the path with increasing love and devotion to the Almighty. But one may read and even memorize all the books of the world, and he may attain all the honours which the world can confer upon him; yet if he fails to come into personal and conscious contact with the sound current, he can make no progress toward the real goal.

As to preparation for the initiation, two or three things may be mentioned. First of all, meat, eggs, fish, and wines or other intoxicating liquors must be given up altogether, as one can make but little progress on this path while he indulges in such things. Perhaps you do not use them anyway. In any case you will not find it difficult to get along without them. There are plenty of wholesome nourishing foods and drinks without them. Even in the worst cases of invalidism, meat and egg products are not necessary.

---

1. This was prior to Partition.

Next begins a rigid system of self-control, enforcing the rule in every detail of life. We are constantly beset by five foes—kam (passion), krodh (anger), lobh (greed), moh (worldly attachments), and ahankar (vanity). All of these must be mastered, brought under control. You can never do that entirely until you have the aid of the Guru and are in harmonic relations with the sound current. But you can begin now, and every effort will be a step on the way.

You may go on studying the teachings as best you can. Read the books you have. Others will be obtained for you, if possible. They will help you to a better understanding of the teachings of the saints, although all books have their limitations and imperfections. By and by, you will be able to write your own books, after you have gained firsthand knowledge. For, you may remember, this is not a system of belief. It is strictly a science. Step by step you will come to *know* for yourself.

~

207.   I am much pleased with the spirit shown in your letter. It is the spirit of a true disciple, and you shall not go unrewarded and unblessed, but your diligent search for the light (spiritual) must bring you to realisation in the proper time. Everything has its time and place, and this cannot be changed, with advantage to all concerned.

You ask why so many hindrances, when one is trying so hard to advance spiritually? Why so many things thrust themselves in to interfere with our best efforts to rise spiritually? There is but one answer—the dark, or negative powers which manage most world affairs do not wish any soul to contact a Satguru who can deliver that soul from the regions of the negative power. He wishes to keep everyone here. And although that negative power is under the Supreme Power, yet within his own territory, he has a certain degree of discretionary power.

It is only when a soul comes in contact with a saint or true Satguru, that he is assured of his complete deliverance from the regions of the negative powers. Of course, those powers will do all they can to keep a soul away from the Satguru. But, in that effort, the negative powers cannot succeed, if one keeps his mind steadfast upon the Guru and persists in his determination to come to the Guru. If he does that, there is no power in the universe which can keep him away from the Guru; and when he is once initiated by the Guru, or even before that, when he has once entrusted his life to the Guru, then and after that the negative power has no more ability to defeat his efforts toward spiritual liberation. He must succeed. A temporary delay like this is no real delay in your spiritual advance, because if you have placed your destiny in the hands of the Guru, he will and must take care of you until the day of your complete and perfect deliverance.

Regarding the meat diet and the advice of your Sufi teacher that eggs and fish and white meat might be advisable, allow me to say that in the study and discipline of Sant Mat, you are not following any system of Hindu philosophy as they are generally known and taught to the world. It is no more like the system of Ramakrishna than the system of the Sufi is like that. It is not like any of the religions or philosophies well known to literature and to the scholars of oriental philosophy. The real Sant Mat, or the teachings of the saints, and the system of yoga which they follow is distinct and individual, and it consists of a definite method of going inside of the Kingdom of Heaven and taking possession of that kingdom. And this is a universal science. It is adaptable to all peoples and all lands, and has absolutely nothing to do with climate or particular condition of any country or people. This much I would strongly emphasize. The view of the Sufi and of his master is a limited view, because they do not know this science and they therefore cannot understand that this is a universal system, suitable for the whole world.

Now, regarding the diet question itself. Most of the old-line physicians adhere to the idea of the necessity of meat and eggs, or at least of eggs, for all who lead a strenuous life, and especially in cold climates. But even that idea is not based upon actual scientific knowledge, but upon an old teaching which they find it hard to discard. Two points must be considered in this study: First, meat and eggs are not necessary for anybody, when looked at from a purely physiological standpoint. There are plenty of good wholesome foods which contain sufficient protein. It is needless to say that one must fully understand where and how to find the proper foods which contain the needed protein content. That must not be overlooked. If that point is overlooked, one may find a deficiency. In a dietary which depends upon meat and eggs for its protein, one may find that he is not getting sufficient. But if one understands where and how to find the protein-bearing foods among vegetables and grains and fruits, he will never have any need whatsoever for meats or eggs. I believe you, as a physician, will understand this.

In the second place, the system of the saints has a very definite method of yoga which reduces the need for excessive quantities of protein. In fact the entire quantity of foods required by the average person—labourer or professional man—will be much reduced; probably fifty percent in some cases, and this will be true no matter in what climate he may live. Besides, the system of yoga which we follow has a very great effect in reducing the effects of the nervous strain of the strenuous life in any climate. If you sit even for an hour as directed at the time of your initiation, you will find that it will still your wandering mind, quieten your nerves, and reduce your heart beat many degrees. All of your life forces will be conserved and you will find yourself growing stronger and less nervous. You will find that you will be able to meet hundreds of people during a strenuous day's work, withstand the discords and the pressure of the most difficult situations, and still keep calm and self-poised.

Now, it is well known to you that meat-eating animals have strength, when put to a sudden test. So also it has been proved in the case of meat-eating men. But they lack endurance. A tiger may exert great strength for a few minutes, but he will never have the endurance that an ox has. What meat-eating animal has the strength of an ox or an elephant?

We have about forty men and women now in America living rigidly under the discipline of this system and they do not complain of any difficulty. Dr Johnson himself declares that he has more strength and endurance now than he had twenty years ago when he was following a meat diet. Miss Bruce here was a vegetarian for many years, in fact almost all of her life, and yet few women can do more hard work than she can do and is doing here now. And hard work for an American woman in this climate is a pretty good test. She is daily doing much hard physical and mental work and feels no need for meat or eggs. It is true that Miss Bruce and Dr Johnson are expert dieticians. They know how to find and prepare a well-balanced diet, without meat or eggs, and that is not so easy a task here as it is in Europe or America. We cannot get just any thing here which we might want, any time of the year. Yet they find plenty to supply every want and keep in health and strength. Miss Bruce says herself that now she is able to do harder work than ever before in her life, and suffers no inconvenience.

So I am sure that upon due trial, you will find no need whatsoever for a meat or egg supplement to your diet. And without meat or eggs, you will at the same time find your strength and calmness of spirit increasing, and your mental powers will increase many fold.

As to any exercises which might help you until the time of your initiation, I can only suggest at this time that you may sit in meditation, in a quiet place, like your own bedroom or some room as secluded as possible, and with spine and body erect, in a comfortable position, fix all the attention at the centre just back of the two eyes, and slowly repeat the words "Radha Soami," fixing the mind on the Supreme Being who is your supreme Father.

This will give you much help and no doubt you will gain some headway. I am sorry the true initiation cannot be given by mail. But this temporary substitute will give you some help—much help in fact. Sit thus as long as you may wish, say one or two hours at a time, at such times as may be most convenient to you. Try to hold your mind from wandering away. Keep it at the centre and force it to rest as nearly still as possible. The soul will rise into greater light, and you will find that your sense of peace and harmony and strength will increase. In this way you will prepare somewhat for the real initiation when you arrive here.

You say you have difficulty with *kam* and *ahankar.* Well, nearly all men have that difficulty. Do not try to fight them, but just subdue them by substituting in their place the opposite virtues as ideals. The old enemies will gradually lose their power over your mind. When the time comes that you actually contact the Shabd Dhun inside, all of the five evils—those troublesome passions—will die out and disappear, because they will find no entertainment in your mind. You will automatically discard them, because you will have a power and a pleasure that supersedes all else.

～

208.   Let me assure you that it is a most fortunate thing in any one's life when he has found a definite purpose and a definite end towards which to work. I am glad you have found that definite end and purpose. You shall not be disappointed.

Regarding your method of sitting, I shall discuss that fully with you when you come here. At present I find no objection to your system, provided that nothing detracts your attention from the centre, back of your eyes, the point at which you are to hold *all attention*—nothing else. Anything that helps you to hold full attention there is good. Anything that in the least detracts from that centre is not good. But, as said before, we will discuss details when you come.

You need not hesitate nor fear to make the trip. Anyone seeking to meet the Satguru, to place his life destiny in the hands of the Guru, has the blessing of the supreme Sat Purush back of him and nothing can defeat that purpose, if the soul persists in deep devotion. Keep your mind on the Satguru who will travel with you, and nothing can hurt you or your beloved wife. Your fate is in the hands of the supreme power.

Of course, you may not expect encouragement in this endeavour. It is quite beyond the grasp of the ordinary man, however worldly wise he may be. But I am much pleased to note what you say—"in the depth of my heart a voice tells me that I must go." Heed that inner voice. It cannot lead you astray. It is true, as your New York friend says, all truth is inside of you. Not only so, but the very Kingdom of Heaven is within you. All wealth is within you. But the difficulty is that you cannot get at that wealth unaided. To all of that the Satguru holds the key. It is given to him by the Supreme Lord, and the method of the Supreme is to work through the Satguru in opening the doors to that inner treasure.

Ask your teacher if he has entered that inner kingdom himself, without a Satguru? No one has ever done so and no one can do so. The rishis, munis, yogis, and sufis, many of them have gone a little way into the subtle worlds, by diligent concentration and rigid self-control. But soon they are stopped—automatically stopped. They can never go far without a real Master to lead the way and take them over difficulties which they can never surmount alone. I am pleased to have you agree that you "cannot consider him as a Satguru." This is extremely fortunate for you. Now your way shall not be blocked by a mistaken devotion to one who is not able to take you very far on the path. Love him by all means, respect and honour him, for all he has done for you. But when a student leaves the freshman class or the primary grades, he looks for a teacher who is himself a Master of Arts if he wishes to win that degree at any later date. On passing to higher grades, one need not cease to love his primary grade teacher. Everyone has his place and his definite work in the Father's school of the soul.

You have reached a high degree in your profession. Now it is due you to reach the highest degree in the university of the spirit. Your face is toward the light. Let nothing hinder or discourage you. You shall drink of the Living Waters, and be thirsty no more. No matter what may be your difficulties and deficiencies; they shall all be overcome, and the divine Shabd whose music never ceases within you shall sooner or later bear you upon its loving waves back to your original home. Have no fear or doubt. So long as one's face is turned uncompromisingly toward the Satguru, he is on his way to perfect realisation. The self-luminous reality, in the form of the audible life stream, when connected by the Satguru, will carry you to the supreme heights. No one can say just how long it will take. But it must be.

~

209.   I am glad to read your progress report. The trembling
and shaking of the body and limbs is not unnatural. It happens with the majority of people who take up this work, but
it stops later on automatically. You may stop it if you can,
otherwise it will stop of itself in time. If a foot or head is suddenly severed from the body, the body will tremble for a time.
The same is the case if the tail of a lizard is cut off from the
body. The soul, which permeates every cell of the body, leaves
it bit by bit in the process of concentration. There is then pain
in the limbs and body and so they shake, sometimes violently.
In every case the agitation is due to the soul leaving the body,
or parts of it. When the withdrawal process has become a routine habit by practice, there is no pain or shaking. When the
concentration is complete and the attention is inside the focus, light will appear, and stray thoughts that now intrude
and interfere will disappear. Then there will come the
realisation that the body is not mine and I am separate from
it; and the body is simply for my use when I wish to function
in this material world.

You are hearing various sounds and have once heard the
bell sound, although not able to hold onto it. It is all a matter
of concentration and of going inside and looking up to catch
it and hold onto it. You have known that there is a bell sound
within, and in time it will be yours.

You may carry on with your practices patiently and
perseveringly, and increase your time slowly, but do not put
yourself under too much strain. Too much strain should be
avoided. The Master is always with you and is giving proper
help and guidance. If at times things go against your wish, it
is for your benefit. For the Master is to do what he thinks
best for you and not what you may think is best for you. Persevere with love and faith, and you will succeed. Guru Nanak
says: "In this path let your foot take a step forward always

and never turn your face backwards. Make good in this very life so that there will be no more rebirth." Says Maulvi Rum: "In this path struggle on and on and do not rest even at the last breath." It is the weakening of the mind that brings failure. Success, even in this material world, comes when one puts himself wholeheartedly into it. Partap, a Rajput prince, carried throughout his life unequal struggle against the great Moghul, Akbar, and then succeeded in the twenty-eighth attack.

Your cancer patient suffered much, but with your help he ended life in peace. His cries and shrieks were due to the awfully bad beatings which the demons of death were giving him. You had Nam. When you came in his presence and held his hands in yours, your current of Nam gave him the protection. The demons left him alone. His attention went in. So he became calm and passed off quietly. The death demons or *yam duts* can never stand in the presence of one who has the power of Nam with him.

$\sim$

210. In your letter you speak of the change in your orientation of life since your return from India and of your attempt to recast your habitat to bring yourself in harmony with this change. When the goal of life is fixed and the means to reach the goal are known, the wise will appreciate the situation and will take full advantage of the leisure and the opportunity that come in their way to reach that goal. To detach the mind from the perishable things of this world and instead to value Nam are signs of special favour of the Creator. You have taken to Sant Mat with the same deep love and faith that this high and invaluable and incomparable philosophy demands. I am glad to see your life moulding to take this new shape.

One and a half hours approximately that you give to simran and a half-hour to dhyan and bhajan is sufficient for the present. Gradual progress is to be preferred. And you have other heavy work to attend to as well. Stilling the wild mind and withdrawing the attention from the body and concentrating it in the eye focus is a slow affair. A Sufi says: "A life-period is required to win and hold the beloved in arms." Concentrating the attention in the eye focus is like the crawl of an ant on a wall. It climbs to fall and falls to rise and to climb again. With perseverance it succeeds and does not fall again. The soul and the mind are very intimately united with matter. We feel pain even when a single hair is pulled from the body surface. But the combination is unreal. Soul and matter are poles asunder. By and by, as the process of separation is continued, you will succeed in detaching the attention from matter. Legs and arms—the extremities of the body—will begin to lose consciousness. The trunk of the body will follow the same course. The whole attention will enter into the eye focus. One will be unconscious of the body and of the material world but fully conscious of a new world within the focus. But one should do simran and bhajan, not as a matter of routine with a heavy heart or as a task, but should take to it with love and eagerness.

Human nature is frail. It is full of weaknesses and one begins to realise the weakness of human nature when one follows Surat Shabd Yoga. Frailties present themselves in almost every conceivable manner and interfere in concentration. But with the help of the Master and the sound current they are overcome, one by one, with every inch of the withdrawal of the current from the body towards the focus. The frailty of human nature is giving place to strength, and when the attention has detached itself from the centres of sense organs, the senses cease to function in this material world haphazardly and are under control.

Mind alone is our enemy. It is with us to keep us out from the eye focus. We realise its power when we practise simran and bhajan. It presents unheard of thoughts and pictures. In this very field the great philosophers and *gyanis* (intellectuals) and theorists fail.

The soul, as it descends from the higher and finer regions into baser and grosser material regions, takes on coverings of these regions to function in them. It could not function there otherwise. These coverings are its weaknesses and the removal of these or, in other words, its going back to higher regions, means regaining its strength. So long as it acts here and is ignorant of other regions, its weakness continues, which cannot be overcome by morality preaching or hearing sermons and reading scriptures, or doing this or that act here.

Do not lose heart but fight courageously. The battle has just begun. Mind is not stronger than the sound current. The Master is with you. He is watching your every movement. He is prepared to fight your battles with you. Take him as your helper. Have faith in him. Fight the mind and you will succeed.

A child grows slowly, but one day becomes a fully grown man. Similarly, daily practice of simran and Nam will bear their fruit in time. When a labourer doing his daily work gets his wages in the evening from his employer, will our Creator withhold his reward from us when we are doing his work? I am glad to learn that you have kept your diet correct and have succeeded in keeping good health on this diet.

I like your idea to keep silent about Sant Mat and Nam so long as you have not made any headway in it. It is not proper to give a medicine to others when one has not experimented with it beforehand and found it useful. Again, the learned and the pundits will ask, "What have you seen?" Then, in the absence of firsthand information, you will have to keep silent. I wish you to give Sant Mat a thorough trial, and if by experience you find it correct, then you can speak of it to others.

You say you do not feel any pain in the limbs as formerly but the left foot aches under the pressure of the right leg after some time; and when the pain becomes unbearable, you change the position. There is nothing wrong in readjusting the position. By and by as the attention will be withdrawn and will collect in the eye focus, the attention will not come down to feel the pain in the leg or foot, and when it has entered the focus and established itself there, all pain will disappear. Do not give any force or pressure or strain on the eyes. The centre of attention is not in the eyes but midway between the eyes. The twitches, shakes and jerks, and balancing motion will all disappear with the withdrawal of attention and the completion of concentration. Have no worries on that account. Such is not the case with all, and with practice even those who suffer from these difficulties get over them.

These very thoughts that come and hinder concentration are to be checked. Since our birth here, we have been daily taking photographs of what we have heard, read, or observed, and storing these in our mind. And the mind is so big that even if we place the whole universe in it, it will be found to be bigger and capable of storing any number of universes and still remain bigger. The thoughts that arise are the same photographs that we have been taking so long and preserving with us. They are not, however, endless. They will finish up in time, with the attention finding its focus. Then this cinema show will end.

As to waking with difficulties, feeling tired and sleepy but after bhajan feeling quite fresh, the mind wants rest. It does not like to go inside, hence plays tricks in the form of feelings of tiresomeness, drowsiness, sleep, and so forth. The soul wants Nam and when it gets it, it pulls up the mind, and the result is peace and joy and freshness. If the soul gets its food, the mind and the body do not feel tired.

You speak of skiing and the snow and the mountains. I have lived in hills during the most part of my service and can well appreciate the scenes depicted in the pictorial cards you have sent me. I congratulate you on your enjoying these mountains and the scenes they present. But these mountains are of this material world and are made up of gross matter. How good and nice it would be if you were to go in, enter the astral plane and see the mountains and so forth there. Then you will be able to see by comparison the difference between these mountains and the mountains within. You also speak of the Master as a saviour. This is yet an idea. There is no doubt that the Master is always with the disciple and gives due guidance and protection. But I wish that your inner eye may open and you may see as a fact what the Master is and what he does for his disciples.

When you were here you may have noticed that all letters, even from India, are not read in public. Most of the letters I open myself; and that which I consider confidential, I ask Rai Sahib to keep in reserve, or I put in my pocket and read out or have it read out privately and then give it to Rai Sahib or some other proper person for reply. American letters I pass on to X for study and for reply after consulting me. Your letter has not been read in public. Special letters are replied in a special way. You may assure Y on my behalf that her correspondence will be kept strictly confidential. If she can send me a typed letter, I will read it myself and will draft a reply. You may please ask her to write to me when she feels like doing so.

Saints do not despise anybody or any system. Whatever they observe inside, they say only that much, and ask others to go inside and verify their statement. They do not ask others to believe them blindly. Their philosophy is not artificial or theoretical. It is going in and observing what is there. No increase or decrease or alteration, no theory or imagination, no construction or destruction—simply observing what is there already. It is a natural science, not manmade. Saints of higher degree, like Shams-i-Tabriz, Maulvi Rum, Khwaja Hafiz, and others, followed the same science. At present there is no higher science or philosophy (whatever you wish to call it) than this. All the saints that speak of Mukam-i-Haq or Sat Nam, no matter in what clime or country or time they appeared, have followed this system—the path of five sound currents. Radha Soami *Mat* (teaching) is not an innovation. It is the same old, old way, given in conformity with the present time.

Dr Johnson was a beginner in this line when he wrote *With a Great Master in India*. It reflects his views of those days. As his experience increased, his ideas changed also, and the manuscript of his coming book which you saw with him will naturally be better than what he wrote before.

In this country the pilgrims take a dip in the waters of the Ganges and think that by so doing their sins are washed off. The river water may cleanse the body but not the mind. They do not know that the nectar that washes off sins is inside of themselves, and the real place for pilgrimage is also inside of themselves. If they were to go inside and connect their souls with the sound current, their sins would be washed off.

~

GLOSSARY

A

abhyas Spiritual practice; spiritual exercise.

abhyasi One who performs spiritual exercise.

adi Primal; first; original.

Adi Granth *or* **Adi Granth Sahib** Literally, primal scripture, also called the "Granth Sahib"; name given to the scripture that enshrines the hymns of the first five Gurus and the ninth Guru in the line of Guru Nanak, and numerous other saints from various parts of India, which makes it a lucid mosaic of esoteric poetry of saints with a variety of religious, cultural, vocational, and geographic backgrounds. The Adi Granth was compiled by Guru Arjun, the fifth Guru, who, representing the universal outlook of all true saints, gave it a broad base and acceptability. Ever since its inception the followers of the Gurus have adopted the Adi Granth as their most sacred scripture.

adi karma Original (*adi*) action causing reaction (*karma*); karma of the beginning, not earned by the individual, but established by the Creator in the beginning. See also: karma.

Agam Lok Inaccessible (*agam*) region (*lok*); the name of the seventh spiritual region. Agam Purush is the Supreme Being presiding over Agam Lok.

ahankar Ego or I-ness; one of the five deadly passions (lust, anger, greed, attachment, ego); pride and vanity; also one of the four divisions of mind, its function is to separate self and self-interests from all else, which leads to erroneous identification with faces and objects of the world. See also: antashkaran.

ahimsa Nonviolence, not hurting any living being, by either word or act.

Ahura Mazda   Ancient Persian name for the lord of life (*ahura*) and lord of wisdom (*mazda*), specially in Zoroastrianism.

Akal   Timeless; beyond birth and death.

Akal Purush   Timeless (*akal*) being (*purush*); the one who is beyond the sphere of birth and death; the supreme positive power, as opposed to Kal, the negative power.

akash   Literally, "sky" or "heaven"; ether, the highest of the five elements, which remains dormant in all living forms except the human. See also: tattwa.

Akash Bani   Sound or voice (*bani*) from the sky (*akash*); heavenly music; Word or Logos; audible life stream. See also: Shabd.

akshar   Indelible; imperishable; Akshar Purush is the appellation for God, the creative power.

Alakh Lok   Invisible (*alakh*) region (*lok*); the sixth spiritual region. Alakh Purush is the Lord of Alakh Lok.

Allah   The Arabic name for God.

Anhad *or* **Anhad Shabd**   Limitless (*anahad*) Sound (*shabd*): the Word or divine creative power. Also called the unstruck sound, logos. See also: Shabd.

Anami Lok   Nameless (*anami*) region (*lok*); the eighth spiritual region, presided over by Anami Purush, Radha Soami, the Supreme Being.

And *or* **Anda**   Literally, "egg"; the astral region, the grand division of the creation lying immediately above the physical realm, Pind.

andi man   astral mind.

antashkaran *or* **antahkaran**   Literally, internal (antar) instruments (karan). Indian philosophy has described four internal-instruments through which cognitive functions are performed: mind (*man*), intellect (*buddhi*), reflective aspect of intellect (*chitt or chit*), and egotism or erroneous identification (*ahankar*).

Anurag Sagar   Believed to be written by Kabir, it is a book of verse in the form of a dialogue between Kabir and his disciple Dharam Das. Modern scholars maintain that this book was written by Dharam Das and not Kabir, and can be described as the sayings of Kabir according to Dharam Das.

Arjun Dev See: Guru Nanak.

Arjuna One of the Pandavas and the hero of the Mahabharata. It was to him that Lord Krishna taught the doctrines known as Bhagvadgita.

asana Posture; in spiritual practice, a meditative pose, with body erect, mind in poise.

Ashtdal Kanwal Eight-petalled (*ashtdal*) lotus (*kanwal*); the name of the centre beyond the eye centre where the disciple first meets the Radiant Form of the Master.

astral region That part of the subtle universe which lies above the physical worlds; the first spiritual region, known as Sahasradal Kanwal.

asura Demons. Asura Lok, the region of demons. In the oldest portions of the Rig Veda, Asura is used for the supreme spirit; later, *sura* came to mean "gods," and *asura*, "demons,"""enemies of God."

atma Soul or spirit. See also: paramatma, jivatma.

atma pad Spirit world, referring generally to the astral plane or first region; more technically, refers to Daswan Dwar, the third spiritual region, where the soul gains self-realization.

aum See: om.

awagawan Coming and going; refers to age-long cycles of births and deaths; transmigration, reincarnation. See also: chaurasi.

B

Baba Jaimal Singh Ji Maharaj The name of the founder of the Radha Soami colony at Beas (Punjab). He was a devoted and highly advanced disciple of Soami Ji Maharaj and was appointed by him in 1877 to carry on the spiritual work with headquarters in the Punjab. He left this world on 29 December, 1903. Several months before he departed, he appointed Huzur Maharaj Baba Sawan Singh Ji as his successor. It was the latter who named the place Dera Baba Jaimal Singh, in honor of his Satguru. In his sacred memory, a *bhandara* is held annually on 29 December at the colony at Beas. He was born in village Ghoman (Punjab) in July, 1839.

Baba Ji Same as Baba Jaimal Singh Ji Maharaj.

babu A title equivalent to Mister or Esquire.

bachan Word; discourse; saying; instruction; order; command.

Bahisht Paradise; the same as Baikunth and Swarg.

Baikunth, Baikuntha, *or* **Baikunth Lok** The abode of Vishnu; the same as Bahisht and Swarg.

Bani Voice, word or teachings; the Voice or Word of God; the audible life stream. See also: Shabd.

Beas The name of a small village, situated on the banks of the Beas river in Punjab.

Bhagvadgita Literally, "The Song of the Lord." It embodies the teachings of Lord Krishna, given in the dialogue between Krishna and Arjuna on the battlefield, and is the most popular book on Hindu philosophy.

bhajan Worship or spiritual practice; listening to the melody of the Shabd within. Also used as an expression of outer devotional songs.

bhakt, bhakta, *or* **bhagat** Devotee.

bhakti Devotion.

bhakti marg The path (*marg*) of devotion (*bhakti*). See also: prem marg.

bhandara Religious feast; large scale feeding of people; esoterically the internal spiritual feast.

Bhanwar Gupha Revolving (*bhanwar*) Cave (*gupha*); the name of the fourth spiritual region.

bibek See: vivek.

bina *or* **been** See: vina.

bodhisattva One who is on the way to attainment of perfect knowledge and has only a certain number of births to undergo before attaining the state of a supreme Buddha.

Brahm The ruler of Trikuti, the second spiritual region; known also as the ruler of Brahm Lok, the name given to the Three Worlds; regarded by many as the Supreme Being.

Brahma God of creation in the Hindu trinity of creator, preserver, destroyer (Brahma, Vishnu, Shiva).

brahmacharya   The practice of celibacy, remaining continent.

Brahmand *or* **Brahmanda**   Literally, "egg of Brahm"; the grand division of the creation extending from Anda up to Bhanwar Gupha; the entire universe over which Brahm has jurisdiction.

brahmandi   Pertaining to Brahmand; universal.

brahmandi manas   Universal mind, which rules the subtle worlds, such as heaven, hell, etc.

brahmin   A member of the highest of the four Hindu castes; a priest.

buddh, budh, *or* **buddhi**   Intellect; one of the four phases of mind. See also: antashkaran.

Buddha   The great sage, Prince Siddhartha of the Sakya clan. The religion of Buddhism is based on his teachings.

C

causal region   See: Trikuti.

chakra   Wheel; centre; ganglion; any of the six energy centres in the human body, with parts resembling the petals of a lotus. See also: kanwal.

chaurasi   Eighty-four; the wheel of eighty-four, or the wheel of transmigration. The name indicates the concept in Indian mythology and Hindu scriptures of eight million, four hundred thousand species in the creation. Mystics have adopted this phrase to tell of the multiplicity of births that souls pass through in the creation, according to the law of karma. See also: karma, awagawan.

chela   Disciple.

chetan   Conscious; awakened; spirit; conscious living as opposed to *jar* (inert or inanimate); reason; soul; self; intelligence; wisdom; also called Chaitanya.

Chetan Akash   The heavenly region above the eyes; part of the first region of spirituality.

Chidakash   The same as Chetan Akash.

chit, chitt, *or* **chitta**   Reflective aspect of intellect; one of the four divisions of mind; the faculty of remembering anddiscerning beauty, form and color. See also: antashkaran.

D

Dadu (1544-1603): A saint of Rajputana, well known for his bold utterances in his beautiful poetry.

dama Restraining or subduing the passions, curbing the mind.

dand Self-discipline; punishment; law of life.

darshan Vision, sight or seeing; implies looking intently at the Master with a deep feeling of respect, devotion and one-pointed attention.

Daswan Dwar Literally, the tenth door; an appellation of the third spiritual region. Trikuti is said to have an inner *garh* (citadel) having ten gates, nine of which are open. The tenth, that leads to the third region, is closed; hence, the third region itself is called Daswan Dwar. In fact, both Sunn and Maha Sunn are referred to as Daswan Dwar—Sunn being the region itself, and Maha Sunn, being the region of intense darkness between Daswan Dwar and Bhanwar Gupha (the fourth region).

daya Mercy; grace.

dayal Compassionate one; a term for the Supreme Being, the positive and merciful power, as opposed to Kal, the lord of judgment, who metes out relentless justice.

Dera Camp or colony. In this book the name refers to the Radha Soami colony, situated on the banks of the river Beas, in the Punjab.

Dera Baba Jaimal Singh P.O. address of Radha Soami colony, Beas.

desh Country or region; inner region. See also: Sat Desh.

Dev Lok Region of the gods.

deva *or* **devta** Shining ones; personifications of the forces of nature; gods, angels.

dham Region or abode; place or home. See also: Radha Soami Dham.

Dharam Rai Literally, "King Judge," the lord of justice, who administers reward or punishment to the soul after death, according to its own actions during life.

dharma   Righteousness or duty; moral and religious duty in life; also used as a synonym for "religion."

dharma megha   A particular state of concentration (*samadhi*) which frees the mind from all activity, inward or outward; a person in such a state is said to radiate a light like a mantle of glory.

dhun   Sound or melody; the Word; the heavenly music. See also: Shabd.

dhunatmak, dhunatmik, or dhunyatmak nam   The inexpressible primal sound, which cannot be written or spoken or heard with the physical ears; the inner music which can be experienced only by the soul. See also: Shabd.

dhyan   Inner contemplation. A meditation technique taught by saints in which the devotee contemplates on the form of the Master within.

din dayal   *Din* means "humble"; *dayal* means "merciful"; hence, "merciful to the humble."

Dwapar Yuga   The Copper Age, the third yuga in the cycle of the ages. See also: yuga.

F

faqir *or* **fakir**   Arabic term for a holy man; an ascetic or a religious mendicant.

G

Ganges *or* **Ganga**   A sacred river in India. Many places of pilgrimage are situated on the banks of this river.

Ghat Ramayana   Name of a book by Tulsi Sahib of Hathras. It is written in beautiful poetry and is strictly an epic of the soul, as distinguished from the Ramayana by Tulsi Das, who lived in another age. Ghat Ramayana pertains to the ascent of the soul within.

Gita   See Bhagvadgita.

Granth   A book, especially a religious scripture; the Sikh scriptures.

Granth Sahib   A title of respect given by the Sikhs to the Adi Granth. See also: Adi Granth.

guna   Attribute or quality; there are three attributes or qualities of primordial matter (*prakriti*) out of which the creation proceeds (harmony, action, and inertia), the source of which is in Trikuti. See also: satogun, rajogun, tamogun.

gurbani   Literally, "teachings of the Guru," esoterically, Nam, Shabd, or Word. Also means what has been written in the Granth Sahib; teachings of the saints; sometimes a particular book, such as the Granth Sahib, Sar Bachan, etc., is also referred to as Gurbani.

gurbhakta   Devotee of a Guru.

gurbhakti   Devotion to a Guru.

Gurdwara   The name used by the Sikhs for their house of worship.

Gurmat   Teachings of the Guru; same as Sant Mat.

gurmukh   One whose face is turned towards the Guru; one who has completely surrendered to the Guru as opposed to one who is slave to the mind (*manmukh*); a highly advanced soul; a term sometimes used for a saint or perfect Master.

gurmukhta   The quality of being a *gurmukh*; devotion and surrender to the Guru; obedience.

Gurmukhi   Punjabi language, so called because it was the language of Guru Nanak.

Guru   Master; teacher; spiritual enlightener.

Guru Granth Sahib   See: Adi Granth.

Guru Nanak (1469-1539):   He was born at Talwandi, near Lahore (now in Pakistan). His parents were Kalu and Tripta. Guru Nanak condemned the orthodox creed of the people with great vigor, and he laid emphasis on the spiritual aspect of religion and on love of God and man. He undertook four major tours to propagate his teachings. The following were his successors to the mastership:

Guru Angad (1504-1552): Second in the line of succession.

Guru Amardas (1479-1574): Third in the line of succession.

Guru Ramdas (1534-1581): Fourth in the line of succession.

Guru Arjan Dev (1563-1606): Fifth in the line of succession.

Guru Hargovind (1595-1644): Sixth in the line of succession.

Guru Har Rai (1630-1661): Seventh in the line of succession.

Guru Harkishan (1656-1664): Eighth in the line of succession.

Guru Tegh Bahadur (1621-1675): Ninth in the line of succession.

Guru Gobind Singh (1666-1708): Tenth in the line of succession.

gyan   Knowledge; True knowledge; spiritual knowledge; spiritual wisdom; spiritual enlightenment.

gyani   A learned person; one who practices or walks on the path of knowledge and wisdom (*gyan*).

gyan marg   The path or way (*marg*) of learning. See also: bhakti marg.

gyan yoga   That form of yoga which attempts to achieve God-realization through the acquisition of knowledge. See also: gyan marg.

H

Hafiz   A famous poet-saint of Persia.

Haq   Literally, truth; Arabic designation of the fifth spiritual region.

Hazrat Mohammed   Prophet and founder of Islam.

hansa   Swan; symbolic of purity, the name given to the highly evolved souls in the regions beyond Brahm; the less-evolved souls are often likened to crows.

Hardwar   A place of pilgrimage. It is from this place that the Ganges, coming from the mountains, gathers volume and flows out into the plains. Orthodox Hindus immerse the ashes of their departed relatives into the river at this place, believing that this will secure salvation for the departed ones.

hatha yoga   One of the Indian systems of yoga, which deals only with the physical body.

Huzur *or* **Hazur**   Term of respect used in addressing or applied to kings, holy men, and high personages.

I

ida *or* **ira**   See: sushumna or Shah Rag.

Ism-i-Azam   The greatest Name; Shabd; Sound; inner music; Word.

J

Japji Sahib   The first portion of the Granth Sahib, which consists of the sayings of Guru Nanak and which contains the essence of the entire Granth Sahib.

jat   A caste in modern India, following mostly the agricultural and military professions.

ji   An honorific term which indicates respect and endearment.

jiv *or* **jiva**   Any living being; the individual or unliberated soul; sometimes used to denote human beings generally.

jivan mukti   Salvation while alive, spiritual liberation during this lifetime.

jivatma   Soul embodied in the physical form.

jnana yoga   See: gyan yoga.

jot *or* **jyoti**   Light, flame; refers to the light of the first spiritual region, Sahasradal Kanwal.

K

Kabir Sahib   A well-known saint (1398-1518) who lived in Benares (Kashi), and preached and practiced Surat Shabd Yoga. He condemned the follies and the external observances of Hindus and Muslims alike. He was succeeded by Dharam Das.

Kal   Time or death; the negative power; the universal mind; the ruler of the three perishable worlds (physical, astral, causal); also called Dharam Rai, the lord of judgment, and Yama, the lord of death. Kal's headquarters are in the second spiritual region, Trikuti, of which he is the ruler. Another name for Brahm.

Kalma   Arabic for Bani; Word; Shabd.

Kalyug *or* **Kalyuga**   The fourth cycle of Time, known as the Dark Age or the Iron Age. It is the age in which we live now. See Yuga.

kam   Lust, passion, desire; one of the five passions (lust, anger, greed, attachment, ego). See also: krodh, lobh, moh, ahankar

karam kanda   Rituals, rites, ceremonies, and outward practices in the various religions.

karan   Causual; cause.

karan man The Casual Mind, which rules the casual region and extends to the top of Brahm.

karan sharir Causal body; also called seed body (*bij sharir*), because the seeds of all karmas reside in it; all such actions or karmas manifest in the lower astral and physical body. The causal bodycorresponds to the causal region. See also: Trikuti.

karma Action; the law of action and reaction; the debits and credits resulting from our deeds, which bring us back to the world in future lives to reap their fruits. There are three types of karma: *pralabdh* or *prarabdh karma,* the fate or destiny we experience in the present life which has been shaped by certain of our past actions; *kriyaman karma,* the debits and credits created by our actions in this life, to be reaped in future lives; *sinchit* or *sanchit karma,* the balance of unpaid karmas from all our past lives, the store of karmas.

Karvat The name of the saw at Benares. The priests in charge claimed that anyone who had his head cut off by it would go to heaven. This practice has been stopped.

khat chakras The six centres of ganglia in the body.

khat sampatti The six types of riches, or moral and spiritual wealth:

1. Sama—balance or equanimity.
2. Dama—self-restraint.
3. Uparati—freedom from ceremonial worship.
4. Titiksha—patience.
5. Sharaddha—faith.
6. Samadhanta—deep meditation.

kanwal *or* **kamal** Lotus; an image used to describe the energy centres, both in the physical body and in the inner regions. See also: chakra; Sahasradal Kanwal.

Koran Same as Quran.

Krishna Lord Krishna, held to be a complete incarnation of Lord Vishnu. He delivered the celebrated Song of the Lord, called Bhagvadgita.

Kritya Yuga Same as Sat Yuga.

kriyaman Karma created in the present life. See also: karma.

krodh Anger; one of the five deadly passions (lust, anger, greed, attachment, and ego). See also: kam, lobh, moh, ahankar.

kundalini Coiled energy situated at the base of the spine, above the lowest centre (*mul chakra*). When aroused, it rises up through the central canal of the spine, unwinding serpentlike; a practice to be shunned by satsangis, as it can easily dissipate spiritual energy and cause illness, insanity or death.

L

laya yoga A form of yoga in which the disciple merges his individuality in that of the Guru or Shabd.

lobh Greed, one of the five deadly passions (lust, anger, greed, attachment, and ego). See also: kam, krodh, moh, ahankar.

lok Region; world.

M

magi The wise men of the East; priests of ancient Persia.

maha Great.

Mahabharat *or* **Mahabharata** The great epic poem of ancient India, the leading subject of which is the great war between the Kauravas and the Pandavas. The object of the great struggle was the kingdom whose capital was Hastinapur, fifty-seven miles northeast of Delhi. See: Pandavas.

Mahadev *or* **Mahadeo** The third of the Hindu Triad; the same as Shiva.

Maha Kal Ruler of the upper part of Brahmand; same as Kal.

maha nada Great music; the inner music, or audible life stream.

Maha Sunn The region of intense darkness, situated above Sunn or Daswan Dwar proper, and below Bhanwar Gupha. It is really one of the six great spiritual regions, but the saints do not refer to it as such so that their disciples, for their own protection, do not start dwelling upon it. It can be crossed only with the help of a spiritual Master. Hence, though there are six great spiritual regions, only five are named as such in Sant Mat literature, and this one is included in the five without mentioning it as a separate region. Therefore, Daswan Dwar is really Sunn and Maha Sunn combined.

Maharaj   Literally, great king; a title of respect.

mahatma   Great soul; also applied to highly spiritual persons.

Maha Yuga   See: Yuga.

Mahesh *or* **Maheshwar**   The same as Shiva.

Man (pronounced mun)   Mind.

manas   Mind; pertaining to the mind.

manmukh   Literally, facing the mind; one who obeys the dictates of the mind; a materialist or worldly person as opposed to a spiritual person. See also: gurmukh.

Mansur   A Muslim saint of Persia (870-923 A.D.).

Manu   An ancient lawgiver who divided Indian society into the four castes.

mardang   A musical instrument, resembling a long drum; also called mridang.

marg   Path or way.

mat   Creed; system; way; religion; teachings.

mauj   Literally, wave; will; especially the will and pleasure of the Sat Guru or the Supreme Being.

Mauj Puri   A place of Hindu pilgrimage.

Maulvi   A Muslim priest; one learned in Islamic religion and theology.

Maulvi Rum, Maulana Rum *or* **Rumi**   A well-known Muslim saint of Persia (1207-1277), who was a devoted disciple of Shamas-i-Tabriz; author of the world-famous *Masnavi*.

maya   Illusion or delusion; deception; unreality, phenomenal universe; all that is not eternal, is not real or true is called maya; it appears but is not. The veil of maya's illusion conceals the vision of God from our sight.

moh   Attachment; worldly attachments or entanglements; one of the five deadly passions (lust, anger, greed, attachment, ego). See also: kam, krodh, lobh, ahankar.

Mohammed   See: Hazrat Mohammed.

moksha   Salvation or liberation from the cycle of transmigration.

Mukam-i-Haq   Same as Sat Lok.

mul chakra   The rectal plexus.

mumuksha   One who desires to attain liberation (*moksha*).

Mundaka   The name of one of the Upanishads.

muni   A sage; holy man; one who contemplates.

murshid   Persian Islamic term for Master.

N

nabhi   Navel.

Nad   Sound; Shabd; Word; inner music.

Nad-bindu   The Sound out of which all things grow; the name of one of the Upanishads.

Nam *or* **Name**   Name; the Shabd, Logos, or Word; the divine creative power.

nam bhakti   Devotion to nam.

Nanak   See: Guru Nanak.

neel chakra *or* **nil chakra**   Blue centre, esoteric term for a certain stage in the ascent of the soul within.

newli karma *or* **neoli karma**   A yogic exercise of lowering the shoulders and flattening the back and, by the force of the breath, moving the abdomen right and left as well as up and down, as curds are churned in the churning vessel.

nij   Literally, means "one's own"; real; higher; innermost.

nij dham   One's own real home.

nijmanas   The inner mind, corresponding to causal body (*karan sharir*).

niranjan   Literally, means pure; an appellation of the Lord of the first spiritual region.

nirat   The soul's power of seeing; the attention inside.

nirguna   Without attributes; appellation for God. See also: guna.

nirvikalpa   Unwavering, concentrated; a state of deep meditation (*samadhi*) in which the disciple cannot distinguish himself from the object of meditation.

nuqta-i-swaida   Black point; third eye; Arabic name for *tisra til* or third eye.

nuri sarup   Light body; the Radiant Form of the Master; the astral form.

O

om   The sound symbol of Brahm; audible life stream or sound of the second spiritual region. See also: Shabd.

Ormuzd   The old Persian and Parsi term for God; an angel; also the planet Jupiter.

P

Padam Puran   A mythological book giving a detailed account of the cycles of the four yugas.

Paltu Sahib *or* **Paltoo Sahib** (1710–1780):   A famous Indian saint noted for his bold and clear description of the path of the Masters, which leads to the highest spiritual region.

Pandavas   The five Pandavas were the sons of Pandu, who was the brother of Dhrita-rashtra, King of Hastinapur. Dhrita-rashtra was blind, and Pandu died at a young age. The sons of Dhrita-rashtra were called the Kauravas. The Pandavas were deprived of their rightful inheritance, which was the cause of the great war between the Pandavas and the Kauravas, known as the Mahabharat.

pandit *or* **pundit**   One learned in Hindu theology and religion; the Hindu priestly class; Brahman priest; any Brahman.

par   Beyond.

Paramatma *or* **Parmatma**   The supreme soul or God. See also: Radha Soami.

param sant   A supreme saint; a saint who has attained the highest spiritual region.

Parbrahm   Beyond Brahm; the regions beyond Brahm Lok.

parmarth   Spiritual way of life; spiritual work; spiritual gain; spiritual effort; spiritual uplift.

parshad, parshadi, *or* **prasad**   Anything sanctified or blessed.

Patanjali   An ancient sage, known for his treatise on yoga.

pie   Smallest Indian coin, lowest in value, no longer in use.

Pind *or* **Pinda**   The physical universe; the physical body of man; the name of the lowest grand division of the creation. See also: Anda, Brahmand, Sach Khand.

pindi man   Physical (lower or material) aspect of the mind which governs the physical frame and senses.

pingala   See: sushumna.

prakriti   Nature; jyoti; maya; female energy or *shakti* of any deity; the essential nature of mind and matter, which projects itself in various forms of emotions and actions, and which also influences the various parts of the body; *prakritis* are twenty-five in number and consist of five principal manifestations of the five elements in the body.

prakritis   These are twenty-five in number and consist of five manifestations of each of the five elements or *tattwas*:

1. ether – Desires, anger, bashfulness, fear, infatuation.
2. air – Running, walking, smelling, contracting, expanding.
3. fire – Hunger, thirst, sleep, personality, laziness.
4. water – Vital fluid, blood, fat, urine, saliva.
5. earth – Bones, flesh, skin, veins, hair.

pralabdh *or* **prarabdh**   The fate karma; our destiny in this life, created by actions in past lives upon which the present life is based. See also: karma.

prana *or* **pran**   Vital force, essence or vital air.

pranayam   Part of the Patanjal yoga system, which attempts to control the vital air (*pran*), mainly through breath control. This practice is not recommended without an adept or Guru as a guide. See also: Guru.

prem marg   The path (*marg*) of love (*prem*); the path of the saints. Also called: bhakti marg.

purush   A being; creative energy; man.

Purusha and Prakriti region   The first spiritual region, where *prakriti* or *jyoti* has merged into Niranjan. *Purusha* and *prakriti* extend up to Brahm; then Brahm alone remains, up to Par Brahm.

Q

Quran *or* **Koran**   The holy book of the Muslims, revealed to Prophet Mohammed.

R

radha   Primal soul.

Radha Soami *or* **Radha Swami**   Lord (*soami*) of the soul (*radha*); appellation of the absolute Supreme Being.

Radha Soami Din Dayal   Literally, "Lord of the Soul, merciful to the humble."

Raheem, Rahim, *or* **Rahman**   Literally, "merciful", "forgiving"; used as a reference to God; Allah.

rajogun *or* **rajas**   The creative or active attribute (guna). See also: tamogun, satogun.

Raj Yoga   A practice that deals with the control of the currents of the mind by increasing the power of the mind through contemplation and certain postures. This practice is not recommended without an adept or Guru as guide.

Ram *or* **Rama**   A name for God; the power that pervades everything: a Hindu god.

Ramayana   The oldest of Sanskrit epic poems, written by the sage Valmiki. The Ramayana by Tulsi Das was written much later.

Ram Chandra   The same as Rama, king of Ayodhya, the seventh incarnation of the god Visnhu, believed to have lived in the Treta Yuga or second age. The story of his life is the subject of the Ramayana in Sanskrit by Valmiki.

Rehman   Same as Rahman.

rishi   One who sees, enlightened one; sage of ancient India, having some level of spiritual attainment, though usually not a saint. See also: sant, yogi.

roop   Form.

S

Sach Khand, Sat Desh, Sat Lok *or* **Nij Dham**   True or imperishable region, the name of the fifth spiritual region (Sat Lok) or the highest grand division of the creation. Region of the true Lord (Sat Purush, Sat Nam).

sadhu *or* **sadh**   One who has controlled the mind; technically, a devotee who has crossed the region of mind and matter and reached the third spiritual region (Daswan Dwar); sometimes applied to one who has gained the second region (Trikuti); generally, a holy man following a path of spiritual discipline.

sadhu seva   Rendering service to *sadhus*.

Sahansdal Kanwal, Sahans Dal Kamal, *or* **Sahasradal Kamal**   The thousand-petalled lotus, the name of the first spiritual region; the astral region.

sahib   Lord; honorable sir; a term of respect.

samadhan   Deep meditation, superconsciousness; a state of rapture.

samadhi   A state of concentration in which all consciousness of the outer world is transcended.

samhita   A code of laws, e.g., the Manu Samhita.

sannyasi   One who has renounced the world, who is free from attachments.

sannyasin   Feminine form of *sannyasi*.

sanskara   Impressions or tendencies from previous births, early upbringing, traditions and social influences, which shape the basic outlook and behavior patterns of a human being.

sanskari   One with a previous background; best fitted spiritually; predestined; a seeker after God.

sant   Saint; one who has attained the fifth spiritual region (Sach Khand); a God-realized soul. See also: Param Sant, Sant Mat.

Sant Mat   The teachings (*mat*) of the saints (*sant*). See also: Surat Shabd Yoga.

Sant Satguru   A saint who is also a spiritual teacher. Everyone who has reached the fifth spiritual region is a saint, but not all of them accept followers or are designated to teach. Hence, every true Master or Satguru is a saint, but not all saints are Satgurus.

sar Essential; important; real; essence; true.

Sar Bachan Literally, essential, true, or important words. The name of a book by Soami Ji.

Sar Shabd *or* **Sar Shabda** The essence (*sar*) of the Word or Sound (*shabd*); the pure Shabd, free from matter, above Trikuti. See also: Anhad Shabd.

sat True, real, everlasting. See also: Satguru, Sat Desh, Sat Lok, Sat Purush.

Sat Desh True (*sat*) home or region (*desh*); another name for Sach Khand. See also: Sat Lok.

Satguru *or* **Satgur** True (*sat*) spiritual teacher (*guru*); perfect Master; true light-giver; a Master who has access to the fifth spiritual region (Sach Khand). A *Satguru* teaches utmost humility, truth and compassion, earns his own living, and never charges for his teachings.

Satguru seva Service to the Satguru; the real way to render him service, and that which he will always accept, is for the disciple to attend to meditation regularly.

Sat Lok True (*sat*) region (*lok*); another name for Sach Khand. See also: Sat Desh.

Sat Nam True (*sat*) Name (*nam*); the unspoken, unwritten Name or Word of God, the supreme Creator, lord of the fifth spiritual region, original source of souls; the true spiritual Father. See also: Sat Purush.

sato guna, satogun, *or* **satwa guna** The quality or attribute of rhythm, harmony, and truth. See also Gunas.

Sat Purush True or eternal (*sat*) being (*purush*); Supreme Being; God: lord of the fifth spiritual region. See also: Sat Nam.

satsang True (*sat*) company (*sang*); association with the true; the company of or association with a perfect Master is external satsang; association of the soul with the Radiant Form of the Master, the Shabd or Nam within, is internal satsang. The highest form

of satsang is to merge in the Shabd. A congregation assembled
to hear a spiritual discourse is also referred to as satsang; even
to think about the Master and his teachings is a form of satsang.

satsangi   One who associates with the true; initiate of a perfect
Master; esoterically, one who has reached the first stage.

Sat Shabd   Literally, True Word; the Divine Sound.

Sat Yuga   True (*sat*) age (*yuga*), the Golden Age, the first of the
four great cycles of time. See also: yuga.

Sawan   The chief rainy month in India, which corresponds with
the latter part of July and the first two weeks of August.

Sawan Singh Ji Maharaj   Known as "the Great Master," he was the
favourite and devoted disciple of Baba Jaimal Singh Ji in the
Punjab. While Baba Jaimal Singh Ji was the one who first settled
in and established what is known as the Radha Soami colony at
Beas, it was Sawan Singh Ji Maharaj who actually built and developed it into the flourishing place which it now is. He attracted
souls from all walks of life and from all corners of the world. He
was born in village Jatana near Mehmansinghwalla, District
Ludhiana (Punjab), his ancestral home, on July 19/20,[1] 1858,
was appointed successor by Baba Jaimal Singh Ji Maharaj in
1903 and assiduously served in that capacity until his departure
on 2 April, 1948.

seva *or* **sewa**   Service; voluntary service to the Master or his disciples.
Of the four types of seva (monetary, physical, mental, spiritual),
the highest form is the spiritual—the meditation practice.

Shabd *or* **Shabda**   Word or Sound; spiritual sound; audible life
stream; sound current. The creative power, the source of all creation, which manifests as sound and light in the spiritual regions. It is the Word or Logos of the Bible; Kalma, Isme-i-Azam,
Bang-i-Asmani, or Kalam-i-Ilahi of the Koran; the Nad of the
Vedas; Nam, Ram Nam, Gurbani, Bani, and Dhun of the Adi

---

1. July 27th had previously been given as the birth date as that is the date on
which it used to be celebrated at the Dera. The actual birth date was 5th Sawan
1915 Bikrami, according to the Indian Calendar, which corresponds to the 19th/
20th July, 1858.

Granth; the Tao of the Chinese; Vadan; and the Saut-i-Surmad of the Sufis. The Zoroastrians call it Shraosha, and it is known by many other names. The secret of hearing the Shabd within oneself can be imparted only by a true Master (*Satguru*). See also: Shabd-dhun, Surat Shabd Yoga, Anhad Shabd.

shabds Hymns; paragraphs or stanzas of sacred texts put to music; often sung by a singer (*pathi*) accompanying a discourse at satsang. These are external sounds, as opposed to inner Sound (*Shabd*). See also: Shabd, satsang.

Shabd Yog Same as Surat Shabd Yog.

Shabd-dhun Music (*Dhun*) of the Word (*shabd*); the Shabd; the audible life stream.

Shabd marg The path (*marg*) of the Word (*shabd*); the path of Shabd Yoga, the path of the saints. See also: Surat Shabd Yoga.

Shah Rag *or* **Shah Rug** Literally, "royal vein," but this does not refer to a vein in the physical body. It is the central current or canal in the finer body, which is located and traversed by means of spiritual practice according to the instructions of a true Master. It is the same as *sushmana* or *sushmuna*, which is the central current. The current on the left is called *ida* or *ira*, and that on the right is known as *pingala*.

shakti Power, ability or strength; the highest form of *maya*, or illusion.

Shamas-i-Tabriz *or* **Shams-i-Tabriz (1206-1248):** Shams-Uddin Mohammed Tabriz, better known as Shams-i-Tabriz, a famous Muslim Saint of Persia, was born in Tabriz, Iran. He was the Master of Maulana Rum who named his composition after the name of his Master—Diwan-i-Shams-Tabriz. He was assassinated by religious fanatics.

Shankaracharya A great commentator of the Vedanta Sutras and the Upanishads.

shanti Peace; peace of mind.

shariat Islamic code of life, religious law, justice; Koranic law and ritual.

Shastras Hindu scriptures; books of philosophy and moral code.

Shiva   God of destruction in the Hindu trinity of creator, preserver, destroyer (Brahma, Vishnu, Shiva).

shraddha   Faith, belief, reverence.

Shraosha   Zarathrustra used the term to refer to the inner Sound, the Shabd. It is referred to as the most majestic aspect or power of Ahura Mazda because it brings eternal life.

sikh *or* **shiskya**   Literally, disciple or follower; the same as chela; the followers of Guru Nanàk and his nine successors are known as Sikhs. The name also applies to one who has reached the first spiritualregion within.

sikhi   The path of discipleship.

simran *or* **sumiran**   Repetition or loving remembrance; repetition of the five holy names according to the instructions of a perfect Master. The simran that a perfect Master gives is charged with his power; disciples concentrate the attention at the third eye (*tisra til*) and carry on repetition with love and one-pointed attention. This practice enables them to withdraw the soul currents from the body to the third eye, from where the real spiritual journey begins.

sinchit *or* **sanchit**   The store of unpaid past karmas. It is from this store that the fate karmas (*pralabdh*) are drawn. See also: karma.

Soami *or* **Swami**   Lord; the Supreme Being; the Master; commonly applied to all spiritual teachers. See also: Radha Soami.

Soami Ji *or* **Swami Ji (1818-1878):**   The Great Saint and founder of what is now known as the Radha Soami faith, science and philosophy. His real name was Seth Shiv Dayal Singh. See Radha Soami Dayal.

Sufi   An adherent of Sufism, which is a mystic sect developed in Persia, who believe in a living Murshid (Guru) and lead a holy life. The term is now being used to denote any holy man among the Muslims.

Sukshm Sarup   Subtle form; astral body.

Sukshm Shahrir   Same as Sukshm Sarup.

Sultan-ul-Azkar   Literally, the king of methods. A reference to the Surat Shabd yoga.

Suméru   Another name for Mount Meru, the place where gods are said to reside; symbolically, the top ofthe spine. It is also called the Golden Mountain, Jewel Park, Lotus Mountain, and Mountain of the gods.

Sunn *or* **Sunna**   Derived from Sanskrit *shunya*, it has usually been translated as void, emptiness, vacuum; but the saints have not used this term in this meaning. According to them it is an inner spiritual region which is devoid of matter in any form. On entering this region the soul becomes free from the bondage of matter, mind and the three attributes.

Surat   Soul; consciousness; inner attention. As consciousness in the body is due to the presence of the soul, hence the soul is also called *surat*.

Surat Shabd Yoga   The practice of joining the soul (*surat*) with the Word (*shabd*) and merging (*yoga*) with it; once the soul merges into the Shabd, it is carried by the Shabd to its source, the Lord.

sushumna *or* **sushmana**   The central current in the finer body, starting from the eye centre and leading upward to the higher spiritual regions, located and traversed by means of the spiritual practice taught by a perfect Master; also known as *Shah Rag*. It is not to be confused with *sushumna* of the yogis, which is the central canal along the spine in the lower body and is to be ignored by satsangis and spiritual practitioners. The *sushumna* divides into two currents, on the left is *ida* and on the right is *pingala*.

swarath   Worldly duties; worldly work; selfishness.

Swarg, Swarga, *or* **Swarg Lok**   Heaven or Paradise in general; the same as Bahisht and Baikunth.

T

tama, tamo-guna, *or* **tamogun**   The attribute of dissolution, inertia, darkness. See also: guna, satogun, rajogun.

Tathagata   One who has attained; a name for the Buddha.

tattwa   Elements, essence; the five elements are present, to various degrees, in all living beings: earth(*prithvi*), water (*jal*), fire (*agni*), air (*vayu*), and ether (*akash*).

til Literally, seed of the sesamum plant; esoterically, the small aperture through which the soul enters Brahmand from Pind; the centre between the eyebrows.

tisra til Third (*tisra*) eye (*til*); a point in the subtle body, between and behind the two eyebrows; the seat of the mind and the soul in the human body, and the point at which the disciples of the saints begin their concentration, and from where they go up. Also called 'the "black point" (*nuqta-i-saveida*) by Sufis and 'the "single eye" in the Bible.

titiksha Endurance, patience; power of enduring hardships with calmness and peace.

Treta Yuga The Silver Age, the second grand cycle of time, immediately following the Golden Age (Sat Yuga). See also: yuga.

Trikuti Three prominences; that part of the subtle universe which lies above the astral world; the name of the second spiritual region; the causal region. Also called: Brahm Lok.

Triloki Three worlds: the physical world (Pind), astral world (Anda) and the causal world (Brahmand), all ruled by Brahm.

Tulsi Das A Saint of medieval times, author of the Ramayana in Hindi.

Tulsi Sahib A great poet-saint of Hathras, and exponent of Sant Mat and the author of *Ghat Ramayana*. He was born in the princely family of Peshwas in 1763 and was heir to the throne of the kingdom of Poona and Sitara. He began to show signs of a devotional trend of mind at a very early age, and had no attachments or desires for worldly pleasures and pursuits. A few days before his coronation was to take place, he left his home and fled towards the North in the garb of a sadhu. He settled in Hathras, near Aligarh, in the U.P., where he was known as Dakkhini Baba (the Sage from the South). Soami Ji's mother was a disciple of Tulsi Sahib long before Soami Ji was born, and Soami Ji himself received Light from him. Tulsi Sahib departed from this world in 1848.

Turiya Pad Another name for Sahansdal Kanwal. The state of superconsciousness where the soul makes its first contact with the real Shabd.

U

Upanishads The philosophical and mystical part of the Vedas relating to esoteric teachings. Upanishad literally means "to sit near or close," and the doctrines were so named because these secrets and mysteries were personally imparted to the disciple by the teacher.

uparati Renunciation; detachment from all worldly desires.

V

Vah Guru *or* **Wahi Guru** The Sikh name for God; the Supreme Lord.

vairagya Detachment, particularly mental detachment from the world and worldly desires; a state of mind—not to be confused with asceticism or physical renunciation of the world.

vairagi One who has attained detachment.

varnatmak Describable; that which can be spoken or written. See also: dhunatmak.

Vedant *or* **Vedanta** A system of Indian philosophy, based particularly on the Upanishads, believing in the unitary existence of God and the identity of the soul with God.

Vedantic Pertaining to Vendanta.

Vedas Literally, knowledge; revealed as embodied in the four holy books of the Hindus: Rig Veda, Sam Veda, Yajur Veda and Atharva Veda.

Vedic Pertaining to the Vedas.

vina, veena *or* **beena, bina** A stringed musical instrument, perhaps the oldest of the classical musical instruments in India, said to be the forerunner of the sitar. While *vina* is the correct name for this stringed instrument referred to in Sant Mat literature, some authors have used the term *bin* or *been*, which should not be confused with the Scottish bagpipe. The exact

sound of the region of Sach Khand cannot be conveyed in terms
of any material musical instrument, as nothing in this world
comes anywhere near that divine melody. In fact, like the light
of that region, its sound also defies terrestrial comparison.

Vishnu   God of preservation in the Hindu trinity of creator, preserver, destroyer (Brahma, Vishnu, Shiva).

vivek   Discrimination; searching inquiry, careful study, as the first
step on the path of the Masters.

W

Wahiguru   Same as Vah Guru.

wheel of   See: chaurasi.

Y

yag, yagya, *or* **yajna**   Sacrifice, a ritual or religious ceremony, which
in ancient times often included the sacrifice of some animal.

Yama   The lord of death, who takes charge of the uninitiated soul
at the time of death. See also: yamdoot.

yamdoot   Messengers or angels (*doot*) of death (*yama*).

yoga   Literally, union; esoterically, spiritual exercises; practice;
meditation in the spiritual sense; any system which leads to or
aims at the union of the soul with God.

yogeshwar   King of yogis, or supreme yogi; one who has reached
the second spiritual region, Brahm Lok, the causal plane.

yogi   One who practices yoga.

yuga   Age; a great cycle of time. Hindu mythology divides time
into four recurring cycles: the Golden Age (Sat Yuga); the Silver
Age (Treta Yuga); the Copper Age (Dwapar Yuga); and the Iron
Age (Kal Yuga), through which we are now passing. One thousand yugas make a Great Age (Maha Yuga), which is equivalent
to one day of Brahm. Saints have adopted this concept to convey the ever-changing nature of life on earth.

INDEX
(According to Letter Numbers)

centre of, 116
during meditation, 23, 168
breaths, number fixed, 70
business, success or failure and
karma, 28

celibacy, responsibility of, 169
ceremonies, participating in, 55
character, need for pure, 177
charity, consequences of, 104
children, parents' duty toward, 28
Christianity, Sant Mat and, 144
companions, real and false, 28
concentration (*see also under*
simran *and* attention)
benefits of, 74, 111, 198
desires interfere with, 69
duty of, *see* duty, disciple's
education and, 104
increasing pleasure of, 168, 194
method of achieving, 28, 117,
145
numbness during, 118
result of complete, 28, 87, 115,
198, 209
sound comes with, 116
states of, 194
strengthens will power, 113
contraception, use of (*see also* sex,
spiritual progress and), 24
cosmology, inner, description of
(*see also under* Creation), 10
Creation
Creator and the, 103
dissolution of, 10
divisions of, 140, 179, 198
history of, 72
transitory nature of, 161

ways of looking at, 20, 99
within man, 68
Creator, path designed by, 95

darshan, impurities of mind im-
pairs inner, 16
death (*see also under* birth)
companions at (*see also* human
form), 65, 69, 118
disposal of body after, 121, 137
form of astral and causal bodies after, 71
of satsangis, 164
process of birth and, 148
protection of Shabd at, 209
relationships and, 139
self-deception of salvation after,
104
suffering at the time of, 80
what happens to satsangis after,
52, 75, 81, 118, 197
Dera, the
attitude towards visiting, 141
during partition of India, 129
origins of, 3
desires (*see also under* birth)
never satisfied, *see* mind, nature of
wealth and, 176
destiny
has to be undergone, 20, 67, 198
inner viewpoint of, 143
predetermined, 11, 28
the Master's attitude towards,
143
we are the makers of our own, 60
detachment (*see also* attachment
and under satsangi)

maturity of, 25
test of, 205
fasting, spiritual progress and, 42
fate, *see* destiny
fear, of going inside, 136
five passions (anger, attachment,
 ego, greed, lust), *see* passions
forms, inner
 bowing to, 39, 55
 challenging, 194
 range of, 134
four lives, *see under* life
free will
 and predestination, 157
 different viewpoints of, *see* Creation, ways of looking at
Freemasonry, limitations of, 147

gender, *see* sex
ghosts, nature of, 183
God, what to ask of (*see also* Sat
 Purush *and under* grace), 21
good and evil, as aspects of mind,
 187
grace
 and effort, 200
 initiation is the Master's, *see*
 under initiation
 of Saints, 3
 signs of God's, 28
Granth Sahib, 122
group soul, *see under* soul
gurmukh
 and manmukh, 161
 definition of, *see under* satsangi

happiness, impossibility of, in
 Creation, 10

harmony,
 achieving, 105
 love and, importance in the
 sangat, 158, 160
healing, spiritual
 dangers of, 57
 wastes spiritual powers, 73
health, care of, 23, 98
human form
 advantages of, 57, 175
 purpose of (*see also under*
 Man), 22, 34, 89, 96, 122
 rare gift of, 73
 soul and mind permeate the, 64
 sustained by soul, 198
human nature, weaknesses of, 105,
 210
humility, *see under* Sant Mat

illness (*see also under* meditation)
 absence of the Master's form
 during, 205
 and treatment is a part of
 karma, 28, 115, 141
 attitude towards, 144, 172
 meditation during, 28
 simran during, 77, 93
India, spirituality of, 168
initiation
 cultivating the seed of, 57, 165
 experiences at time of, 54
 is the Master's grace, 7
 is pre-ordained, 143
 must bear fruit, 144, 205, 206
 object of, 57, 158
 only by a living Master, 120
 only for chosen souls, 28
 permanence of, 152

25

aim of, 74
alone that counts, 65, 113
antidote to karma, 28
anxiety at missing, 43
attitude towards, 210
control of the mind during, 81
discomfort in, 36, 81, 198
explanation of, 145
failure in, 116
first duty is, *see under* duty
first step of, 168
giving time to, 32, 83, 85, 94, 156
missing, importance of not, 181
natural and as ancient as man (*see also* Creator), 96
phases of, 10
posture in, 29, 79
problems in, 48
progress in, lack of, 122
record of, 113, 181
results of, 8, 31, 38, 87, 152
rewards, certainty of, 210
sensations during, 147
shaking during, 209
sleep during, 156
social service, compared to, *see* social service
strain during, 74, 95, 145, 198, 210
stress, reduces, 207
struggle of, 41, 118
mediums, 168, 170
memories, attitude towards, 91
mercy, *see* grace
mind
actions recorded in (*see also under* karma), 20

calmness of, 45, 140
cleansing of, 210
concentration of, 20, 29, 36, 116, 123
consequences of the actions of, *see* karma, law of
consequences of wavering of, 28, 140, 173
controlling (*see also under* meditation), 68, 74, 142
deception of (*see also* simran, function of), 12, 21, 84, 174
detachment of, difficulty with (*see also* detachment), 25
dictates what we do, 7
enmity of, 202, 210
forms of, 20, 22, 106, 147, 165
guarding over, 98
heart centre, focused at, 20
Kal, relationship with, 116
learning, effect of worldly on, 122, 131
meditation, effect of on, *see* under meditation
nature of, 64, 114, 115, 142
origin of, 12, 25
power of, 60, 117, 131
powers, use of (*see also under* miracles), 104, 134
restlessness of, 64
Shabd, tranquillised by, 34
shaking of, 25
states of, 150
struggle with, 20, 30, 82, 116, 143, 148
training of, 32
tricks of, 210
vastness of, 210

veil of (*see also* mind, controlling), 34, 86
worshipped by the world, 12
miracles
Masters' attitude toward, *see*
Master, immense power of
no value in, 205
penalties of performing, 134
moods, factors affecting, 136
motive, important in karma, 20
music, effect of worldly, 50

Nam, *see* Shabd
Nanak, Guru, spread of Sant Mat
by, *see under* Sant Mat
nirat, necessity for developing, 13
non-resistance, doctrine of, 202

obedience, advantages of, 136

pain
and pleasure controlled by the
Master, 49
during meditation, 23, 25, 116
parents, *see* children
passions, five (anger, attachment,
ego, greed, lust)
association with and defeat of,
28
bravery in overcoming kam
and krodh, 19
controlling (*see also under*
Shabd), 50, 118, 207
giving up, 198
met within as young boys, 28
Patanjali, Sant Mat and, 10
patience, 205
path, the, *see* Creator

peace
finding lasting, 67
inside us, 82, 149
the search for, 148
perseverance, 209
photographs, dhyan on, *see under*
dhyan
posture (*see also under* meditation),
29, 74, 88, 100, 142, 147
advice on, 197, 198
during illness, *see under* illness
power, spiritual (*see also under*
mind *and* Master), 34, 40,
54, 184, 194
prayer wheel, 200
prayer
attention and, 182
limitations of, 28
progress, spiritual (*see also under*
meditation)
after death of the Master, 71, 139
factors affecting, 26, 90, 118
physical defects and, 80
rate of, 23, 25, 37, 115, 147,
174, 210
reason for lack of, 143
repayment of karma and, 40, 41
psychic plane, *see* regions, inner
psychic power, *see* power

Radha Soami, meaning of, 1, 197
Radiant Form (*see also under*
Master)
awakens souls, 200
meeting, 28, 37, 38, 152, 157, 198
resemblance to the Master, 84
talking with, 122
reality, obscured by mind, 144

power of, 182, 195, 198
protection of (*see also under* death), 96
pulling power of, 200
real form of the Master, *see under* Master
real wealth of, *see under* wealth
relationship to soul and God, 34
St John's Gospel explains, *see* St John
separation from, consequences of, 147
separated from soul by mind, *see* mind, veil of
superiority of (*see also* Shabd, protection of), 104, 105, 115, 118, 130
technique of listening to, 51
tranquilises the mind, *see under* mind
two kinds of, 10, 161
unable to hear or see, *see* mind, shaking of
value of, 152
shocks, desirability of, 46
simran (*see also under* concentration *and* meditation)
advice on, 124, 198, 200
concentration achieved by, 200
function of, 21, 64, 156, 198
method of, 23, 73, 101, 171
natural process of, 82, 95
nature of, 117
protects against spirits, *see under* spirits
result of, 20, 33, 157, 202
testing visions of Master, *see under* Master

value of holy Names in, 54, 154
when not meditating, 124, 156, 173
sin
blame lower mind for, 21
Master's attitude towards, 21
slander, consequences of, 162
sleep (*see also under* meditation)
attention and (*see also under* eye centre), 145, 146, 147
location of soul during, *see* consciousness, states of
visions in (*see also* visions), 42
social customs, Sant Mat and, 28
social service, compared with meditation, 43
Socrates familiar with Shabd, 24
soldier, career of, 200, 202
solitude
advantages of, 108, 118, 123
our natural state, 76
soul
ascent of, *see under* journey
ascent of mind and, 140
becomes active in the embryo, *see under* embryo
cages of, 104
change of one's viewpoint with rise of, 106
coverings of (*see also* mind, forms of), 210
deliverance from Kal of, 207
descent of the mind and, 105
effects of meditation on, *see under* meditation
entanglements of, 198
freedom from mind and matter, 159
gradual withdrawal of, 171

group, 184
hunger of, 44
light of, 10, 12
natural tendency to rise of, 147
origin of, 12, 25
pain of withdrawal of, 209
potential of, 157
present condition of (*see also
   under* karma *and* progress),
   25, 57, 145, 172, 198
rate of rise of, 200
re-establishing the supremacy
   of, 26
relationship to Shabd, *see under*
   Shabd
separated from Shabd, *see*
   mind, veil of
suffering of, 174
time for needs of, 157
two faculties of, 10, 198
wanderings in birth and death
   of, 143
sound current, *see* Shabd
spirit, *see* soul
spirits, evil (*see also* forms, inner)
   casting out, 190
   deception by, 62
   protects against, 38
   simran protects against, 194
spiritual powers, *see* powers
spiritual progress, *see* progress
spiritual uplift, three steps of, 198
spiritual wealth, *see* wealth
stories, allegories and metaphors
   about Baba Jaimal Singh, 1, 3
   Baba Jaimal Singh paying
      karmic debt of initiate, 24
   Bhai Lalo and destiny, 143

boy goes to school, 115
death of mother of Maharaj
   Sawan Singh, 205
deceiving vision, 15
horse and Persian wheel, 11
lamp covered with cloths, 54
Moses and the bird, 8
the ox, 18
reaping what you sow, 20
thorny shrub and silk cloth, 145
stress, *see under* meditation
suffering (*see also under* karma)
   attitude towards, 93
   a blessing in disguise, 28
   pre-ordained, 70, 138
Swami Ji, Maharaj
   five sounds taught by, 56
   translation of a shabd by, 143

tattwas (elements), *see under* Creation
teachings, *see under* Master
Theosophy, Sant Mat and, 22
time, as experienced outside the
   eye centre, 72
third eye, *see* eye centre
transmigration (*see also* reincarnation)
   actions leading to, 169
   cycle of, 123
   escaping, 20, 25, 57, 81
   the soul and, 147
   understanding, 200
Trinity, the, 104
truth
   study of, 151
   value of, 36
   where found, 145

LOCAL ADDRESSES
FOR INFORMATION AND BOOKS

INDIAN SUB-CONTINENT

INDIA
The Secretary
Radha Soami Satsang Beas
P.O. Dera Baba Jaimal Singh 143204
District Amritsar, Punjab

Mr. Krishin Babani
Buona Casa Bldg., 2nd Floor
Sir P.M. Road, Fort
Bombay 400 001

NEPAL
Mr. V.K. Bhandari
Bhandari Builder & Sons (Contractor)
Ramshah Path
or (P.O. Box 1778), Kathmandu

Mr. Kedar Gayawali
Radha Soami Satsang Beas
Khairahani, Chitwan, Narayani Zone

SRI LANKA
Mr. D. H. Jiwat
c/o Geekay Ltd.
33 Bankshall Street, Colombo 11

SOUTHEAST ASIA

INDONESIA
Mr. Gope L. Nanwani
Jl. Kelinci Raya No. 32A
Jakarta Pusat 10710

Mr. Tarachand Chotrani
Jl. Bubutan 51
or (P.O. Box 144), Surabaya

MALAYSIA
Dr. Narjit Singh Dhaliwal
Kumpulan Perubatan SMP
18 Lorong Sempadan, Jalan 16/7
or (P.O. Box 7081)
Shah Alam 40702, Selangor

SINGAPORE
Mr. Sajan Shankardas Nanwani
Beas Enterprises
111 North Bridge Road
#04-04 Peninsula Plaza
Singapore 0617

THAILAND
Mr. Harmahinder Singh Sethi
Sawan Textiles Ltd.
154 Serm Sin Kha
Sampheng, Bangkok

ASIA PACIFIC

AUSTRALIA
Mrs. Janet Bland
P.O. Box 3, Oaklands Park
Adelaide, S. Australia 5046

HONG KONG
Mrs. Cami Moss
T.S.T., P.O. Box 97739, Kowloon

Mr. Mohan Das Chatlani
T.S.T., P.O. Box 90745, Kowloon

JAPAN
Mr. Jani Mohinani
1-1-10 Akamatsu-cho, Nada-ku
Kobe 657

393

NEW ZEALAND
Mr. Tony Waddicor
10 Maxine Place, Tauranga

PHILIPPINES
Mr. Kay Sham
P.O. Box 2346
MCC Makati, Metro Manila

TAIWAN R.O.C.
Mr. Larry T. Nanwani
No. 57 Tun Hwa South Road Sec. 1
Room 808, Choo Woo House
or (P.O. Box 68-1414), Taipei

NORTH AMERICA

CANADA
Mr. John W. Abel
701-1012 Beach Ave.
Vancouver, B.C. V6E 1T7

Dr. Peter Grayson
177 Division Street South
Kingsville, Ontario N9Y 1R1

UNITED STATES
Dr. Eugene Ivash
4701 Shadow Lane
Austin, TX 78731

Dr. Vincent P. Savarese
3507 Saint Elizabeth Road
Glendale, CA 91206

Dr. John Templer
114 Verdier Road
Beaufort, SC 29902

Dr. Frank Vogel
7 Pelham Terrace
Arlington, MA 02174

CARIBBEAN ISLANDS

CARIBBEAN ISLANDS
Mr. Sean Finnigan
Villa Rosa, Canape Vert.
or (P.O. Box 2314)
Port-au-Prince, Haiti

BARBADOS
Mr. Bhagwandas Kessaram Gopwani
c/o Kiddies Corner, 43 Swan Street
or (P.O. Box 603)
Bridgetown

TRINIDAD (WEST INDIES)
Mr. Thakurdas Chatlani
8A Saddle Road, Maraval

CENTRAL AMERICA

MEXICO
Mr. Jorge Angel Santana
Cometa 2821, Jardines del Bosque
Guadalajara, JAL 44520

For the following countries, contact:
Mr. Jorge Angel Santana, MEXICO

BELIZE
COSTA RICA
GUATEMALA
HONDURAS
NICARAGUA
PANAMA
SAN SALVADOR

SOUTH AMERICA

BRAZIL
Mr. Alberto Cancio Ferreira
See PORTUGAL.

ECUADOR
Mr. Gonzalo Vargas Noriega
Calle Montalvo No. 200, Oficina 201
Edificio Ponce Larrea
or (P.O. Box 17-21-1477)
Quito

GUYANA
Mrs. Rajni B. Manglani
c/o Bhagwan's Store
18 Water Street, Georgetown

PERU
Mr. Gonzalo Vargas Noriega
See ECUADOR.

VENEZUELA
Mr. Jose Antonio Penaherrera
Calle Mohedano Con Sucre
Edif. Don Jose, Local 2
Apartado Postal 63-436
Chacaito, Caracas 1.016

EUROPE

AUSTRIA
Mr. Hansjorg Hammerer
Sezenweingasse 10
Salzburg A-5020

BELGIUM
Mr. Jacob Hofstra
See NETHERLANDS.

BULGARIA
Mr. Emil Saev
P.O. Box 342, Sofia 1000

CYPRUS
Mr. Heraclis Achilleos
18 Kyriacou Matsi, Flat 101
or (P.O. Box 9077)
Pallouriotissa, Nicosia 116

CZECH REPUBLIC
Mr. Vladimir Skalsky
Maratkova 916, Prague 4, 142 00

DENMARK
Mr. Rudolf Walberg
See GERMANY.

FRANCE
Mr. Pierre de Proyart
7 Quai Voltaire, Paris 75007

GERMANY
Mr. Rudolf Walberg
P.O. Box 1544
D-65800 Bad Soden/Taunus

GIBRALTAR
Mr. Sunder T. Mahtani
Radha Soami Satsang Beas
401 Ocean Heights

GREECE
Mr. Dimitrios Sotiriou
Moschoula 4, Penteli
Athens 152-36

ITALY
Mrs. Wilma Salvatori Torri
Via Bacchiglione 3-00199, Rome

**NETHERLANDS, THE
(HOLLAND)**
Mr. Jacob Hofstra
Geulwijk 6, Leusden 3831 LM

396 ADDRESSES FOR INFORMATION AND BOOKS

NORWAY
Mr. Rudolf Walberg
See GERMANY.

PORTUGAL
Mr. Alberto Cancio Ferreira
Urb. do Buzano
Av. Comandante Gilberto
Duarte e Duarte, Lote 2, 3 Esq.
S. Domingos de Rana 2775

SLOVENIA
Mr. Marko Bedina
Brezje PRI, Trzicu 68, 64290 Trzic

SPAIN
Mr. Hiro W. Balani
Radha Soami Satsang Beas
Loma Del Valle, Cruce del Pinar
Alhaurin de la Torre
or (P.O. Box 486)
Malaga 29012

SWEDEN
Mr. Lennart Zachen
Norra Sonnarpsvagen 29
S-286 72 Asljunga

SWITZERLAND
Mr. Olivier de Coulon
Rue du Centre
Tolochenaz (VD) CH-1131

UNITED KINGDOM
Mrs. Flora E. Wood
Haynes Park
Haynes, Bedford MK45 3BL

AFRICA

BENIN
Mrs. Priya J. Vaswani
c/o Mr. Jaikumar Vaswani
B.P. 951, Cotonou

GHANA
Mr. James Osei Kojo Sekyi
P.O. Box 4615, Accra

KENYA
Mr. Surinder Singh Ghir
P.O. Box 39993, Nairobi

MAURITIUS
Mrs. Doolaree Nuckcheddy
17 Leconte de Lisle Ave.
Quatre Bornes

MOROCCO
Mr. Hiro W. Balani
See SPAIN.

NIGERIA
Mr. Nanik N. Balani
Nim House, 22, Idowu Taylor Street
2nd Floor, Rooms 15 & 16
Victoria Island, Lagos

SOUTH AFRICA
Mr. Sam Busa
P.O. Box 41355, Craighall 2024

TANZANIA
Mr. Diljeet Nath Pandit
83 Lugalo Rd., East Upanga
or (P.O. Box 1963), Dar-es-Salaam

UGANDA
Mr. Sylvester Kakooza
Alanda Ltd., Plot 64, William Street
or (P.O. Box 31381), Kampala

ZIMBABWE
Mrs. Dorothy Roodt
102 Suffolk Rd., Strathaven
or (P.O. Box 7095), Harare

MIDDLE EAST

DUBAI, U.A.E
Mr. Chander Bhatia
Shabnam Trading Co.
P.O. Box 2296

ISRAEL
Mrs. H. Mandelbaum
P.O. Box 22121, Tel Aviv 61221

BOOKS ON THIS SCIENCE

SOAMI JI MAHARAJ
    Sar Bachan

BABA JAIMAL SINGH
    Spiritual Letters (to Huzur Maharaj Sawan Singh: 1896-1903)

HUZUR MAHARAJ SAWAN SINGH
    The Dawn of Light (letters to Western disciples: 1911-1934)
    Discourses on Sant Mat
    My Submission (introduction to *Philosophy of the Masters*)
    Philosophy of the Masters (*Gurmat Sidhant*), 5 vols.
        (an encyclopedia on the teachings of the Saints)
    Philosophy of the Masters (abridged)
    Spiritual Gems (letters to Western disciples: 1919-1948)
    Tales of the Mystic East (as narrated in satsangs)

SARDAR BAHADUR MAHARAJ JAGAT SINGH
    The Science of the Soul (discourses and letters: 1948-1951)

HUZUR MAHARAJ CHARAN SINGH
    Die to Live (answers to questions on meditation)
    Divine Light (discourses and letters: 1959-1964)
    Light on Saint John
    Light on Saint Matthew
    Light on Sant Mat (discourses and letters: 1952-1958)
    The Master Answers (to audiences in America: 1964)
    The Path (first part of *Divine Light*)
    Quest for Light (letters: 1965-1971)
    Spiritual Discourses
    Spiritual Heritage (from tape-recorded talks)
    Teachings of the Saints (first chapter of *Die to Live*)
    Thus Saith the Master (to audiences in America: 1970)
    Truth Eternal (a discourse)

BOOKS ABOUT THE MASTERS
Call of the Great Master—Diwan Daryai Lal Kapur
Heaven on Earth—Diwan Daryai Lal Kapur
Treasure Beyond Measure—Shanti Sethi
With a Great Master in India—Julian P. Johnson
With the Three Masters, 3 volumes—from the diary of Rai Sahib
    Munshi Ram

BOOKS ON SANT MAT IN GENERAL
The Holy Name—Miriam Bokser Caravella
In Search of the Way—Flora E. Wood
The Inner Voice—Colonel C. W. Sanders
Liberation of the Soul—J. Stanley White
Message Divine—Shanti Sethi
Mystic Bible—Randolph Stone
The Mystic Philosophy of Sant Mat—Peter Fripp
Mysticism, The Spiritual Path, 2 volumes—Lekh Raj Puri
The Path of the Masters—Julian P. Johnson
Radha Soami Teachings— Lekh Raj Puri
A Soul's Safari—Netta Pfeifer
Teachings of the Gurus— Lekh Raj Puri
Yoga and the Bible—Joseph Leeming

MYSTICS OF THE EAST SERIES
Bulleh Shah—J. R. Puri and T.R. Shangari
Dadu, The Compassionate Mystic—K. N. Upadhyaya
Dariya Sahib, Saint of Bihar—K. N. Upadhyaya
Guru Nanak, His Mystic Teachings—J. R. Puri
Guru Ravidas, Life and Teachings—K. N. Upadhyaya
Kabir, The Great Mystic—Isaac A. Ezekiel
Kabir, The Weaver of God's Name—V. K. Sethi
Mira, The Divine Lover—V. K. Sethi
Saint Namdev, His Life and Teachings—J. R. Puri and V. K. Sethi
Saint Paltu—Isaac A. Ezekiel
Sant Charan Das—T. R. Shangari
Sarmad, Jewish Saint of India—Isaac A. Ezekiel
Sultan Bahu—J. R. Puri
Tukaram, Saint of Maharashtra—C. Rajwade
Tulsi Sahib, Saint of Hathras—J. R. Puri and V. K. Sethi